Thinking:
From Association to Gestalt

PERSPECTIVES IN PSYCHOLOGY

William Kessen
George Mandler
General Editors

George A. Miller
Mathematics and Psychology

Jean Matter Mandler and George Mandler
Thinking: From Association to Gestalt

Thinking: From Association to Gestalt

**Jean Matter Mandler
and George Mandler**

University of Toronto

GREENWOOD PRESS, PUBLISHERS
WESTPORT, CONNECTICUT

Library of Congress Cataloging in Publication Data

Main entry under title:

Thinking, from association to gestalt.

   Reprint. Originally published: New York : Wiley,
1964. (Perspectives in psychology)
   Includes bibliographical references and index.
   1. Thought and thinking. 2. Association of
ideas. I. Mandler, Jean Matter. II. Mandler, George.
III. Series: Perspectives in psychology.
BF455.T528   1982   153.4   81-13347
ISBN 0-313-23261-X (lib. bdg.)   AACR2

Copyright by George and Jean Mandler.

All Rights Reserved.
This book or any part thereof must not be reproduced
in any form without written permission from the authors.

Reprinted with the permission of Professors George and
Jean Mandler.

Reprinted in 1981 by Greenwood Press,
A division of Congressional Information Service, Inc.
88 Post Road West, Westport, Connecticut 06881

Printed in the United States of America

10 9 8 7 6 5 4 3 2 1

Foreword

Perspectives in Psychology is a series of original books written for psychologists and students who are concerned with the history of ideas in psychology.

It is our intention to present fresh and thoughtful assessments of the current psychological scene in the context of relevant historical changes. Many authors of the *Perspectives* books will examine a selected slice of the history of psychology by way of selected and annotated readings. This is not to say that *Perspectives* is a uniform or systematic encyclopedia of the history of psychology. Psychologists, by disposition and training, are reluctant to work their ideas into a standard weave—homespun or exotic—and *Perspectives* represents well the happy diversity of the discipline.

Some books in the series are scholarly disquisitions on the historical antecedents of a current problem in psychological analysis, some books move—after a brief glance at historical antecedents—directly toward a discussion of contemporary psychology and its future, some books deal with the past largely as a platform for polemical exposition. And, occasionally, *Perspectives* will present an original work in psychology that escapes the historical definition altogether.

Perspectives in Psychology, by using the avenues of documented history and informed discussions of current as well as classical issues, will emphasize that psychology has a history as well as a past and that it advances as it grows.

WILLIAM KESSEN
GEORGE MANDLER

Preface

When we first undertook to edit this book the project appeared to be both straightforward and challenging. Straightforward, because like most of our colleagues, we had assimilated an outline of the history of psychology that left few dark corners and in most cases seemed to follow a straight line of succession. Challenging, because we believed that it might be possible to put a different emphasis on some well-known facts. In addition, we thought that a single volume would adequately serve as a documented introduction to the history of thinking. But, as authors frequently are, we were caught up by the naiveté of our expectations.

In the first instance, it became obvious that a single volume could not possibly do justice to the field. Too many essential thoughts and thinkers demanded inclusion. The possibility then arose to cut the field in terms of early and late history. This, however, involved the assumption that there was in fact a single line of historical development. Once we were convinced that this assumption too was faulty, our final decision to attempt two volumes and to describe two more or less distinct streams of development was practically automatic.

In the present book we have concentrated on the traditional historical line. However, we believe that reasons other than tradition will be apparent in our selections. Another historical line, from German philosophy and phenomenology to the behaviorist reaction and revolution which recapitulated the associationists, and from the re-emergence of structuralism in the "French school" to modern developments, must await the next volume.

Within the family tree discussed here we have emphasized first the relative sophistication of early associationism and second the Würzburg school. The latter emphasis made it desirable to present a number of previously untranslated selections. In the process we uncovered a new hero, as we became impressed with the importance—and previous slighting—of Otto Selz, and we rediscovered an old villain—Wilhelm Wundt. In general, however, a compilation such as the present one is necessarily inadequate. We could have employed, and did consider, different emphases, different authors, and different selections. In a sense the final choices simply represent an artificial conclusion to our own indecisions; they stress theory rather than data, ours rather than other people's prejudices.

A word about the translations. Whenever possible we have tried to use a language that will be comprehensible to the contemporary psychologist, while retaining the flavor of the original material. To allay the reader's, and our own, uncertainties, we have occasionally added bracketed elucidations.

We must stress that this book is not a history of thinking; it has neither the depth nor the length. However, we have tried to be historically accurate to the extent that our coverage has permitted. It is our hope that the student who reads this volume as an addendum to current work on thinking and the teacher who uses it to refresh his recollections may use it as a starting point for a true exploration of that history.

We are most grateful to George A. Miller and William Kessen who read and commented on our manuscript and shared some of our indecisions, and to Daniel E. Berlyne for reading the manuscript and for many useful discussions while the work was in progress. Adrian De Groot kindly lent us a most valuable draft of parts of his forthcoming book on the thinking process. Whatever errors of omission or commission still occur among our selections and comments are, of course, entirely our responsibility. Finally, we would like to thank Pearl Ashworth and Maude Merrill who diligently suffered through the task of typing translations and original material.

Toronto, Canada   JEAN M. MANDLER
June 1964   GEORGE MANDLER

Contents

1 **Introduction** 1

2 **Early Associationism: The Philosophers** 7
   Aristotle Thinking, 9 • Recollection, 10
   Thomas Hobbes Thought, 15 • Of the Train of Imaginations, 18
   John Locke Ideas and Their Origin, 26 • Simple Ideas, 30 • Perception, 32 • Memory, 36 • Naming and Abstraction, 38 • Complex Ideas, 39 • The Association of Ideas, 40 • Reason, 43
   David Hume Of Ideas, Their Origin, Composition, Connexion, Abstraction, etc., 51

3 **Early Associationism: Philosophical Psychology** 70
   David Hartley The Doctrines of Vibrations and Association in General, 72 • Words and the Ideas Associated with Them, 87
   James Mill The Association of Ideas, 94 • Ratiocination, 113 • The Will, 115
   Alexander Bain Compound Association, 126 • The Singling Out of One Among Many Trains, 127

4 **Thinking and the New Psychology: Imageless Thought** 132
   A. Mayer and J. Orth The Qualitative Investigation of Associations, 135
   Karl Marbe The Psychology of Judgments, 143

August Messer Experimental-Psychological Investigations on Thinking, 148
Narziss Ach Awareness, 152
Edward Bradford Titchener Imagery and Sensationalism, 167 • The Psychology of Thought, 176 • The Problem of Meaning, 179

5 The New Psychology: Directed Thinking 186

Henry J. Watt Experimental Contribution to a Theory of Thinking, 189
Narziss Ach Determining Tendencies, 201
Oswald Külpe The Modern Psychology of Thinking, 208
Georg Elias Müller In Defense of Association Psychology, 217

6 The Unit of Thought 222

Otto Selz The Revision of the Fundamental Conceptions of Intellectual Processes, 225
Kurt Koffka The Distinction between Descriptive and Functional Concepts, 236
Max Wertheimer The Syllogism and Productive Thinking, 250
Karl Duncker The Solution of Practical Problems, 262 • On Total Insight or Evidence, 270 • On Learning and Partial Insight, 287 • On Solutions through Resonance, 291

Name Index 299

**Thinking:
From Association
to Gestalt**

1

Introduction

If one were to estimate the major activities that take up man's time from the amount of space devoted to various topics in most textbooks of psychology in the twentieth century, one would have to conclude that human activity primarily consists of seeing, hearing, learning new behavior patterns, acquiring verbal skills, or being mentally ill. The reader would hardly conclude that much of our time is spent in judging, contemplating, cogitating, imagining, considering—in short, thinking. And yet, the topic has fascinated psychologists in and out of the laboratory. They have worried it as a dog worries a precious bone. It was always there, sometimes buried, sometimes dug up again and brought to a high sheen, never quite cracked or digested, and never forgotten. Even the Wundts and the Hulls promised themselves to get back to the problem sooner or later while they counseled patience and attention to simpler problems that seemed to contain the principles needed to unlock the complexities of human thought. The failure of that program cannot be blamed on its advocates, since the simpler problems turned out to be complex—and as yet short of even partial resolution. But for every Wundt psychology has had a Bühler, for every Hull a Wertheimer—psychologists impatient with the programmatic building-block approach, unwilling to wait for the solution of the simple, and eager to plunge into the complexities and wonders of full-blown human thought.

Thus the psychology of thinking has frequently had the character of a resistance movement against the mainstreams of hard-headed experimental psychology. Considerations of intricate thought processes were often introduced by the gadflies, the radicals, the way-out-in-left-fielders. Not unexpectedly these excursions frequently resulted in abortive adventures, errant speculation, unsubstantiated conclusions, and—all too often—they bogged down in the quicksand of subjectivism and obscurantist epistemology. In contrast to these abortive attempts, we shall try to demonstrate in this volume that the psychology of thought does have a respectable history.

It seems to be particularly appropriate to publish in the 1960's a selection of some of the choicepoints in the psychology of thinking. To attempt that most dangerous of generalizations—a historical evaluation of the present—it appears that in mid-twentieth century the experimental psychology of thinking is coming of age. We believe that the advent of the modern computer has given psychologists the tools with which to handle the intricate transformations involved in thought, that the departure from the Ebbinghaus tradition in human learning has opened the doors to new considerations of memory, that the marriage of modern linguistics with experimental methods has given us new insights into the power and structure of language, and that the new mathematical psychology has taught us to look afresh at our data. At the beginning of a new era—if such in fact it is—it seems apposite to reacquaint ourselves with the early history of the field.

The psychology of thinking has probably suffered more than any other branch from the major disability of all psychologizing—the failure to make the logical distinction between the subject and the investigator.* Whereas in other areas of psychology the failure to make the subject-scientist distinction produced primarily a confusion of languages, in the psychology of thinking the private "mental" events of the philosophical psychologist continuously

---

* For a general discussion of this topic, see G. Mandler and W. Kessen, *The language of psychology*. New York: Wiley, 1959, Chap. 2.

misled him to confuse his introspections with a theory of thought. The confusion was actually twofold. In the first place there was the usual confusion of languages, the tendency to interpret the protocol statement "I have an image" with the descriptive, scientific statement "He has an image." There is obviously a world of difference between the latter statement and the proper description: "He said, 'I have an image.'" However, if we are forced to build a theory of thought on our own introspections, the error is practically inescapable. And to the extent that our introspective evidence is a miniature private theory in the first place, we will try to order these private events in terms of our own predilections and past experiences. It was not until 1912 that the problem was clearly stated for psychologists, when Kurt Koffka pointed out that the image that we experience ($Image_1$) and the image that we invoke as an explanatory construct to understand human thinking ($Image_2$) are two different concepts.

Hand in hand with this confusion of languages went a commitment to tie the theory of thinking to the experiences that seemed to accompany it. Thinking obviously occurred "in the head" and theories of thinking only slowly moved from the processes that went on "in the head" and were accessible to inspection, to processes that were still "in the head," only not so accessible, and finally to the theoretical notions of today that rarely have such an exalted locus, but primarily serve the mundane functions of prediction and explanation.

The business of most theories of psychology—even as early as the time of Hobbes—is to explain the transformations that take place between the facts presented by the environment and the behavior of the organism. Whether this problem is put into the framework of input-output transformations or stimulus-response connections or the representation of the world in ideas, the problem remains the same. Our philosophical historical heritage as well as common sense has usually insisted that in order to find out what goes on between these two poles, all we have to do is look and listen. The belief that the thought processes are freely open to inspection even led Locke to elevate this peeping tomism to a special sensory virtue. In contrast it can be argued that psychology became productive and creative when it broke away from this canon, and it will be a theme of this volume that the history of the psychology of thinking is the history of the departure from the common-sense theory of thought. Not only did the subject-scientist identity have to be renounced, but the identification of thinking with introspectively available experiences had to be given up as well.

It is beyond the scope of our comments to cite current evidence showing that the correlation between what a subject does and what he thinks he is doing is frequently zero or even negative. Psychology has come of age to the extent that we accept what the eighteenth century found unthinkable: that one can speak grammatically without being able to articulate a grammar, that one can add without a mastery of number theory, and that one can think constructively without being able to observe the construction. Any theory of thought constructs a theory of the structure of mind, of the transformations that give rise to creative, rational, contemplative products. It has long become obvious that to restrict such theories to concepts provided by the introspections of the thinker is hopelessly inadequate. It is hoped that the selections to follow will contribute not only to an appreciation of the development of the psychology of thinking, but in the process also illustrate how such a conclusion became "obvious."

This volume is not intended to be a history of the psychology of thinking—it has neither the space nor the pretensions to be that. Rather, a selection of some important milestones in such a history should provide the reader with an appreciation of the development of the field up to the beginning of the current era. We have—somewhat arbitrarily—dated that point somewhere in the early twentieth century, the stage of development at which British associationism had been abandoned, the Würzburgers had made their impact, and Gestalt psychology reached its flowering. It would take another such volume to pursue the story through the behaviorist revolution to the current scene.

In planning the scope of a volume such as this, decisions had to be made concerning areas of the psychology of thinking that were *not* to be covered. Our final selections were primarily guided by the arguments just outlined. Perusal of the literature made it seem reasonable to identify one line of development in the history of thinking that ranges from Aristotle to the British associationists, then jumps the Channel to Germany—particularly to Würzburg— and continues via the immediate results of the Würzburger revolution to the early days of Gestalt psychology. This particular tradition battled with the problems of imagery, directed thinking, and the unit of thought.

In choosing to pursue this particular line of investigation we deliberately left aside three major developments. One of them stretches from Kant to Dilthey, Husserl, and to the apriorism of the Gestalt school. Another, in the French tradition, covers Binet, Claparède, and Piaget in modern times. The psychology of thinking in these particular lines of succession was somewhat less concerned with the particular problems plumbed by the writers of our selections. We have also bypassed the development of behaviorism from Pavlov, Thorndike, and Watson to the present, simply because these considerations left no impact on the tradition we have explored. These chains of development belong more properly to a study of contemporary investigations of thinking. It is our hope that the relevance of these traditions to modern psychology of thinking can be explored in a subsequent volume.

Finally, we have put aside Freud and the psychoanalytic movement. It seemed more appropriate to explore the nonconscious factors in thinking within the line of thought that had originally espoused it. It will be quite obvious that notions of nonconscious thought were never alien to such men as Ach, Messer, and Selz. Furthermore, the contributions of the psychoanalytic school have been concentrated on motivational aspects of thought and relatively infrequently on the mechanisms of thinking as such.

The place of the psychology of thinking within the general history of psychology is not within our scope. However, it would have been impossible to collect the present volume without the guidelines presented by Boring's* and Brett's† histories. The

---

* E. G. Boring, *A history of experimental psychology*, 2nd ed. New York: Appleton-Century-Crofts, 1950.
† G. S. Brett, *A history of psychology*, 3 vols. London: Allen, 1912–1921; and R. S. Peters, *Brett's history of psychology*, rev. ed. London: Allen and Unwin, 1962.

reader must—as we did—go to these sources to find the place of thinking in the general scheme of things. And no treatment of the problem of thinking can even start without Humphrey's masterly introduction.* Although we sometimes disagree with Humphrey's interpretations, his exposition remains a milestone for any exploration of the psychology thinking.

* G. Humphrey, *Thinking*. London: Methuen, 1951.

2

Early Associationism: The Philosophers

Man's exploration of the nature of thought, like the rest of psychology, began life in the philosopher's armchair. The study of thought processes, however, took even longer than many other areas of psychology to pull loose from philosophy. It not only had to get up out of the armchair but out of the very head of the man nestled therein. Because of the elusive, private, intensely personal nature of thought, on the one hand, and because of its relation to "truth," "knowledge," and "judgment" on the other, the philosopher has been reluctant to part with this province of the study of man, and he has not entirely given it up today. Nevertheless the study of thinking has gradually moved out of the philosopher's library into the laboratory, out of the philosopher's head into the scientist's.

The introduction of "thought" to the laboratory was accomplished only at the beginning of this century. Before that time the psychology of thinking was strictly the philosopher's province, and so its history is studded with names of the great and near-great, especially in the centuries during which empirical philosophy flourished in Great Britain. We can only sample from among them: Hobbes, Locke, Berkeley, Hume, the Mills, Spencer. When reference is made to the writings of the British empiricists, they are often called the British associationists because their work is based on a fundamental principle of mental life, the association of ideas.

This phrase was invented by Locke late in the seventeenth century, but he did not originate the principles it subsumes. Thomas Hobbes, a half century earlier, was the first writer of modern times to describe the way in which one idea follows another, whether the process be occurring in memory, thought, or imagination. And his formulation in turn can be traced to that of Aristotle, writing almost 2000 years earlier.

Thus, as with much of the rest of psychology, we find ourselves beginning our history with Aristotle. His priority cannot be gainsaid; indeed, some of his most ardent defenders denied any subsequent accretion to his fundamental ideas. The following passage by Sir William Hamilton shows that as late as the middle of the last century, a heated—if not altogether enlightening—defense of Aristotle proceeded to deny the British philosophical tradition any success with or even any contribution to the doctrine of association:

> ... [In] truth, it might be broadly asserted, that every statement in regard to the history of this doctrine [of the association of ideas] hazarded by British philosophers, to say nothing of others, is more or less erroneous.—Priestley, for example, assigns to *Locke* the honour of having *first* observed the fact of association . . . ; and Hume, . . . arrogates to *himself* the glory of *first* generalizing its laws. . . . Mr. Stewart . . . says that *"something like an attempt* to enumerate the laws of Association is to be found in Aristotle."—Sir James Mackintosh, again, . . . affirms that Aristotle and his disciples . . . confine the application of the law of association *"exclusively to the phaenomena of recollection,* without any glimpse of a more general operation, extending to all the connections of *thought and feeling";* while the enouncement of a general theory of Association thus denied to the genius of Aristotle is all, and more than all, accorded to the sagacity of *Hobbes.* The truth, however, is that in his whole doctrine upon this subject, name and thing, Hobbes is simply a silent follower of the Stagirite; inferior to his master in the comprehension and accuracy of his general views; and not superior, even on the special points selected, either to Aristotle or to Vives.*

As our first selection we have chosen two of the most influential passages from Aristotle. The first from *De Anima* postulates the

---

* Hamilton, W. (Ed.), *The works of Thomas Reid,* Vol. 2, 8th ed. Edinburgh: Maclachlan and Stewart, 1880. (First edition: 1846). The quote is from Sir William Hamilton's appendix D**, p. 890, original italics.

mind ("in its world of images") as being constituted of images as elements. How this notion persisted to the twentieth century will be apparent in later passages; for the time being we are more concerned with the doctrine of association taken from the section entitled *De Memoria* in the *Parva Naturalia*. In this section Aristotle postulates the orderly sequence of experience and the three laws of association, those of similarity, contrast, and contiguity. Sir William Hamilton's diatribe can best be evaluated by contrasting these first steps with the later selections from the British philosophers.

* * *

Aristotle

Thinking

The reasoning mind thinks its ideas in the form of images; and as the mind determines the objects it should pursue or avoid in terms of these images, even in the absence of sensation, so it is stimulated to action when occupied with them. For example, when one sees that a beacon is lighted, and observes by means of the "common sense" that it is in motion, one comprehends that an enemy is near. Sometimes by means of the images or ideas in the soul the mind reasons as a seeing person, and takes thought for the future in terms of things before one's eyes. When the mind there in its world of images says that a thing is pleasant or painful, here in the world of things it pursues or avoids—in a word, it acts. Apart from action the true and false belong to the same category as the good and bad. They differ, however, in the absolute character of the one and the relative character of the other.

W. A. Hammond, (Ed.), *Aristotle's psychology: A treatise on the principle of life*, transl. by W. A. Hammond. London: Swan Sonnenschein, 1902, pp. 124–125, 203–208.

10   Aristotle

The mind thinks abstractions, as e.g. when it thinks the snub-nosed, which in one sense is a snub-nose, and in another sense, if one thinks it actually, one would think it as a curvature without the flesh in which the curvature is found. So too with mathematical figures, though in actuality not separate from bodies, the mind thinks them as separated, when it thinks them. In a word the mind *is* the thing when actually thinking it. Whether or not it is possible to think any abstraction when the mind itself is not separate from magnitude, must be investigated later.

Recollection

The subject of recollection remains to be treated. First of all we must take as presuppositions the truths which were established in the treatise *On Argumentation*. Accordingly, recollection is neither the recovery nor acquirement of a memory. For when one learns or acquires an impression for the first time, one does not recover any memory (for none has preceded), nor does one acquire an initial memory. But when a persistent mental condition and impression is fixed in the soul, then we have memory. Consequently, memory is not produced simultaneously with the production of an impression. Further, in the indivisible complete moment when the impression is first received, the impression and the knowledge are recorded in the affected subject, if one can call this mental condition and impression, knowledge (and there is nothing to prevent our remembering, in the sense of accident, a certain thing which we know conceptually). But memory as such is not possible until after the lapse of time. For what we remember now, we have previously known or experienced, but what we experience now is not in the present moment remembered. Further, it is evidently possible to have in memory what we do not now recollect, but what was once perceived or experienced. When one reacquires knowledge or sensation (or whatever the mental possession be to which we apply the term memory), it is then that one recollects one of the aforesaid mental possessions. The process of memory takes place, and memory ensues. Neither do the phenomena of recollection, if their occurrence is the repetition of a previous recollection, follow absolutely the same order, but sometimes they occur in one way and sometimes in another. It is possible for the same individual to learn and discover the same thing twice. Recollection, then, must differ from learning and discovery, and there is need of greater initial latitude here than is the case with learning.

Recollection is effected, when one suggestion succeeds another in natural order. If the succession is a necessary one, it is plain that when the antecedent suggestion is given, it will excite the succeeding one. If, however, the succession is not a necessary one, but only customary, the recollection will be stirred generally. But it is a fact that some persons by being impressed only once are trained in a given way more than others after frequent impressions. And so there are some things which after we have seen once, we remember better than others do who have seen them frequently. When, therefore, we recollect, we awaken certain antecedent processes and continue this until we call up that particular experience, after which the desired one is wont to appear. That is the reason why we hunt through a series in thought, beginning with an object presently before us, or with something else, or with an object that is similar, or opposite, or contiguous. In this way, recollection is awakened. For mental movements in these instances are identical in some cases, in others simultaneous, with the desired experience, and in other cases they involve a portion of it, so that there is a small remainder whose stimulation ensues. This then, is the way in which people try to recollect, and without conscious effort they recollect in this way, when the desired experience is recalled as the sequence of another experience. For the most part, however, the desired experience is recalled only after several different suggestions, such as we have described, have preceded. One does not at all need to look at the remote and ask how we remember it, but at what lies near before us. For the same method applies to both cases—I mean the method of sequences—without any prior effort to find this sequence and without recalling it. For mental movements follow one another, this one after that, by habituation. When a person wants to recall a thing, he will do the following: he will try to gain a starting-point in the process, in sequence to which the desired experience was had. Consequently, recollections which are awakened from the starting-point are most quickly and best effected. For just as things are mutually related in their order of succession, so also are the mental processes. And such things as have a fixed order are easily remembered, as e.g. mathematical truths. Other things are remembered poorly and with difficulty. Recollection differs from re-learning in this, that there can be in the former case a sort of self-movement back to that which follows upon the original experience. When this is not done, but the recollection is prompted by another person, then it is no longer memory. Oftentimes one is unable to recollect a thing, but after searching succeeds in finding it. This seeking and finding is what happens when one awakens a number of experiences and continues to do so until one sets that particular experience in motion upon which the desired thing is attendant. Memory is the possession of an experience potentially revivable. This process is effected, as was said above, in such way that it comes from the person's own effort and from the movements in his power. One must, however, have a starting-point. And so persons appear sometimes to recall things from local suggestions. The reason is that one passes rapidly from one thing to another, e.g. from milk to the suggested idea of white, from white to air, from air to the moist, and from this one recalls the late autumn, which is the season one was trying to think of. In general, it is the middle, too, of the entire series that seems to be the starting-point for memory. For when a person does not remember earlier, then he does so when he comes to the middle point, or when he does not remember here, then at no other point at all, as is the case e.g. when one passes through the series $ABCDEFGH$. If one does not remember at H, one remembers when one comes to E, provided one is in quest of F or G. For from that point the movement of suggestion is possible in both directions, towards the point D as well as towards the point F. If, however, a person is not in quest of one of these, he will remember on reaching C, and if not then, he will remember on reaching A, and this is the case always. But from the same point of suggestion one sometimes remembers and sometimes does not, the reason for which lies in the possibility of movement in more than one direction from the initial point, e.g. from E to F or from E to D. If the movement is influenced by an old suggestion, it takes place in the direction of the more fixed habit. For habit is second nature. Consequently, we remember easily what we often ponder. For as one definite thing succeeds another in nature, so it is also in our activity. Frequent repetition produces nature. Since we find in the realm of nature occurrences that violate her laws and are due to chance, much more do we find this in the realm of custom, to which the term nature cannot be applied in the same sense. The consequence is that a movement here sometimes takes place in one direction and sometimes in another, especially when the mind is distracted from a particular point to something else. Therefore, when one has to remember a name, and remembers one like it, one commits a solecism in regard to it. This then is the way in which recollection takes place.

* * *

A thin line of scholarship connects these pages with the work of the British associationists so many centuries later. Aristotle's formulations of the laws of thought were essentially unimproved upon for two millennia, and they are still in use in recognizable form today. As we shall see in the following selections, the essence of his famous passages is to be found in all the British philosophers' works, although much elaborated and expanded in the last two centuries.

The association theory of thought can be said to have been founded by Aristotle, but the mantle might be more reasonably placed, if placed it must be, upon the shoulders of Thomas Hobbes in the seventeenth century (Sir William Hamilton notwithstanding). Although Hobbes worked no great elaboration or improvement upon Aristotle's notions, nonetheless he started British psychology on the road it was to follow for many years. In the first place, his work led psychology away from the doctrine of innate ideas which Descartes was propounding at that time, thus beginning a tradition of his own which was to dog the footsteps of the British associationists and to exert a powerful influence on German psychology. Hobbes, however, turned his back on the rationalist position and stressed instead the empirical basis of mental life. All our ideas come from the senses, in fact they are but the decaying remains of sensations. Hobbes was fascinated by the physical problem of how the world comes to be represented inside our heads. His attempts to solve this problem led to another important influence on psychology, namely the interest in the psychophysical basis of sensation and thought. Following a trip to the continent to visit Galileo, he became fascinated with the concept of motion as a powerful explanatory principle not only of the workings of the physical world but also of the mind. Motion was to be the "cause of all things," since if everything were at rest or moved at the same rate, discrimination would be impossible. Rarely would it be possible during the next two centuries for a philosopher to disengage himself from this preoccupation and to write about thought without also adding some speculations about its physical basis.

The following two selections present Hobbes' major notions about thinking and the train of thought. The selection from *Human Nature,* written in 1640 but not published until ten years later, follows a discussion of the senses and the way in which ideas or conceptions are built up from sensations. Hobbes also enunciates contiguity as the basic principle of association, or—as he calls it—coherence of the original experiences. The details of the system still await amplification. Hobbes recognizes in passing that imagination or thinking, or even memory, do not exactly recreate past experience, and he also recognizes the problem that an experience may have been paired with more than one other, yet sometimes one and sometimes the other is brought to mind. However, no solutions to these problems are offered.

In the selection from *Leviathan,* published in 1651, some hints for such further developments are presented in the discussions of motivated (directed) thinking and the influence of "desire" upon the succession of thought. This topic did not receive its full appreciation until the late nineteenth and early twentieth centuries, and was generally underplayed by the early associationists who obviously found it difficult to fit such notions into a scheme of mental life reduced to the associations of elementary sensations and ideas.

* * *

Thomas Hobbes

Thought

1 The *succession* of conceptions in the mind, series or consequence of one after another, may be *casual* and incoherent, as in dreams for the most part; and it may be *orderly,* as when the former thought introduceth the latter; and this is *discourse* of the mind. But because the word discourse is commonly taken for the *coherence* and consequence of words, I will, to avoid equivocation, call it *discursion.*

2 The *cause* of the *coherence* or consequence of one conception to another, is their first *coherence* or consequence at that *time* when they are produced by sense: as for example, from St. Andrew the mind runneth to St. Peter, because their names are read together; from St. Peter to a *stone,* for the same cause; from *stone* to *foundation,* because we see them together; and for the same cause, from foundation to *church,* and from church to *people,* and from people to *tumult:* and according to this example, the mind may run almost from anything to anything. But as in the *sense* the conception of cause and effect may succeed one another;

W. Molesworth (Ed.), *The English works of Thomas Hobbes. Human nature* from Vol. 4, London: Bohn, 1840, pp. 14–19; *Leviathan* from Vol. 3, London: Bohn, 1839, pp. 11–17. First published in 1650 and 1651 respectively. Above selection from *Human Nature.*

so may they after sense in the *imagination:* and for the most part they do so; the *cause* whereof is the *appetite* of them, who, having a conception of the *end,* have next unto it a conception of the next *means* to that end: as, when a man, from a thought of *honour* to which he hath an appetite, cometh to the thought of *wisdom,* which is the next means thereunto; and from thence to the thought of *study,* which is the next means to wisdom.

3 To omit that kind of discursion by which we proceed from anything to anything, there are of the *other* kind *divers* sorts: as first, in the *senses* there are certain coherences of conceptions, which we may call *ranging;* examples whereof are; a man casteth his *eye* upon the *ground,* to look about for some *small* thing lost; the *hounds* casting about at a fault in hunting; and the *ranging* of spaniels: and herein we take a beginning arbitrary.

4 Another sort of discursion is, when the *appetite* giveth a man his beginning, as in the example before, where honour to which a man hath appetite, maketh him think upon the next means of attaining it, and that again of the next, etc. And this the Latins call *sagacitas,* and we may call *hunting* or *tracing,* as dogs trace beasts by the smell, and men hunt them by their footsteps; or as men hunt after riches, place, or knowledge.

5 There is yet another kind of discursion beginning with the appetite to *recover* something lost, proceeding from the *present backward,* from thought of the place where we *miss* at, to the thought of the place from whence we came *last;* and from the thought of that, to the thought of a place *before,* till we have in our mind some place, wherein we had the thing we miss: and this is called *reminiscence.*

6 The *remembrance* of succession of one thing to another, that is, of what was *antecedent,* and what *consequent,* and what *concomitant,* is called an *experiment;* whether the same be made by us *voluntarily,* as when a man putteth any thing into the fire, to see what effect the fire will produce upon it: or *not* made by us, as when we remember a fair morning after a red evening. To have had many *experiments,* is that we call *experience,* which is nothing else but *remembrance* of what antecedents have been followed by what consequents.

7 No man can have in his mind a conception of the *future*, for the future is *not yet:* but of our conceptions of the *past*, we make a *future;* or rather, call *past, future* relatively. Thus after a man hath been accustomed to see like antecedents followed by like consequents, whensoever he seeth the like come to pass to any thing he had seen before, he looks there should follow it the same that followed then: as for example, because a man hath often seen offences followed by punishment, when he seeth an offence in present, he thinketh punishment to be consequent thereto; but consequent unto that which is present, men call future; and thus we make *remembrance* to be the *prevision* of things to come, or *expectation* or presumption of the future.
8 In the same manner, if a man seeth in present that which he hath seen before, he thinks that that which was antecedent to that which he saw before, is also antecedent to that he presently seeth: as for example, he that hath seen the ashes remain after the fire, and now again seeth ashes, concludeth again there hath been fire: and this is called again *conjecture* of the past, or presumption of the fact.
9 When a man hath *so often* observed like antecedents to be followed by like consequents, that *whensoever* he seeth the antecedent, he looketh again for the consequent; or when he seeth the consequent, maketh account there hath been the like antecedent; then he calleth both the antecedent and the consequent, *signs* one of another, as clouds are signs of rain to come, and rain of clouds past.
10 This taking of signs by *experience*, is that wherein men do ordinarily think, the difference stands between man and man in *wisdom*, by which they commonly understand a man's whole ability or *power cognitive;* but this is an *error*: for the signs are but *conjectural;* and according as they have often or seldom failed, so their *assurance* is more or less; but *never full* and *evident:* for though a man have always seen the day and night to follow one another hitherto; yet can he not thence conclude they shall do so, or that they have done so eternally: *experience concludeth nothing universally.* If the signs hit twenty times for one missing, a man may lay a wager of twenty to one of the event; but

may not conclude it for a truth. But by this it is plain, that they shall *conjecture best,* that have *most experience,* because they have most signs to conjecture by: which is the reason *old men* are more *prudent,* that is, conjecture better, *cæteris paribus,* than young: for, being old, they remember more; and experience is but remembrance. And *men* of *quick* imagination, *cæteris paribus,* are more *prudent* than those whose imaginations are slow: for they observe *more* in *less* time. Prudence is nothing but conjecture from experience, or taking of signs from experience warily, that is, that the experiments from which he taketh such signs be all remembered; for else the cases are not alike that seem so.

11 As in conjecture concerning things past and future, it is prudence to conclude from experience, what is like to come to pass, or to have passed already; so it is an error to conclude from it, that *it is* so or so *called;* that is to say, we cannot from experience conclude, that any thing is to be called *just* or *unjust, true* or *false,* or any proposition *universal* whatsoever, except it be from remembrance of the use of names imposed arbitrarily by men: for example, to have heard a sentence given in the like case, the like sentence a thousand times is not enough to conclude that the sentence is just; though most men have no other means to conclude by: but it is *necessary,* for the drawing of such conclusion, to *trace* and *find out,* by many experiences, what men do mean by calling things just and unjust. Further, there is another *caveat* to be taken in concluding by experience, from the tenth section of the second chapter; that is, that we conclude such things to be without, that are within us.

Of the Train of Imaginations

By *consequence,* or *train* of thoughts, I understand that succession of one thought to another, which is called, to distinguish it from discourse in words, *mental discourse.*

From Leviathan.

When a man thinketh on any thing whatsoever, his next thought after is not altogether so casual as it seems to be. Not every thought to every thought succeeds indifferently. But as we have no imagination, whereof we have not formerly had sense, in whole, or in parts; so we have no transition from one imagination to another, whereof we never had the like before in our senses. The reason whereof is this. All fancies are motions within us, relics of those made in the sense: and those motions that immediately succeeded one another in the sense, continue also together after sense: insomuch as the former coming again to take place, and be predominant, the latter followeth, by coherence of the matter moved, in such manner, as water upon a plane table is drawn which way any one part of it is guided by the finger. But because in sense, to one and the same thing perceived, sometimes one thing, sometimes another succeedeth, it comes to pass in time, that in the imagining of any thing, there is no certainty what we shall imagine next; only this is certain, it shall be something that succeeded the same before, at one time or another.

This train of thoughts, or mental discourse, is of two sorts. The first is *unguided, without design,* and inconstant; wherein there is no passionate thought, to govern and direct those that follow, to itself, as the end and scope of some desire, or other passion: in which case the thoughts are said to wander, and seem impertinent one to another, as in a dream. Such are commonly the thoughts of men, that are not only without company, but also without care of any thing; though even then their thoughts are as busy as at other times, but without harmony; as the sound which a lute out of tune would yield to any man; or in tune, to one that could not play. And yet in this wild ranging of the mind, a man may oft-times perceive the way of it, and the dependance of one thought upon another. For in a discourse of our present civil war, what could seem more impertinent, than to ask, as one did, what was the value of a Roman penny? Yet the coherence to me was manifest enough. For the thought of the war, introduced the thought of the delivering up the king to his enemies; the thought of that, brought in the thought of the delivering up of Christ; and that again the thought of the thirty pence, which was the price of that treason; and thence easily followed that malicious question, and all this in a moment of time; for thought is quick.

The second is more constant; as being *regulated* by some desire, and design. For the impression made by such things as we desire, or fear, is strong, and permanent, or, if it cease for a time, of quick return: so strong it is sometimes, as to hinder and break our sleep. From desire, ariseth the thought of some means we have seen produce the like of that which we aim at; and from the thought of that, the thought of means to that mean; and so continually, till we come to some beginning within our own power. And because the end, by the greatness of the impression, comes often to mind, in case our thoughts begin to wander, they are quickly again reduced into the way: which observed by one of the seven wise men, made him give men this precept, which is now worn out, *Respice finem;* that is to say, in all your actions, look often upon what you would have, as the thing that directs all your thoughts in the way to attain it.

The train of regulated thoughts is of two kinds; one, when of an effect imagined we seek the causes, or means that produce it: and this is common to man and beast. The other is, when imagining any thing whatsoever, we seek all the possible effects, that can by it be produced; that is to say, we imagine what we can do with it, when we have it. Of which I have not at any time seen any sign, but in man only; for this is a curiosity hardly incident to the nature of any living creature that has no other passion but sensual, such as are hunger, thirst, lust, and anger. In sum, the discourse of the mind, when it is governed by design, is nothing but *seeking,* or the faculty of invention, which the Latins called *sagacitas,* and *solertia;* a hunting out of the causes, of some effect, present or past; or of the effects, of some present or past cause. Sometimes a man seeks what he hath lost; and from that place, and time, wherein he misses it, his mind runs back, from place to place, and time to time, to find where, and when he had it; that is to say, to find some certain, and limited time and place, in which to begin a method of seeking. Again, from thence, his thoughts run over the same places and times, to find what action, or other occasion might make him lose it. This we call *remembrance,* or calling to mind: the Latins call it *reminiscentia,* as it were a *re-conning* of our former actions.

Sometimes a man knows a place determinate, within the compass whereof he is to seek; and then his thoughts run over all the parts thereof, in the same manner as one would sweep a room, to find a jewel; or as a spaniel ranges the field, till he find a scent; or as a man should run over the alphabet, to start a rhyme.

Sometimes a man desires to know the event of an action; and then he thinketh of some like action past, and the events thereof one after another; supposing like events will follow like actions. As he that foresees what will become of a criminal, recons what he has seen follow on the like crime before; having this order of thoughts, the crime, the officer, the prison, the judge, and the gallows. Which kind of thoughts, is called *foresight*, and *prudence*, or *providence;* and sometimes *wisdom;* though such conjecture, through the difficulty of observing all circumstances, be very fallacious. But this is certain; by how much one man has more experience of things past, than another, by so much also he is more prudent, and his expectations the seldomer fail him. The *present* only has a being in nature; things *past* have a being in the memory only, but things *to come* have no being at all; the *future* being but a fiction of the mind, applying the sequels of actions past, to the actions that are present; which with most certainty is done by him that has most experience, but not with certainty enough. And though it be called prudence, when the event answereth our expectation; yet in its own nature, it is but presumption. For the foresight of things to come, which is providence, belongs only to him by whose will they are to come. From him only, and supernaturally, proceeds prophecy. The best prophet naturally is the best guesser; and the best guesser, he that is most versed and studied in the matters he guesses at: for he hath most *signs* to guess by.

A *sign* is the evident antecedent of the consequent; and contrarily, the consequent of the antecedent, when the like consequences have been observed, before: and the oftener they have been observed, the less uncertain is the sign. And therefore he that has most experience in any kind of business, has most signs, whereby to guess at the future time; and consequently is the most prudent: and so much more prudent than he that is new in that kind of business, as not to be equalled by any advantage of natural and extemporary wit: though perhaps many young men think the contrary.

Nevertheless it is not prudence that distinguisheth man from beast. There be beasts, that at a year old observe more, and pursue that which is for their good, more prudently, than a child can do at ten.

As prudence is a *presumption* of the *future,* contracted from the *experience* of time *past:* so there is a presumption of things past taken from other things, not future, but past also. For he that hath seen by what courses and degrees a flourishing state hath first come into civil war, and then to ruin; upon the sight of the ruins of any other state, will guess, the like war, and the like courses have been there also. But this conjecture, has the same uncertainty almost with the conjecture of the future; both being grounded only upon experience.

There is no other act of man's mind, that I can remember, naturally planted in him, so as to need no other thing, to the exercise of it, but to be born a man, and live with the use of his five senses. Those other faculties, of which I shall speak by and by, and which seem proper to man only, are acquired and increased by study and industry; and of most men learned by instruction, and discipline; and proceed all from the invention of words, and speech. For besides sense, and thoughts, and the train of thoughts, the mind of man has no other motion; though by the help of speech, and method, the same faculties may be improved to such a height, as to distinguish men from all other living creatures.

Whatsoever we imagine is *finite*. Therefore there is no idea, or conception of any thing we call *infinite*. No man can have in his mind an image of infinite magnitude; nor conceive infinite swiftness, infinite time, or infinite force, or infinite power. When we say any thing is infinite, we signify only, that we are not able to conceive the ends, and bounds of the things named; having no conception of the thing, but of our own inability. And therefore the name of God is used, not to make us conceive him, for he is incomprehensible; and his greatness, and power are unconceivable; but that we may honour him. Also because, whatsoever, as I said before, we conceive, has been perceived first by sense, either all at once, or by parts; a man can have no thought, representing any thing, not subject to sense. No man therefore can conceive any thing, but he must conceive it in some place; and indued with some determinate magnitude; and which may be divided into parts; nor that any thing is all in this place, and all in another place at the same time; nor that two, or more things can be in one, and the same place at once: for none of these things ever have, nor can be incident to sense; but are absurd speeches, taken upon credit, without any signification at all, from deceived philosophers, and deceived, or deceiving schoolmen.

* * *

One of the problems left untreated by Hobbes—the way in which complex ideas are compounded from simple sensations—was taken up fifty years later, in 1690, by Locke in his *Essay Concerning Human Understanding*.

It is difficult to place Locke in his own school. We say "his" advisedly, because many writers have placed him as the founder of associationism. Although it is true that he did coin the phrase, in fact he contributed little to the doctrine. His interests were threefold: epistemological, psychological, and pedagogical, and his work on the association of ideas primarily served the last of these. He recognized, for example, the effects of habit on our thinking, that various associations of ideas could be firmly ingrained in the mind, whether they be "true" or not, and thus hinder the acquisition of new ideas. But he did not contribute in detail to the elaboration of an associationist theory of thinking.

Locke's main purpose in the *Essay* is to develop a theory of knowledge, and the psychological aspects of the work subserve this epistemological purpose. Like the other philosophers of his time, Locke's interest in psychology was secondary to his interest in philosophical problems. One explored the nature of the mind as a necessary step in the quest for the limits of human knowledge. The ontological and epistemological problems of what there is in the world and to what degree of certainty we can know about it were the ultimate goals. It was to aid this quest for validity of belief that Locke attempted to follow the development of "understanding" from its simplest beginnings in sensation to the most complex operations of reasoning.

Like Hobbes, Locke takes pains to refute the notion of innate or intuitively known ideas and stresses that all the stuff that our minds have to work with comes from experience. He goes about this empiricism in a slightly different way, however. Our ideas come from two sources, the first sensation, the second reflection or "internal sense," which consists of the mind's perception of its own operations. The nature of reflection is not entirely clear; it seems to contain elements of the modern term "introspection," but it is primarily related to the active powers of the mind. The distinction is made, for example, between the passive reception of simple ideas of sense and the perception of more complex ideas. He mentions in a discussion which reverberates into the twentieth century that judgment, which involves reflection, influences much of our perception of the world. Reflection is not developed as a psychological term; it too serves Locke's theory of knowledge, which he considers to consist of the perception of the connection and agreement, or disagreement, of our ideas. Although the role of reflection remains psychologically vague, Locke moved a step away from the simple sensationism of Hobbes and raised the problem of how the mind takes the simple ideas passively received and combines and compares them to form the more complex ideas with which it customarily deals. The identification of Locke with the *tabula rasa*, which carries overtones of the passive reception of input, has overshadowed his notions about the active processing character of the mind. In that direction, Locke's use of "reflection" was an important step toward a more sophisticated theory of thinking.

For Locke the term "idea" is a general one; it is his unit of analysis; perception, thinking, doubting, reasoning, willing, pleasure, and pain are all different sets of ideas. Using "idea" as a basic unit paves the way for the development of associationism: ideas can be compounded, compared, and strung together. Here lies probably the origin of the "atomistic" flavor of later association theory. There is nothing experiential about this concept. Psychologically different processes are built up from these neutral units, deriving their distinctive character from the way in which they are combined.

In the following excerpts from Book II of Locke's *Essay Concerning Human Understanding*, we can follow the system from these simple building stones of his psychology—the ideas—through a discussion of perception and memory to the statements of the associative doctrine. The final selection, from Book IV, discusses reasoning and clearly illustrates the distinction between a modern psychology of thinking and the early philosophical attempts. The early discussions are permeated by a preoccupation with content —the ideas and their associations. The process of thought—reasoning, for example—is circumnavigated in most instances by simply calling it a property of the human organism; it just happens. Note though that Locke parts company with the leftover Aristotelian notion that all reasoning requires syllogistic skills, and that he is willing at least to speculate what the reasoning processes might be.

It is also useful to keep in mind during a perusal of these pages what the method of the empirical philosophers was. Locke describes and defends it himself in the following passage from one of the chapters primarily concerned with epistemological problems:

And thus I have given a short and, I think, true *history of the first beginnings of human knowledge;* whence the mind has its first objects, and by what steps it makes its progress to the laying in and storing up those ideas out of which is to be framed all the knowledge it is capable of; wherein I must appeal to experience and observation whether I am in the right. This is the only way that I can discover whereby the ideas of things are brought into the understanding. If other men have either innate ideas or infused principles, they have reason to enjoy them; and if they are sure of it, it is impossible for others to deny them the privilege that they have above their neighbours. I can speak but of what I find in myself.*

It would take another two hundred years before psychologists would be able to speak of processes found "in others."

---

* J. Locke, *An essay concerning human understanding,* abridged and edited by A. S. Pringle-Pattison. Oxford: Clarendon Press, 1924, p. 91.

John Locke

Ideas and Their Origin

IDEA IS THE OBJECT OF THINKING. Every man being conscious to himself that he thinks, and that which his mind is applied about whilst thinking being the ideas that are there, it is past doubt that men have in their minds several ideas, such as are those expressed by the words, "whiteness, hardness, sweetness, thinking, motion, man, elephant, army, drunkenness," and others. It is in the first place then to be enquired, How he comes by them? I know it is a received doctrine, that men have native ideas and original characters stamped upon their minds in their very first being. This opinion I have at large examined already; and, I suppose, what I have said in the foregoing Book will be much more easily admitted, when I have shown whence the understanding may get all the ideas it has, and by what ways and degrees they may come into the mind; for which I shall appeal to every one's own observation and experience.

ALL IDEAS COME FROM SENSATION OR REFLECTION. Let us then suppose the mind to be, as we say, white paper, void of all characters, without any ideas; how comes it to be furnished? Whence comes it by that vast store, which the busy and boundless fancy of man has painted on it with an almost endless variety? Whence has it all the materials of reason and knowledge? To this I answer, in one word, from EXPERIENCE; in that all our knowledge is founded, and from that it ultimately derives itself. Our observa-

---

J. Locke, *An essay concerning human understanding*, abridged and edited by A. S. Pringle-Pattison. Oxford: Clarendon Press, 1924, pp. 42–351 passim. First edition: London, T. Basset, 1690. Above selection from Book II, Chap. 1.

tion, employed either about external sensible objects, or about the internal operations of our minds, perceived and reflected on by ourselves, is that which supplies our understandings with all the materials of thinking. These two are the fountains of knowledge, from whence all the ideas we have, or can naturally have, do spring.

THE OBJECTS OF SENSATION ONE SOURCE OF IDEAS. First, our senses, conversant about particular sensible objects, do convey into the mind several distinct perceptions of things, according to those various ways wherein those objects do affect them; and thus we come by those *ideas* we have of yellow, white, heat, cold, soft, hard, bitter, sweet, and all those which we call sensible qualities; which when I say the senses convey into the mind, I mean, they from external objects convey into the mind what produces there those perceptions. This great source of most of the ideas we have, depending wholly upon our senses, and derived by them to the understanding, I call, SENSATION.

THE OPERATIONS OF OUR MINDS THE OTHER SOURCE OF THEM. Secondly, the other fountain, from which experience furnisheth the understanding with ideas, is the perception of the operations of our own minds within us, as it is employed about the ideas it has got; which operations, when the soul comes to reflect on and consider, do furnish the understanding with another set of ideas which could not be had from things without: and such are perception, thinking, doubting, believing, reasoning, knowing, willing, and all the different actings of our own minds; which we being conscious of, and observing in ourselves, do from these receive into our understanding as distinct ideas, as we do from bodies affecting our senses. This source of ideas every man has wholly in himself: and though it be not sense, as having nothing to do with external objects, yet it is very like it, and might properly enough be called internal sense. But as I call the other Sensation, so I call this REFLECTION, the ideas it affords being such only as the mind gets by reflecting on its own operations within itself. By Reflection, then, in the following part of this discourse, I would be understood to mean that notice which the mind takes of its own operations, and the manner of them, by reason whereof there come to be ideas of these operations in the understanding. These two, I say, viz., external material things as the objects of Sensation, and the operations of our own minds within as the objects of Reflection, are, to me, the only originals from whence all our ideas take their beginnings. The term *operations* here, I use in a large sense, as comprehending not barely the actions of the mind about its ideas, but some sort of passions arising sometimes from them, such as is the satisfaction or uneasiness arising from any thought.

ALL OUR IDEAS ARE OF THE ONE OR THE OTHER OF THESE. The understanding seems to me not to have the least glimmering of any ideas which it doth not receive from one of these two. *External objects* furnish the mind with the ideas of sensible qualities, which are all those different perceptions they produce in us; and *the mind* furnishes the understanding with ideas of its own operations. These, when we have taken a full survey of them, and their several modes, combinations, and relations, we shall find to contain all our whole stock of ideas; and that we have nothing in our minds which did not come in one of these two ways. Let any one examine his own thoughts, and thoroughly search into his understanding, and then let him tell me, whether all the original ideas he has there, are any other than of the objects of his senses, or of the operations of his mind considered as objects of his reflection; and how great a mass of knowledge soever he imagines to be lodged there, he will, upon taking a strict view, see that he has not any idea in his mind but what one of these two have imprinted, though perhaps with infinite variety compounded and enlarged by the understanding, as we shall see hereafter.

OBSERVABLE IN CHILDREN. He that attentively considers the state of a child at his first coming into the world, will have little reason to think him stored with plenty of ideas that are to be the matter of his future knowledge. It is by degrees he comes to be furnished with them: and though the ideas of obvious and familiar qualities imprint themselves before the memory begins to keep a register of time and order, yet it is often so late before some unusual qualities come in the way, that there are few men that

Ideas and Their Origin 29

cannot recollect the beginning of their acquaintance with them: and if it were worth while, no doubt a child might be so ordered as to have but a very few even of the ordinary ideas till he were grown up to a man. But all that are born into the world being surrounded with bodies that perpetually and diversely affect them, variety of ideas, whether care be taken about it or no, are imprinted on the minds of children. Light and colours are busy and at hand everywhere when the eye is but open; sounds and some tangible qualities fail not to solicit their proper senses, and force an entrance to the mind; but yet I think it will be granted easily, that if a child were kept in a place where he never saw any other but black and white till he were a man; he would have no more ideas of scarlet or green, than he that from his childhood never tasted an oyster or a pine-apple has of those particular relishes.

MEN ARE DIFFERENTLY FURNISHED WITH THESE ACCORDING TO THE DIFFERENT OBJECTS THEY CONVERSE WITH. Men then come to be furnished with fewer or more simple ideas from without, according as the objects they converse with afford greater or less variety; and from the operations of their minds within, according as they more or less reflect on them. For, though he that contemplates the operations of his mind cannot but have plain and clear ideas of them; yet, unless he turn his thoughts that way, and considers them *attentively*, he will no more have clear and distinct ideas of all the operations of his mind, and all that may be observed therein, than he will have all the particular ideas of any landscape, or of the parts and motions of a clock, who will not turn his eyes to it, and with attention heed all the parts of it. The picture or clock may be so placed, that they may come in his way every day; but yet he will have but a confused idea of all the parts they are made up of, till he applies himself with attention to consider them each in particular.

IDEAS OF REFLECTION LATER, BECAUSE THEY NEED ATTENTION. And hence we see the reason why it is pretty late before most children get ideas of the operations of their own minds; and some have not any very clear or perfect ideas of the greatest part of them all their lives. Because, though they pass there continually, yet, like floating visions, they make not deep impressions enough to leave in the mind clear, distinct, lasting ideas, till the understanding turns inwards upon itself, reflects on its own operations, and makes them the object of its own contemplation. Children, when they come first into it, are surrounded with a world of new things, which, by a constant solicitation of their senses, draw the mind constantly to them, forward to take notice of new, and apt to be delighted with the variety of changing objects. Thus the first years are usually employed and diverted in looking abroad. Men's business in them is to acquaint themselves with what is to be found without; and so, growing up in a constant attention to outward sensations, seldom make any considerable reflection on what passes within them till they come to be of riper years; and some scarce ever at all.

THE SOUL BEGINS TO HAVE IDEAS WHEN IT BEGINS TO PERCEIVE. To ask, at what *time* a man has first any ideas, is to ask when he begins to perceive; having ideas, and perception, being the same thing. I know it is an opinion, that the soul always thinks; and that it has the actual perception of ideas in itself constantly, as long as it exists; and that actual thinking is as inseparable from the soul, as actual extension is from the body: which if true, to enquire after the beginning of a man's ideas is the same as to enquire after the beginning of his soul. For by this account, soul and its ideas, as body and its extension, will begin to exist both at the same time.

Simple Ideas

UNCOMPOUNDED APPEARANCES. The better to understand the nature, manner, and extent of our knowledge, one thing is carefully to be observed concerning the ideas we have; and that is, that some of them are *simple*, and some *complex*.

Though the qualities that affect our senses are, in the things themselves, so united and blended that there is no separation, no distance between them; yet it is plain the ideas they produce in the mind enter by the senses simple and unmixed. For though the sight and touch often take in from the same object at the same time different ideas; as a man sees at once motion and colour, the hand feels softness and warmth in the same piece of wax; yet the simple ideas thus united in the same subject are as perfectly distinct as those that come in by different senses. The coldness and hardness which a man feels in a piece of ice being as distinct ideas in the mind as the smell and whiteness of a lily, or as the taste of sugar and smell of a rose: and there is nothing can be plainer to a man than the clear and distinct perception he has of those simple ideas; which, being each in itself uncompounded, contains in it nothing but one uniform appearance or conception in the mind, and is not distinguishable into different ideas.

THE MIND CAN NEITHER MAKE NOR DESTROY THEM. These simple ideas, the materials of all our knowledge, are suggested and furnished to the mind only by those two ways above mentioned, viz., sensation and reflection. When the understanding is once stored with these simple ideas, it has the power to repeat, compare, and unite them, even to an almost infinite variety, and so can make at pleasure new complex ideas. But it is not in the power of the most exalted wit or enlarged understanding, by any quickness or variety of thought, to invent or frame one new simple idea in the mind, not taken in by the ways before mentioned; nor can any force of the understanding destroy those that are there. The dominion of man in this little world of his own understanding, being muchwhat the same as it is in the great world of visible things, wherein his power, however managed by art and skill, reaches no farther than to compound and divide the materials that are made to his hand, but can do nothing towards the making the least particle of new matter, or destroying one atom of what is already in being. The same inability will every one find in himself, who shall go about to fashion in his understanding any simple idea not received in by his senses from external objects, or by reflection from the operations of his own mind about them. I would have any one try to fancy any taste which had never affected his palate, or frame the idea of a scent he had never smelt; and when he can do this, I will also conclude, that a blind man hath ideas of colours, and a deaf man true distinct notions of sounds.

Perception

IT IS THE FIRST SIMPLE IDEA OF REFLECTION. Perception, as it is the first faculty of the mind exercised about our ideas, so it is the first and simplest idea we have from reflection, and is by some called thinking in general. Though thinking, in the propriety of the English tongue, signifies that sort of operation of the mind about its ideas wherein the mind is active; where it, with some degree of voluntary attention, considers anything. For in bare, naked perception, the mind is, for the most part, only passive; and what it perceives, it cannot avoid perceiving.

IS ONLY WHEN THE MIND RECEIVES THE IMPRESSION. What perception is, every one will know better by reflecting on what he does himself, when he sees, hears, feels, etc., or thinks, than by any discourse of mine. Whoever reflects on what passes in his own mind, cannot miss it: and if he does not reflect, all the words in the world cannot make him have any notion of it. This is certain, that whatever alterations are made in the body, if they reach not the mind; whatever impressions are made on the outward parts, if they are not taken notice of within, there is no perception. Fire may burn our bodies with no other effect than it does a billet, unless the motion be continued to the brain, and there the sense of heat or idea of pain be produced in the mind, wherein consists actual perception. How often may a man observe in himself, that whilst his mind is intently employed in the contemplation of some objects, and curiously surveying some ideas that are there, it takes no notice of impressions of sounding bodies made upon the organ of

From Book II, Chap. 9.

hearing with the same alteration that uses to be for the producing the idea of sound? Want of sensation in this case is not through any defect in the organ, or that the man's ears are less affected than at other times when he does hear; but that which uses to produce the idea, though conveyed in by the usual organ, not being taken notice of in the understanding, and so imprinting no idea on the mind, there follows no sensation.

CHILDREN, THOUGH THEY HAVE IDEAS IN THE WOMB, HAVE NONE INNATE. Therefore, I doubt not but children, by the exercise of their senses about objects that affect them in the womb, receive some few ideas before they are born, as the unavoidable effects either of the bodies that environ them, or else of those wants or diseases they suffer; amongst which (if one may conjecture concerning things not very capable of examination) I think the ideas of hunger and warmth are two, which probably are some of the first that children have, and which they scarce ever part with again. Yet these simple ideas are far from those innate principles which some contend for, and we above have rejected, being the effects of sensation, and no otherwise differing in their manner of production from other ideas derived from sense, but only in the precedency of time. So, after they are born, those ideas are the earliest imprinted which happen to be the sensible qualities which first occur to them: amongst which, light is not the least considerable, nor of the weakest efficacy. And how covetous the mind is to be furnished with all such ideas as have no pain accompanying them, may be a little guessed by what is observable in children new born, who always turn their eyes to that part from whence the light comes, lay them how you please.

IDEAS OF SENSATION OFTEN CHANGED BY THE JUDGEMENT. We are farther to consider concerning perception, that the ideas we receive by sensation are often in grown people altered by the judgement without our taking notice of it. When we set before our eyes a round globe of any uniform colour, v.g. gold, alabaster, or jet, it is certain that the idea thereby imprinted in our mind is of a flat circle variously shadowed with several degrees of light and brightness coming to our eyes. But we having by use been accustomed to perceive what kind of appearance convex bodies are wont to make in us, what alterations are made in the reflections of light by the difference of the sensible figures of bodies, the judgement presently, by an habitual custom, alters the appearances into their causes: so that, from that which truly is variety of shadow or colour collecting the figure, it makes it pass for a mark of figure, and frames to itself the perception of a convex figure and an uniform colour; when the idea we receive from thence is only a plane variously coloured, as is evident in painting. (To which purpose I shall here insert a problem of that very ingenious and studious promoter of real knowledge, the learned and worthy Mr. Molineux, which he was pleased to send me in a letter some months since; and it is this: "Suppose a man born blind, and now adult, and taught by his touch to distinguish between a cube and a sphere of the same metal, and nighly of the same bigness, so as to tell, when he felt one and the other, which is the cube, which the sphere. Suppose then the cube and sphere placed on a table, and the blind man to be made to see; *quaere*, Whether by his sight, before he touched them, he could now distinguish and tell which is the globe, which the cube?" To which the acute and judicious proposer answers: "Not. For though he has obtained the experience of how a globe, how a cube, affects his touch; yet he has not yet attained the experience, that what affects his touch so or so, must affect his sight so or so; or that a protuberant angle in the cube, that pressed his hand unequally, shall appear to his eye at it does in the cube." I agree with this thinking gentleman, whom I am proud to call my friend, in his answer to this his problem; and am of opinion, that the blind man, at first sight, would not be able with certainty to say which was the globe, which the cube, whilst he only saw them; though he could unerringly name them by his touch, and certainly distinguish them by the difference of their figures felt. This I have set down, and leave with my reader, as an occasion for him to consider how much he may be beholden to experience, improvement, and acquired notions, where he thinks he has not the least use of, or help from them; and the rather, because this observing gentleman farther adds, that having upon the occasion of my book proposed this to divers very ingenious men, he hardly ever met with one that at first gave the answer to it which he thinks true, till by hearing his reasons they were convinced.)

But this is not, I think, usual in any of our ideas but those received by sight; because sight, the most comprehensive of all our senses, conveying to our minds the ideas of light and colours which are peculiar only to that sense; and also the far different ideas of space, figure, and motion, the several varieties whereof change the appearances of its proper object, viz., light and colours; we bring ourselves by use to judge of the one by the other. This, in many cases, by a settled habit, in things whereof we have frequent experience, is performed so constantly and so quick, that we take that for the perception of our sensation which is an idea formed by our judgement; so that one, viz., that of sensation, serves only to excite the other, and is scarce taken notice of itself; as a man who reads or hears with attention and understanding, takes little notice of the characters or sounds, but of the ideas that are excited in him by them.

Nor need we wonder that this is done with so little notice, if we consider how very quick the actions of the mind are performed: for as itself is thought to take up no space, to have no extension, so its actions seem to require no time, but many of them seem to be crowded into an instant. I speak this in comparison to the actions of the body. Any one may easily observe this in his own thoughts who will take the pains to reflect on them. How, as it were in an instant, do our minds with one glance see all the parts of a demonstration, which may very well be called a long one, if we consider the time it will require to put it into words, and step by step show it another? Secondly, we shall not be so much surprised that this is done in us with so little notice, if we consider how the facility which we get of doing things, by a custom of doing, makes them often pass in us without our notice. Habits, especially such as are begun very early, come at last to produce actions in us which often escape our observation. How frequently do we in a day cover our eyes with our eyelids, without perceiving that we are at all in the dark? Men, that by custom have got the use of a byword, do almost in every sentence pronounce sounds which, though taken notice of by others, they themselves neither hear nor observe. And therefore it is not so strange that our mind should often change the idea of its sensation into that of its judgement, and make one serve only to excite the other, without our taking notice of it.

Memory

CONTEMPLATION. The next faculty of the mind, whereby it makes a farther progress towards knowledge, is that which I call *retention,* or the keeping of those simple ideas which from sensation or reflection it hath received. This is done two ways. First, by keeping the idea which is brought into it, for some time actually in view, which is called *contemplation.*

MEMORY. The other way of retention is the power to revive again in our minds those ideas which, after imprinting, have disappeared, or have been as it were laid aside out of sight. And thus we do, when we conceive heat or light, yellow or sweet, the object being removed. This is *memory,* which is, as it were, the storehouse of our ideas. For the narrow mind of man not being capable of having many ideas under view and consideration at once, it was necessary to have a repository to lay up those ideas, which at another time it might have use of. (But our ideas being nothing but actual perceptions in the mind, which cease to be anything when there is no perception of them, this laying up of our ideas in the repository of the memory, signifies no more but this, that the mind has a power, in many cases, to revive perceptions which it has once had, with this additional perception annexed to them,—that it has had them before. And in this sense it is that our ideas are said to be in our memories, when indeed they are actually nowhere, but only there is an ability in the mind, when it will, to revive them again, and, as it were, paint them anew on itself, though some with more, some with less difficulty; some more lively, and others more obscurely.) And thus it is by the assistance of this faculty that we are said to have all those ideas in our understandings, which though we do not actually contemplate, yet we can bring in sight, and make appear again and be the objects of our thoughts, without the help of those sensible qualities which first imprinted them there.

ATTENTION, REPETITION, PLEASURE, AND PAIN FIX IDEAS. Attention and repetition help much to the fixing any ideas in the memory: but those which naturally at first make the deepest and most lasting impression, are those which are accompanied with pleasure or pain. The great business of the senses being to make us take notice of what hurts or advantages the body, it is wisely ordered by nature (as has been shown) that pain should accompany the reception of several ideas; which, supplying the place of consideration and reasoning in children, and acting quicker than consideration in grown men, makes both the young and old avoid painful objects with that haste which is necessary for their preservation, and in both settles in the memory a caution for the future.

CONSTANTLY REPEATED IDEAS CAN SCARCE BE LOST. But concerning the ideas themselves it is easy to remark, that those that are oftenest refreshed (amongst which are those that are conveyed into the mind by more ways than one) by a frequent return of the objects or actions that produce them, fix themselves best in the memory, and remain clearest and longest there; and therefore those which are of the original qualities of bodies, viz., solidity, extension, figure, motion, and rest; and those that almost constantly affect our bodies, as heat and cold; and those which are the affections of all kinds of beings, as existence, duration, and number, which almost every object that affects our senses, every thought which employs our minds, bring along with them: these, I say, and the like ideas, are seldom quite lost whilst the mind retains any ideas at all.

IN REMEMBERING, THE MIND IS OFTEN ACTIVE. In this secondary perception, as I may so call it, or viewing again the ideas that are lodged in the memory, the mind is oftentimes more than barely passive, the appearance of those dormant pictures depending sometimes on the will. The mind very often sets itself on work in search of some hidden idea, and turns, as it were, the eye of the soul upon it; though sometimes too they start up in our minds of their own accord, and offer themselves to the understanding, and very often are roused and tumbled out of their dark cells into open daylight by some turbulent and tempestuous passion; our affections bringing ideas to our memory which had otherwise lain quiet and unregarded. (This farther is to be observed concerning ideas lodged in the memory, and upon occasion revived by the mind, that they are not only (as the word revive imports) none of them new ones, but also that the mind takes notice of them as of a former impression, and renews its acquaintance with them as with ideas it had known before. So that though ideas formerly imprinted are not all constantly in view, yet in remembrance they are constantly known to be such as have been formerly imprinted, i.e., in view, and taken notice of before by the understanding.)

Naming and Abstraction

NAMING. When children have by repeated sensations got ideas fixed in their memories, they begin by degrees to learn the use of signs. And when they have got the skill to apply the organs of speech to the framing of articulate sounds, they begin to make use of words to signify their ideas to others. These verbal signs they sometimes borrow from others, and sometimes make themselves, as one may observe among the new and unusual names children often give to things in their first use of language.

ABSTRACTION. The use of words then being to stand as outward marks of our internal ideas, and those ideas being taken from particular things, if every particular idea that we take in should have a distinct name, names must be endless. To prevent this, the mind makes the particular ideas, received from particular objects, to become general; which is done by considering them as they are in the mind such appearances, separate from all other existences and the circumstances of real existence, as time, place, or any other concomitant ideas. This is called *abstraction*, whereby ideas taken

From Book II, Chap. 11.

from particular beings become general representatives of all of the same kind; and their names general names, applicable to whatever exists conformable to such abstract ideas. Such precise, naked appearances in the mind, without considering how, whence, or with what others they came there, the understanding lays up (with names commonly annexed to them) as the standards to rank real existences into sorts, as they agree with these patterns, and to denominate them accordingly. Thus, the same colour being observed to-day in chalk or snow, which the mind yesterday received from milk, it considers that appearance alone, makes it a representative of all of that kind; and having given it the name whiteness, it by that sound signifies the same quality wheresoever to be imagined or met with; and thus universals, whether ideas or terms, are made.

Complex Ideas

MADE BY THE MIND OUT OF SIMPLE ONES. We have hitherto considered those ideas, in the reception whereof the mind is only passive, which are those simple ones received from sensation and reflection before mentioned, whereof the mind cannot make one to itself, nor have any idea which does not wholly consist of them. (But as the mind is wholly passive in the reception of all its simple ideas, so it exerts several acts of its own, whereby out of its simple ideas, as the materials and foundations of the rest, the other are framed. The acts of the mind wherein it exerts its power over its simple ideas are chiefly these three: (1) Combining several simple ideas into one compound one; and thus all complex ideas are made. (2) The second is bringing two ideas, whether simple or complex, together, and setting them by one another, so as to take a view of them at once, without uniting them into one; by which it gets all its ideas of relations. (3) The third is separating them from all other ideas that accompany them in their real existence; this is called abstraction: and thus all its general ideas are made. This shows man's power and its way of operation to be much-what the same in the material and intellectual world. For, the materials in both being such as he has no power over, either to make or destroy, all that man can do is either to unite them together, or to set them by one another, or wholly separate them. I shall here begin with the first of these in the consideration of complex ideas, and come to the other two in their due places.) As simple ideas are observed to exist in several combinations united together, so the mind has a power to consider several of them united together as one idea; and that not only as they are united in external objects, but as itself has joined them. Ideas thus made up of several simple ones put together I call *complex;* such as are beauty, gratitude, a man, an army, the universe; which, though complicated of various simple ideas or complex ideas made up of simple ones, yet are, when the mind pleases, considered each by itself as one entire thing, and signified by one name.

MADE VOLUNTARILY. In this faculty of repeating and joining together its ideas, the mind has great power in varying and multiplying the objects of its thoughts infinitely beyond what sensation or reflection furnished it with: but all this still confined to those simple ideas which it received from those two sources, and which are the ultimate materials of all its compositions. For simple ideas are all from things themselves; and of these the mind can have no more nor other than what are suggested to it. It can have no other ideas of sensible qualities than what come from without by the senses, nor any ideas of other kind of operations of a thinking substance than what it finds in itself: but when it has once got these simple ideas, it is not confined barely to observation, and what offers itself from without; it can, by its own power, put together those ideas it has, and make new complex ones which it never received so united.

The Association of Ideas

SOMETHING UNREASONABLE IN MOST MEN. There is scarce any one that does not observe something that seems odd to him, and is in itself really extravagant, in the opinions, reasonings, and actions of other men. The least flaw of this kind, if at all different from his own, every one is quick-sighted enough to espy in another, and will by the authority of reason forwardly condemn, though he be guilty of much greater unreasonableness in his own tenets and conduct, which he never perceives, and will very hardly, if at all, be convinced of.

FROM A WRONG CONNEXION OF IDEAS. Some of our ideas have a natural correspondence and connexion one with another; it is the office and excellency of our reason to trace these, and hold them together in that union and correspondence which is founded in their peculiar beings. Besides this, there is another connexion of ideas wholly owing to chance or custom: ideas that in themselves are not at all of kin, come to be so united in some men's minds that it is very hard to separate them; they always keep in company, and the one no sooner at any time comes into the understanding, but its associate appears with it; and if they are more than two which are thus united, the whole gang, always inseparable, show themselves together.

THIS CONNEXION HOW MADE. This strong combination of ideas, not allied by nature, the mind makes in itself either voluntarily or by chance; and hence it comes in different men to be very different, according to their different inclinations, educations, interests, etc. Custom settles habits of thinking in the understanding, as well as of determining in the will, and of motions in the body; all which seems to be but trains of motion in the animal spirits, which, once set agoing, continue in the same steps they have been used to, which, by often treading, are worn into a smooth path, and the motion in it becomes easy, and as it were natural. As far as we can comprehend thinking, thus ideas seem to be produced in our minds; or if they are not, this may serve to explain their following one another in an habitual train, when once they are put into that track, as well as it does to explain such motions of the body. A musician used to any tune will find that, let it but once begin in his head, the ideas of the several notes of it will follow one another orderly in his understanding, without any care or attention, as regularly as his fingers move orderly over the keys of the organ to play out the tune he has begun, though his unattentive thoughts be elsewhere a-wandering. Whether the natural cause of these ideas, as well as of that regular dancing of his fingers, be the motion of his animal spirits, I will not determine, how probable soever by this instance it appears to be so: but this may help us a little to conceive of intellectual habits, and of the tying together of ideas.

SOME ANTIPATHIES AN EFFECT OF IT. That there are such associations of them made by custom in the minds of most men, I think nobody will question who has well considered himself or others; and to this, perhaps, might be justly attributed most of the sympathies and antipathies observable in men, which work as strongly, and produce as regular effects, as if they were natural, and are therefore called so, though they at first had no other original but the accidental connexion of two ideas which either the strength of the first impression, or future indulgence so united, that they always afterwards kept company together in that man's mind, as if they were but one idea. I say, most of the antipathies, I do not say all; for some of them are truly natural, depend upon our original constitution, and are born with us.

I mention this not out of any great necessity there is, in this present argument, to distinguish nicely between natural and acquired antipathies; but I take notice of it for another purpose, viz., that those who have children, or the charge of their education, would think it worth their while diligently to watch, and carefully to prevent the undue connexion of ideas in the minds of young people. This wrong connexion in our minds of ideas, in themselves loose and independent one of another, is of so great force to set us awry in our actions, as well moral as natural, passions, reasonings, and notions themselves, that perhaps there is not any one thing that deserves more to be looked after. The ideas of goblins and sprites have really no more to do with darkness than light; yet let but a foolish maid inculcate these often on the mind of a child, and raise them there together, possibly he shall never be able to separate them again so long as he lives.

A man receives a sensible injury from another, thinks on the man and that action over and over, and by ruminating on them strongly or much in his mind, so cements those two ideas together, that he makes them almost one; never thinks on the man, but the pain and displeasure he suffered comes into his mind with it, so that he scarce distinguishes them, but has as much an aversion for the one as the other. Thus hatreds are often begotten from slight and almost innocent occasions, and quarrels propagated and continued in the world. A man has suffered pain or sickness in any place; he saw his friend die in such a room. Though these have in nature nothing to do with one another, yet when the idea of the place occurs to his mind, it brings that of the pain and displeasure with it; he confounds them in his mind, and can as little bear the one as the other.

Reason

VARIOUS SIGNIFICATIONS OF THE WORD REASON. The word *reason*, in the English language, has different significations: sometimes it is taken for true and clear principles; sometimes for clear and fair deductions from those principles; and sometimes for the cause, and particularly the final cause. But the consideration I shall have of it here is in a signification different from all these; and that is, as it stands for a faculty in man, that faculty whereby man is supposed to be distinguished from beasts, and wherein it is evident he much surpasses them.

WHEREIN REASONING CONSISTS. If general knowledge, as has been shown, consists in a perception of the agreement or disagreement of our own ideas; and the knowledge of the existence of all things without us (except only of a God) be had only by our senses; what room then is there for the exercise of any other faculty but outward sense and inward perception? What need is there of reason? Very much; both for the enlargement of our knowledge and regulating our assent: for it hath to do both in knowledge and opinion, and is necessary and assisting to all our other intellectual faculties, and indeed contains two of them, viz., *sagacity* and *illation*. By the one it finds out, and by the other it so orders, the intermediate ideas as to discover what connexion there is in each link of the chain, whereby the extremes are held together; and thereby, as it were, to draw into view the truth sought for, which is that we call *illation* or *inference,* and consists in nothing but the perception of the connexion there is between the ideas in each step of the deduction; whereby the mind comes to see either the certain agreement or disagreement of any two ideas, as in demonstration, in which it arrives at knowledge, or their probable connexion, on which it gives or withholds its assent, as in opinion. Sense and intuition reach but a very little way. The greatest part of our knowledge depends upon deductions and intermediate ideas: and in those cases where we are fain to substitute assent instead of knowledge, and take propositions for true without being certain they are so, we have need to find out, examine, and compare the grounds of their probability. In both these cases the faculty which finds out the means, and rightly applies them to discover certainty in the one, and probability in the other, is that which we call reason.

So that we may in reason consider these *four degrees:* The first and highest is the discovering and finding out of proofs; the second, the regular and methodical disposition of them, and laying them in a clear and fit order, to make their connexion and force be plainly and easily perceived; the third is the perceiving their connexion; and the fourth, the making a right conclusion. These several degrees may be observed in any mathematical demonstration: it being one thing, to perceive the connexion of each part, as the demonstration is made by another; another, to perceive the dependence of the conclusion on all the parts; a third, to make out a demonstration clearly and neatly one's self; and something different from all these, to have first found out those intermediate ideas or proofs by which it is made.

SYLLOGISM NOT THE GREAT INSTRUMENT OF REASON. There is one thing more which I shall desire to be considered concerning reason; and that is, whether *syllogism,* as is generally thought, be the proper instrument of it, and the usefullest way of exercising this faculty. The causes I have to doubt are these:

Because syllogism serves our reason but in one only of the forementioned parts of it; and that is, to show the connexion of the proofs in any one instance, and no more; but in this it is of no great use, since the mind can perceive such connexion where it really is, as easily, nay perhaps better, without it.

If we will observe the actings of our own minds, we shall find that we reason best and clearest, when we only observe the connexion of the proof, without reducing our thoughts to any rule of syllogism. And therefore we may take notice that there are many men that reason exceeding clear and rightly, who know not how to make a syllogism; and I believe scarce any one ever makes syllogisms in reasoning within himself. Indeed, syllogism is made use of, on occasion, to discover a fallacy hid in a rhetorical flourish, or cunningly wrapped up in a smooth period; and stripping an absurdity of the cover of wit and good language, show it in its naked deformity. (But the weakness or fallacy of such a loose discourse it shows, by the artificial form it is put into, only to those who have thoroughly studied *mode* and *figure,* and have so examined the many ways that three propositions may be put together, as to know which of them does certainly conclude right, and which not, and upon what grounds it is that they do so. If syllogisms must be taken for the only proper instrument of reason and means of knowledge, it will follow that before Aristotle there was not one man that did or could know anything by reason; and that, since the invention of syllogisms, there is not one of ten thousand that doth.

But God has not been so sparing to men to make them barely two-legged creatures, and left it to Aristotle to make them rational. God has been more bountiful to mankind than so. He has given them a mind that can reason, without being instructed in methods of syllogizing. The understanding is not taught to reason by these rules; it has a native faculty to perceive the coherence or incoherence of its ideas, and can range them right, without any such perplexing repetitions. I say not this any way to lessen Aristotle, whom I look on as one of the greatest men amongst the ancients; whose large views, acuteness and penetration of thought, and strength of judgement, few have equalled; and who, in this very invention of forms of argumentation, wherein the conclusion may be shown to be rightly inferred, did great service against those who were not ashamed to deny anything. And I readily own that all right reasoning may be reduced to his forms of syllogism. But yet I think, without any diminution to him, I may truly say, that they are not the only, nor the best way of reasoning, for the leading of those into truth who are willing to find it. And he himself, it is plain, found out some forms to be conclusive and others not, not by the forms themselves, but by the original way of knowledge, i.e., by the visible agreement of ideas.) Tell a country gentlewoman that the wind is south-west, and the weather louring and like to rain, and she will easily understand it is not safe for her to go abroad thin clad in such a day, after a fever: she clearly sees the probable connexion of all these, viz., south-west wind, and clouds, rain, wetting, taking cold, relapse, and danger of death, without tying them together in those artificial and cumbersome fetters of several syllogisms, that clog and hinder the mind, which proceeds from one part to another quicker and clearer without them. And I think every one will perceive in mathematical demonstrations, that the knowledge gained thereby comes shortest and clearest without syllogism.

(To infer is nothing but by virtue of one proposition laid down as true, to draw in another as true; v.g., let this be the proposition laid down, "Men shall be punished in another world," and from thence be inferred this other, "Then men can determine themselves." The question now is, to know whether the mind has made this inference right or no; if it has made it by finding out the intermediate ideas, and taking a view of the connexion of them, placed in a due order, it has proceeded rationally, and made a right inference. If it has done it without such a view, it has not so much made an inference that will hold, as shown a willingness to have it be, or be taken for such. But in neither case is it syllogism that discovered those ideas, or showed the connexion of them; for they must be both found out, and the connexion everywhere perceived, before they can rationally be made use of in syllogism: unless it can be said that any idea, without considering what connexion it hath with the two other, whose agreement should be shown by it, will do well enough in a syllogism, and may be taken at a venture for the *medius terminus* to prove any conclusion. But this nobody will say; because it is by virtue of the perceived agreement of the intermediate idea with the extremes, that the extremes are concluded to agree; and therefore each intermediate idea must be such as, in the whole chain, hath a visible connexion with those two it is placed between. In the instance above mentioned the mind, seeing the connexion there is between the idea of men's punishment in the other world and the idea of God punishing, between God punishing and the justice of the punishment, between justice of punishment and guilt, between guilt and a power to do otherwise, between a power to do otherwise and freedom, and between freedom and self-determination, sees the connexion between men and self-determination.

Now I ask whether the connexion of the extremes be not more clearly seen in this simple and natural disposition than in the perplexed repetitions and jumble of five or six syllogisms. For the natural order of the connecting ideas must direct the order of the syllogisms, and a man must see the connexion of each intermediate idea with those that it connects, before he can with reason make use of it in a syllogism. And when all those syllogisms are made, neither those that are nor those that are not logicians will see the force of the argumentation, i.e., the connexion of the extremes, one jot the better.

Of what use, then, are syllogisms? I answer, Their chief and main use is in the Schools, where men are allowed without shame to deny the agreement of ideas that do manifestly agree; or out of the Schools, to those who from thence have learned without shame to deny the connexion of ideas, which even to themselves is visible. But to an ingenuous searcher after truth, who has no other aim but to find it, there is no need of any such form to force the allowing of the inference; the truth and reasonableness of it is better seen in ranging of the ideas in a simple and plain order. And hence it is that men, in their own enquiries after truth, never use syllogisms to convince themselves, because, before they can put them into a syllogism, they must see the connexion that is between the intermediate idea and the two other ideas it is set between and applied to, to show their agreement; and when they see that, they see whether the inference be good or no; and so syllogism comes too late to settle it.

I have had experience how ready some men are, when all the use which they have been wont to ascribe to anything is not allowed, to cry out, that I am for laying it wholly aside. But to prevent such unjust and groundless imputations, I tell them, that I am not for taking away any helps to the understanding in the attainment of knowledge. And if men skilled in and used to syllogisms find them assisting to their reason in the discovery of truth, I think they ought to make use of them. All that I aim at is, that they should not ascribe more to these forms than belongs to them. Some eyes want spectacles to see things clearly and distinctly; but let not those that use them therefore say, nobody can see clearly without them.)

SERVES NOT TO INCREASE OUR KNOWLEDGE, BUT FENCE WITH IT. But let it help us (as perhaps may be said) in convincing men of their errors and mistakes; (and yet I would fain see the man that was forced out of his opinion by dint of syllogism) yet still it fails our reason in that part which, if not its highest perfection, is yet certainly its hardest task, and that which we most need its help in; and that is, *the finding out of proofs, and making new discoveries.* The rules of syllogism serve not to furnish the mind with those intermediate ideas that may show the connexion of remote ones. This way of reasoning discovers no new proofs, but is the art of marshalling and ranging the old ones we have already. The forty-seventh proposition of the First Book of Euclid is very true; but the discovery of it, I think, not owing to any rules of common logic. A man knows first, and then he is able to prove syllogistically. So that syllogism comes after knowledge, and then a man has little or no need of it. But it is chiefly by the finding out those ideas that show the connexion of distant ones, that our stock of knowledge is increased, and that useful arts and sciences are advanced. Syllogism, at best, is but the art of fencing with the little knowledge we have, without making any addition to it. And if a man should employ his reason all this way, he will not do much otherwise than he who, having got some iron out of the bowels of the earth, should have it beaten up all into swords, and put it into his servants' hands to fence with and bang one another. And I am apt to think, that he who shall employ all the force of his reason only in brandishing of syllogisms, will discover very little of that mass of knowledge which lies yet concealed in the secret recesses of nature; and which, I am apt to think, native rustic reason (as it formerly has done) is likelier to open a way to, and add to the common stock of mankind.

* * *

The use of the "idea" as a basic unit did not find an easy niche in psychology, and fifty years later we find Hume declaiming that Locke's usage perverted the notion.

David Hume was, like John Locke, a philosopher interested in epistemological questions. In his search for what man can know with certainty he thought it necessary to trace the history of this or that idea back to its foundation, to discover how it arose in the human mind in the first place. Consequently a good deal of his main work, *A Treatise of Human Nature,* published in 1739, searches into psychological problems, especially the nature of thought. His philosophical conclusions are primarily negative, his treatise developing into a radical scepticism as to what man can know with certainty. In fact, his conclusion is that he can know so little that we had really better give up the philosophy game and stick to pyschology: "We may well ask, *What causes us to believe in the existence of the body?* but it is in vain to ask, *Whether there be body or not?* That is a point we must take for granted in all our reasonings." In spite of this conclusion it is well to remember when reading the *Treatise* that Hume was first of all a philosopher and only secondarily interested in the problems that today are called "psychological."

Hume uses the term "idea" in a more commonsense form than did Locke. Hume divides all the "perceptions" of the human mind into two classes: impressions, which correspond to sensations and emotions, and "ideas," which are faint images of these, occurring during thinking and reasoning. His differentiation between these two on the basis of force, liveliness, or vividness is not a very satisfactory distinction, but it is probably not central to his psychology. What is important is that every simple idea is preceded by a simple impression, of which the idea is an exact copy. Thus he has the source of the mind's ideas solidly located in the empirical world—perhaps a little too solidly. He went to great pains to stress this isomorphic relationship, but it reinforced the atomistic conception of the mind that was continually to plague the association school. The complexities of thought are built up out of elementary sensations, and for us to know the certainty of any idea requires that we find the sensations from which it was derived. It is from this basis that Hume ultimately deduces his famous argument that we cannot prove a causal relationship. The most we can derive from our sensations are such relationships as contiguity, priority in time, and constant conjunction, but nowhere can we find a sensation (and therefore the idea) of necessary connection or power or influence of one object on another, which was held to be the crucial element in a causal relationship. The ideas we have of such a relation must stem from our habitual associations; the repetition of an association between two events arouses an expectation in the mind; but the conclusion of causal connection is an inference, not a direct perception.

The failure to find an immediate perception of causality was irrefutable, and Hume could find no way to prove the validity of a causal inference. The philosopher might note that Hume's argument moved the problem of causality solidly into psychology. The perception of causality—within the framework of modern psychology*—is an empirical problem of human thought; Hume's *Treatise* taught us not to confuse it with physical causality.

As far as the elements of his psychology are concerned, Hume himself noted at least one apparent exception to his statement that for every simple idea there is a corresponding previous impression—the example of a person having a clear idea of a certain shade of blue he has never seen—but he thought this such a minor exception as to be not worth bothering with, and he proceeded apace. Other conclusions follow from this conception of the mind, and Hume, unlike his predecessor Locke, was not afraid to draw

---

* See, for example, *A. Michotte, *La perception de la causalité*, 2nd ed. Louvain: Public. Univers. de Louvain, 1954.

them. One such conclusion is that the mind can hold no abstract or general ideas, in the sense that it is impossible to imagine "any quantity or quality without forming a precise notion of its degrees." The inability to admit to his system any vague or blurred images stems from his premise that every simple idea is a copy of the original sense impression. Locke had been willing to say that we can form the general idea of a triangle that is neither oblique nor equilateral, but more or less both at the same time. The gauntlet was taken up by Bishop Berkeley, and in turn by Hume, who swore they could imagine no such thing, and this strange and wondrous controversy continued into the twentieth century, when we find Titchener still wrestling with the problem. As we shall note later, in the selection from Külpe, the problem of how the mind forms and uses abstract ideas is insoluble within the image theory of ideas, a framework of psychology that ties thinking solely to images and conscious processes.

In the following selection from Hume's *Treatise of Human Nature*, we can trace his development of the general theme of his psychology from the origin of ideas to the notion of abstract concepts.

* * *

David Hume

Of Ideas, Their Origin, Composition, Connexion, Abstraction, etc.

SECTION I: OF THE ORIGIN OF OUR IDEAS. All the perceptions of the human mind resolve themselves into two distinct kinds, which I shall call IMPRESSIONS and IDEAS. The difference betwixt these consists in the degrees of force and liveliness with which they strike

D. Hume, *A treatise of human nature*, edited by L. A. Selby-Bigge. Oxford: Clarendon Press, 1888, pp. 1–21. First edition: London, John Noon, 1739.

upon the mind, and make their way into our thought or consciousness. Those perceptions, which enter with most force and violence, we may name *impressions;* and under this name I comprehend all our sensations, passions and emotions, as they make their first appearance in the soul. By *ideas* I mean the faint images of these in thinking and reasoning; such as, for instance, are all the perceptions excited by the present discourse, excepting only, those which arise from the sight and touch, and excepting the immediate pleasure or uneasiness it may occasion. I believe it will not be very necessary to employ many words in explaining this distinction. Every one of himself will readily perceive the difference betwixt feeling and thinking. The common degrees of these are easily distinguished; tho' it is not impossible but in particular instances they may very nearly approach to each other. Thus in sleep, in a fever, in madness, or in any very violent emotions of soul, our ideas may approach to our impressions: As on the other hand it sometimes happens, that our impressions are so faint and low, that we cannot distinguish them from our ideas. But notwithstanding this near resemblance in a few instances, they are in general so very different, that no-one can make a scruple to rank them under distinct heads, and assign to each a peculiar name to mark the difference. [1]

There is another division of our perceptions, which it will be convenient to observe, and which extends itself both to our impressions and ideas. This division is into SIMPLE and COMPLEX. Simple perceptions or impressions and ideas are such as admit of no distinction nor separation. The complex are the contrary to these, and may be distinguished into parts. Tho' a particular colour, taste, and smell are qualities all united together in this apple, 'tis easy to perceive they are not the same, but are at least distinguishable from each other.

---

[1] I here make use of these terms *impression* and *idea*, in a sense different from what is usual, and I hope this liberty will be allowed me. Perhaps I rather restore the word, idea, to its original sense, from which Mr. *Locke* had perverted it, in making it stand for all our perceptions. By the term of impression I would not be understood to express the manner, in which our lively perceptions are produced in the soul, but merely the perceptions themselves; for which there is no particular name either in the *English* or any other language, that I know of.

Of Ideas, Their Origin, Composition 53

Having by these divisions given an order and arrangement to our objects, we may now apply ourselves to consider with the more accuracy their qualities and relations. The first circumstance, that strikes my eye, is the great resemblance betwixt our impressions and ideas in every other particular, except their degree of force and vivacity. The one seem to be in a manner the reflexion of the other; so that all the perceptions of the mind are double, and appear both as impressions and ideas. When I shut my eyes and think of my chamber, the ideas I form are exact representations of the impressions I felt; nor is there any circumstance of the one, which is not to be found in the other. In running over my other perceptions, I find still the same resemblance and representation. Ideas and impressions appear always to correspond to each other. This circumstance seems to me remarkable, and engages my attention for a moment.

Upon a more accurate survey I find I have been carried away too far by the first appearance, and that I must make use of the distinction of perceptions into *simple and complex*, to limit this general decision, *that all our ideas and impressions are resembling*. I observe, that many of our complex ideas never had impressions, that corresponded to them, and that many of our complex impressions never are exactly copied in ideas. I can imagine to myself such a city as the *New Jerusalem*, whose pavement is gold and walls are rubies, tho' I never saw any such. I have seen *Paris*; but shall I affirm I can form such an idea of that city, as will perfectly represent all its streets and houses in their real and just proportions?

I perceive, therefore, that tho' there is in general a great resemblance betwixt our *complex* impressions and ideas, yet the rule is not universally true, that they are exact copies of each other. We may next consider how the case stands with our *simple* perceptions. After the most accurate examination, of which I am capable, I venture to affirm, that the rule here holds without any exception, and that every simple idea has a simple impression, which resembles it; and every simple impression a correspondent idea. That idea of red, which we form in the dark, and that impression, which strikes our eyes in sun-shine, differ only in degree, not in nature. That the case is the same with all our simple impressions and ideas, 'tis impossible to prove by a particular enumeration of them. Every one may satisfy himself in this point by running over as many as he pleases. But if any one should deny this universal resemblance, I know no way of convincing him, but by desiring him to shew a simple impression, that has not a correspondent idea, or a simple idea, that has not a correspondent impression. If he does not answer this challenge, as 'tis certain he cannot, we may from his silence and our own observation establish our conclusion.

Thus we find, that all simple ideas and impressions resemble each other; and as the complex are formed from them, we may affirm in general, that these two species of perception are exactly correspondent. Having discover'd this relation, which requires no farther examination, I am curious to find some other of their qualities. Let us consider how they stand with regard to their existence, and which of the impressions and ideas are causes, and which effects.

The *full* examination of this question is the subject of the present treatise; and therefore we shall here content ourselves with establishing one general proposition, *That all our simple ideas in their first appearance are deriv'd from simple impressions, which are correspondent to them, and which they exactly represent.*

In seeking for phænomena to prove this proposition, I find only those of two kinds; but in each kind the phænomena are obvious, numerous, and conclusive. I first make myself certain, by a new review, of what I have already asserted, that every simple impression is attended with a correspondent idea, and every simple idea with a correspondent impression. From this constant conjunction of resembling perceptions I immediately conclude, that there is a great connexion betwixt our correspondent impressions and ideas, and that the existence of the one has a considerable influence upon that of the other. Such a constant conjunction, in such an infinite number of instances, can never arise from chance; but clearly proves a dependence of the impressions on the ideas, or of the ideas on the impressions. That I may know on which side this dependence lies, I consider the order of their *first appearance;* and find by constant experience, that the simple impressions always take the precedence of their correspondent ideas, but never appear in the contrary order. To give a child an idea of scarlet or orange, of sweet or bitter, I present the objects, or in other words, convey to him these impressions; but proceed not so absurdly, as to endeavour to produce the impressions by exciting the ideas. Our ideas upon their appearance produce not their correspondent impressions, nor do we perceive any colour, or feel any sensation merely upon thinking of them. On the other hand we find, that any impressions either of the mind or body is constantly followed by an idea, which resembles it, and is only different in the degrees of force and liveliness. The constant conjunction of our resembling perceptions, is a convincing proof, that the one are the causes of the other; and this priority of the impressions is an equal proof, that our impressions are the causes of our ideas, not our ideas of our impressions.

To confirm this I consider another plain and convincing phænomenon; which is, that where-ever by any accident the faculties, which give rise to any impressions, are obstructed in their operations, as when one is born blind or deaf; not only the impressions are lost, but also their correspondent ideas; so that there never appear in the mind the least traces of either of them. Nor is this only true, where the organs of sensation are entirely destroy'd, but likewise where they have never been put in action to produce a particular impression. We cannot form to ourselves a just idea of the taste of a pine-apple, without having actually tasted it.

There is however one contradictory phænomenon, which may prove, that 'tis not absolutely impossible for ideas to go before their correspondent impressions. I believe it will readily be allow'd, that the several distinct ideas of colours, which enter by the eyes, or those of sounds, which are convey'd by the hearing, are really different from each other, tho' at the same time resembling. Now if this be true of different colours, it must be no less so of the different shades of the same colour, that each of them produces a distinct idea, independent of the rest. For if this shou'd be deny'd, 'tis possible, by the continual gradation of shades, to run a colour insensibly into what is most remote from it; and if you will not allow any of the means to be different, you cannot without absurdity deny the extremes to be the same. Suppose therefore a person to have enjoyed his sight for thirty years, and to have become perfectly well acquainted with colours of all kinds, excepting one particular shade of blue, for instance, which it never has been his fortune to meet with. Let all the different shades of that colour, except that single one, be plac'd before him, descending gradually from the deepest to the lightest; 'tis plain, that he will perceive a blank, where that shade is wanting, and will be sensible, that there is a greater distance in that place betwixt the contiguous colours, than in any other. Now I ask, whether 'tis possible for him, from his own imagination, to supply this deficiency, and raise up to himself the idea of that particular shade, tho' it had never been conveyed to him by his senses? I believe there are few but will be of opinion that he can; and this may serve as a proof, that the simple ideas are not always derived from the correspondent impressions; tho' the instance is so particular and singular, that 'tis scarce worth our observing, and does not merit that for it alone we should alter our general maxim.

But besides this exception, it may not be amiss to remark on this head, that the principle of the priority of impressions to ideas must be understood with another limitation, *viz.* that as our ideas are images of our impressions, so we can form secondary ideas, which are images of the primary; as appears from this very reasoning concerning them. This is not, properly speaking, an exception to the rule so much as an explanation of it. Ideas produce the images of themselves in new ideas; but as the first ideas are supposed to be derived from impressions, it still remains true, that all our simple ideas proceed either mediately or immediately from their correspondent impressions.

This then is the first principle I establish in the science of human nature; nor ought we to despise it because of the simplicity of its appearance. For 'tis remarkable, that the present question concerning the precedency of our impressions or ideas, is the same with what has made so much noise in other terms, when it has been disputed whether there be any *innate ideas*, or whether all ideas be derived from sensation and reflexion. We may observe, that in order to prove the ideas of extension and colour not to be innate, philosophers do nothing but shew, that they are conveyed by our senses. To prove the ideas of passion and desire not to be innate, they observe that we have a preceding experience of these emotions in ourselves. Now if we carefully examine these arguments, we shall find that they prove nothing but that ideas are preceded by other more lively perceptions, from which they are derived, and which they represent. I hope this clear stating of the question will remove all disputes concerning it, and will render this principle of more use in our reasonings, than it seems hitherto to have been.

SECTION II: DIVISION OF THE SUBJECT. Since it appears, that our simple impressions are prior to their correspondent ideas, and that the exceptions are very rare, method seems to require we should examine our impressions, before we consider our ideas. Impressions may be divided into two kinds, those of SENSATION and those of REFLEXION. The first kind arises in the soul originally, from unknown causes. The second is derived in a great measure from our ideas, and that in the following order. An impression first strikes upon the senses, and makes us perceive heat or cold, thirst or hunger, pleasure or pain of some kind or other. Of this impression there is a copy taken by the mind, which remains after the impression ceases; and this we call an idea. This idea of pleasure or pain, when it returns upon the soul, produces the new impressions of desire and aversion, hope and fear, which may properly be called impressions of reflexion, because derived from it. These again are copied by the memory and imagination, and become ideas; which perhaps in their turn give rise to other impressions and ideas. So that the impressions of reflexion are only antecedent to their correspondent ideas; but posterior to those of sensation, and deriv'd from them. The examination of our sensations belongs more to anatomists and natural philosophers than to moral; and therefore shall not at present be enter'd upon. And as the impressions of reflection, *viz.* passions, desires, and emotions, which principally deserve our attention, arise mostly from ideas, 'twill be necessary to reverse that method, which at first sight seems most natural; and in order to explain the nature and principles of the human mind, give a particular account of ideas, before we proceed to impressions. For this reason I have here chosen to begin with ideas.

SECTION III: OF THE IDEAS OF THE MEMORY AND IMAGINATION. We find by experience, that when any impression has been present with the mind, it again makes its appearance there as an idea; and this it may do after two different ways; either when in its new appearance it retains a considerable degree of its first vivacity, and is somewhat intermediate betwixt an impression and an idea; or when it intirely loses that vivacity, and is a perfect idea. The faculty, by which we repeat our impressions in the first manner, is called the MEMORY, and the other the IMAGINATION. 'Tis evident at first sight, that the ideas of the memory are much more lively and strong than those of the imagination, and that the former faculty paints its objects in more distinct colours, than any which are employ'd by the latter. When we remember any past event, the idea of it flows in upon the mind in a forcible manner; whereas in the imagination the perception is faint and languid, and cannot without difficulty be preserv'd by the mind steady and uniform for any considerable time. Here then is a sensible difference betwixt one species of ideas and another. . . .

There is another difference betwixt these two kinds of ideas, which is no less evident, namely that tho' neither the ideas of the memory nor imagination, neither the lively nor faint ideas can make their appearance in the mind, unless their correspondent impressions have gone before to prepare the way for them, yet the imagination is not restrain'd to the same order and form with the original impressions; while the memory is in a manner ty'd down in that respect, without any power of variation.

'Tis evident, that the memory preserves the original form, in which its objects were presented, and that where-ever we depart from it in recollecting any thing, it proceeds from some defect or imperfection in that faculty. An historian may, perhaps, for the more convenient carrying on of his narration, relate an event before another, to which it was in fact posterior; but then he takes notice of this disorder, if he be exact; and by that means replaces the idea in its due position. 'Tis the same case in our recollection of those places and persons, with which we were formerly acquainted. The chief exercise of the memory is not to preserve the simple ideas, but their order and position. In short, this principle is supported by such a number of common and vulgar phænomena, that we may spare ourselves the trouble of insisting on it any farther.

The same evidence follows us in our second principle, *of the liberty of the imagination to transpose and change its ideas.* The fables we meet with in poems and romances put this entirely out of question. Nature there is totally confounded, and nothing mentioned but winged horses, fiery dragons, and monstrous giants. Nor will this liberty of the fancy appear strange, when we consider, that all our ideas are copy'd from our impressions, and that there are not any two impressions which are perfectly inseparable. Not to mention, that this is an evident consequence of the division of ideas into simple and complex. Where-ever the imagination perceives a difference among ideas, it can easily produce a separation.

SECTION IV: OF THE CONNEXION OR ASSOCIATION OF IDEAS. As all simple ideas may be separated by the imagination, and may be united again in what form it pleases, nothing wou'd be more unaccountable than the operations of that faculty, were it not guided by some universal principles, which render it, in some measure, uniform with itself in all times and places. Were ideas entirely loose and unconnected, chance alone wou'd join them; and 'tis impossible the same simple ideas should fall regularly into complex ones (as they commonly do) without some bond of union among them, some associating quality, by which one idea naturally introduces another. This uniting principle among ideas is not to be consider'd as an inseparable connexion; for that has been already excluded from the imagination; Nor yet are we to conclude, that without it the mind cannot join two ideas; for nothing is more free than that faculty: but we are only to regard it as a gentle force, which commonly prevails, and is the cause why, among other things, languages so nearly correspond to each other; nature in a manner pointing out to every one those simple ideas, which are most proper to be united into a complex one. The qualities, from which this association arises, and by which the mind is after this manner convey'd from one idea to another, are three, *viz.* RESEMBLANCE, CONTIGUITY in time or place, and CAUSE and EFFECT.

I believe it will not be very necessary to prove, that these qualities produce an association among ideas, and upon the appearance of one idea naturally introduce another. 'Tis plain, that in the course of our thinking, and in the constant revolution of our ideas, our imagination runs easily from one idea to any other that *resembles* it, and that this quality alone is to the fancy a sufficient bond and association. 'Tis likewise evident, that as the senses, in changing their objects, are necessitated to change them regularly, and take them as they lie *contiguous* to each other, the imagination must by long custom acquire the same method of thinking, and run along the parts of space and time in conceiving its objects. As to the connexion, that is made by the relation of *cause and effect*, we shall have occasion afterwards to examine it to the bottom, and therefore shall not at present insist upon it. 'Tis sufficient to observe, that there is no relation, which produces a stronger connexion in the fancy, and makes one idea more readily recall another, than the relation of cause and effect betwixt their objects.

That we may understand the full extent of these relations, we must consider, that two objects are connected together in the imagination, not only when the one is immediately resembling, contiguous to, or the cause of the other, but also when there is interposed betwixt them a third object, which bears to both of them any of these relations. This may be carried on to a great length; tho' at the same time we may observe, that each remove considerably weakens the relation. Cousins in the fourth degree are connected by *causation,* if I may be allowed to use that term; but not so closely as brothers, much less as child and parent. In general we may observe, that all the relations of blood depend upon cause and effect, and are esteemed near or remote, according to the number of connecting causes interpos'd betwixt the persons.

Of the three relations above-mention'd this of causation is the most extensive. Two objects may be consider'd as plac'd in this relation, as well when one is the cause of any of the actions or motions of the other, as when the former is the cause of the existence of the latter. For as that action or motion is nothing but the object itself, consider'd in a certain light, and as the object continues the same in all its different situations, 'tis easy to imagine how such an influence of objects upon one another may connect them in the imagination.

We may carry this farther, and remark, not only that two objects are connected by the relation of cause and effect, when the one produces a motion or any action in the other, but also when it has a power of producing it. And this we may observe to be the source of all the relations of interest and duty, by which men influence each other in society, and are plac'd in the ties of government and subordination. A master is such-a-one as by his situation, arising either from force or agreement, has a power of directing in certain particulars the actions of another, whom we call servant. A judge is one, who in all disputed cases can fix by his opinion the possession or property of any thing betwixt any members of the society. When a person is possess'd of any power, there is no more required to convert it into action, but the exertion of the will; and *that* in every case is consider'd as possible, and in many as probable; especially in the case of authority, where the obedience of the subject is a pleasure and advantage to the superior.

These are therefore the principles of union or cohesion among our simple ideas, and in the imagination supply the place of that inseparable connexion, by which they are united in our memory. Here is a kind of ATTRACTION, which in the mental world will be found to have as extraordinary effects as in the natural, and to shew itself in as many and as various forms. Its effects are every where conspicuous; but as to its causes, they are mostly unknown, and must be resolv'd into *original* qualities of human nature, which I pretend not to explain. Nothing is more requisite for a true philosopher, than to restrain the intemperate desire of searching into causes, and having establish'd any doctrine upon a sufficient number of experiments, rest contented with that, when he sees a farther examination would lead him into obscure and uncertain speculations. In that case his enquiry wou'd be much better employ'd in examining the effects than the causes of his principle.

Amongst the effects of this union or association of ideas, there are none more remarkable, than those complex ideas, which are the common subjects of our thoughts and reasoning, and generally arise from some principle of union among our simple ideas. These complex ideas may be divided into *Relations, Modes,* and *Substances.* We shall briefly examine each of these in order, and shall subjoin some considerations concerning our *general* and *particular* ideas, before we leave the present subject, which may be consider'd as the elements of this philosophy.

SECTION V: OF RELATIONS. The word RELATION is commonly used in two senses considerably different from each other. Either for that quality, by which two ideas are connected together in the imagination, and the one naturally introduces the other, after the manner above-explained; or for that particular circumstance, in which, even upon the arbitrary union of two ideas in the fancy, we may think proper to compare them. In common language the former is always the sense, in which we use the word, relation; and 'tis only in philosophy, that we extend it to mean any particular subject of comparison, without a connecting principle. Thus distance will be allowed by philosophers to be a true relation, because we acquire an idea of it by the comparing of objects: But in a common way we say, *that nothing can be more distant than such or such things from each other, nothing can have less relation;* as if distance and relation were incompatible.

It may perhaps be esteemed an endless task to enumerate all those qualities, which make objects admit of comparison, and by which the ideas of *philosophical* relation are produced. But if we diligently consider them, we shall find that without difficulty they may be compriz'd under seven general heads, which may be considered as the sources of all *philosophical* relation.

1. The first is *resemblance*: And this is a relation, without which no philosophical relation can exist; since no objects will admit of comparison, but what have some degree of resemblance. But tho' resemblance be necessary to all philosophical relation, it does not follow, that it always produces a connexion or association of ideas. When a quality becomes very general, and is common to a great many individuals, it leads not the mind

directly to any one of them; but by presenting at once too great a choice, does thereby prevent the imagination from fixing on any single object.

2. *Identity* may be esteem'd a second species of relation. This relation I here consider as apply'd in its strictest sense to constant and unchangeable objects; without examining the nature and foundation of personal identity, which shall find its place afterwards. Of all relations the most universal is that of identity, being common to every being, whose existence has any duration.

3. After identity the most universal and comprehensive relations are those of *Space* and *Time*, which are the sources of an infinite number of comparisons, such as *distant, contiguous, above, below, before, after,* etc.

4. All those objects, which admit of *quantity*, or *number*, may be compar'd in that particular; which is another very fertile source of relation.

5. When any two objects possess the same *quality* in common, the *degrees*, in which they possess it, form a fifth species of relation. Thus of two objects, which are both heavy, the one may be either of greater, or less weight than with the other. Two colours, that are of the same kind, may yet be of different shades, and in that respect admit of comparison.

6. The relation of *contrariety* may at first sight be regarded as an exception to the rule, *that no relation of any kind can subsist without some degree of resemblance*. But let us consider, that no two ideas are in themselves contrary, except those of existence and non-existence, which are plainly resembling, as implying both of them an idea of the object; tho' the latter excludes the object from all times and places, in which it is supposed not to exist.

7. All other objects, such as fire and water, heat, and cold, are only found to be contrary from experience, and from the contrariety of their *causes* or *effects*; which relation of cause and effect is a seventh philosophical relation, as well as a natural one. The resemblance implied in this relation, shall be explain'd afterwards.

It might naturally be expected, that I should join *difference* to the other relations. But that I consider rather as a negation of relation, than as any thing real or positive. Difference is of two kinds as oppos'd either to identity or resemblance. The first is called a difference of *number;* the other of *kind.*

SECTION VI: OF MODES AND SUBSTANCES. I wou'd fain ask those philosophers, who found so much of their reasonings on the distinction of substance and accident, and imagine we have clear ideas of each, whether the idea of *substance* be deriv'd from the impressions of sensation or reflection? If it be convey'd to us by our senses, I ask, which of them; and after what manner? If it be perceiv'd by the eyes, it must be a colour; if by the ears, a sound; if by the palate, a taste; and so of the other senses. But I believe none will assert, that substance is either a colour, or sound, or a taste. The idea of substance must therefore be deriv'd from an impression of reflection, if it really exist. But the impressions of reflection resolve themselves into our passions and emotions; none of which can possibly represent a substance. We have therefore no idea of substance, distinct from that of a collection of particular qualities, nor have we any other meaning when we either talk or reason concerning it.

The idea of a substance as well as that of a mode, is nothing but a collection of simple ideas, that are united by the imagination, and have a particular name assigned them, by which we are able to recall, either to ourselves or others, that collection. But the difference betwixt these ideas consists in this, that the particular qualities, which form a substance, are commonly refer'd to an unknown *something,* in which they are supposed to inhere; or granting this fiction should not take place, are at least supposed to be closely and inseparably connected by the relations of contiguity and causation. The effect of this is, that whatever new simple quality we discover to have the same connexion with the rest, we immediately comprehend it among them, even tho' it did not enter into the first conception of the substance. Thus our idea of gold may at first be a yellow colour, weight, malleableness, fusibility; but upon the discovery of its dissolubility in *aqua regia,* we join that to the other qualities, and suppose it to belong to the substance as much as if its idea had from the beginning made a part of the compound one. The principle of union being regarded as the chief part of the complex idea, gives entrance to whatever quality afterwards occurs, and is equally comprehended by it, as are the others, which first presented themselves.

That this cannot take place in modes, is evident from considering their nature. The simple ideas of which modes are formed, either represent qualities, which are not united by contiguity and causation, but are dispers'd in different subjects; or if they be all united together, the uniting principle is not regarded as the foundation of the complex idea. The idea of a dance is an instance of the first kind of modes; that of beauty of the second. The reason is obvious, why such complex ideas cannot receive any new idea, without changing the name, which distinguishes the mode.

SECTION VII: OF ABSTRACT IDEAS. A very material question has been started concerning *abstract* or *general* ideas, *whether they be general or particular in the mind's conception of them.* A great philosopher[2] has disputed the receiv'd opinion in this particular, and has asserted, that all general ideas are nothing but particular ones, annexed to a certain term, which gives them a more extensive signification, and makes them recall upon occasion other individuals, which are similar to them. As I look upon this to be one of the greatest and most valuable discoveries that has been made of late years in the republic of letters, I shall here endeavour to confirm it by some arguments, which I hope will put it beyond all doubt and controversy.

'Tis evident, that in forming most of our general ideas, if not all of them, we abstract from every particular degree of quantity and quality, and that an object ceases not to be of any particular species on account of every small alteration in its extension, duration and other properties. It may therefore be thought, that here is a plain dilemma, that decides concerning the nature of those abstract ideas, which have afforded so much speculation to philosophers. The abstract idea of a man represents men of all sizes and all qualities; which 'tis concluded it cannot do, but either by representing at once all possible sizes and all possible

[2] Dr. *Berkeley.*

qualities, or by representing no particular one at all. Now it having been esteemed absurd to defend the former proposition, as implying an infinite capacity in the mind, it has been commonly infer'd in favour of the latter; and our abstract ideas have been suppos'd to represent no particular degree either of quantity or quality. But that this inference is erroneous, I shall endeavour to make appear, *first*, by proving, that 'tis utterly impossible to conceive any quantity or quality, without forming a precise notion of its degrees: And *secondly* by showing, that tho' the capacity of the mind be not infinite, yet we can at once form a notion of all possible degrees of quantity and quality, in such a manner at least, as, however imperfect, may serve all the purposes of reflection and conversation.

To begin with the first proposition, *that the mind cannot form any notion of quantity or quality without forming a precise notion of degrees of each;* we may prove this by the three following arguments. First, We have observ'd, that whatever objects are different are distinguishable, and that whatever objects are distinguishable are separable by the thought and imagination. And we may here add, that these propositions are equally true in the *inverse,* and that whatever objects are separable are also distinguishable, and that whatever objects are distinguishable are also different. For how is it possible we can separate what is not distinguishable, or distinguish what is not different? In order therefore to know, whether abstraction implies a separation, we need only consider it in this view, and examine, whether all the circumstances, which we abstract from in our general ideas, be such as are distinguishable and different from those, which we retain as essential parts of them. But 'tis evident at first sight, that the precise length of a line is not different nor distinguishable from the line itself; nor the precise degree of any quality from the quality. These ideas, therefore, admit no more of separation than they do of distinction and difference. They are consequently conjoined with each other in the conception; and the general idea of a line, notwithstanding all our abstractions and refinements, has in its appearance in the mind a precise degree of quantity and quality; however it may be made to represent others, which have different degrees of both.

Secondly, 'tis confest, that no object can appear to the senses; or in other words, that no impression can become present to the mind, without being determin'd in its degrees both of quantity and quality. The confusion, in which impressions are sometimes involv'd, proceeds only from their faintness and unsteadiness, not from any capacity in the mind to receive any impression, which in its real existence has no particular degree nor proportion. That is a contradiction in terms; and even implies the flattest of all contradictions, *viz.* that 'tis possible for the same thing both to be and not to be.

Now since all ideas are deriv'd from impressions, and are nothing but copies and representations of them, whatever is true of the one must be acknowledg'd concerning the other. Impressions and ideas differ only in their strength and vivacity. The foregoing conclusion is not founded on any particular degree of vivacity. It cannot therefore be affected by any variation in that particular. An idea is a weaker impression; and as a strong impression must necessarily have a determinate quantity and quality, the case must be the same with its copy or representative.

Thirdly, 'tis a principle generally receiv'd in philosophy, that every thing in nature is individual, and that 'tis utterly absurd to suppose a triangle really existent, which has no precise proportion of sides and angles. If this therefore be absurd in *fact and reality*, it must also be absurd *in idea;* since nothing of which we can form a clear and distinct idea is absurd and impossible. But to form the idea of an object, and to form an idea simply is the same thing; the reference of the idea to an object being an extraneous denomination, of which in itself it bears no mark or character. Now as 'tis impossible to form an idea of an object, that is possest of quantity and quality, and yet is possest of no precise degree of either; it follows, that there is an equal impossibility of forming an idea, that is not limited and confin'd in both these particulars. Abstract ideas are therefore in themselves individual, however they may become general in their representation. The image in the mind is only that of a particular object, tho' the application of it in our reasoning be the same, as if it were universal.

This application of ideas beyond their nature proceeds from

our collecting all their possible degrees of quantity and quality in such an imperfect manner as may serve the purposes of life, which is the second proposition I propos'd to explain. When we have found a resemblance among several objects, that often occur to us, we apply the same name to all of them, whatever differences we may observe in the degrees of their quantity and quality, and whatever other differences may appear among them. After we have acquired a custom of this kind, the hearing of that name revives the idea of one of these objects, and makes the imagination conceive it with all its particular circumstances and proportions. But as the same word is suppos'd to have been frequently applied to other individuals, that are different in many respects from that idea, which is immediately present to the mind; the word not being able to revive the idea of all these individuals, only touches the soul, if I may be allow'd so to speak, and revives that custom, which we have acquir'd by surveying them. They are not really and in fact present to the mind, but only in power; nor do we draw them all out distinctly in the imagination, but keep ourselves in a readiness to survey any of them, as we may be prompted by a present design or necessity. The word raises up an individual idea, along with a certain custom; and that custom produces any other individual one, for which we may have occasion. But as the production of all the ideas, to which the name may be apply'd, is in most cases impossible, we abridge that work by a more partial consideration, and find but few inconveniences to arise in our reasoning from that abridgment.

For this is one of the most extraordinary circumstances in the present affair, that after the mind has produc'd an individual idea, upon which we reason, the attendant custom, reviv'd by the general or abstract term, readily suggests any other individual, if by chance we form any reasoning, that agrees not with it. Thus shou'd we mention the word, triangle, and form the idea of a particular equilateral one to correspond to it, and shou'd we afterwards assert, *that the three angles of a triangle are equal to each other,* the other individuals of a scalenum and isosceles, which we overlook'd at first, immediately crowd in upon us, and make us perceive the falsehood of this proposition, tho' it be true with relation to that idea, which we had form'd. If the mind suggests not always these ideas upon occasion, it proceeds from some imperfection in its faculties; and such a one as is often the source of false reasoning and sophistry. But this is principally the case with those ideas which are abstruse and compounded. On other occasions the custom is more entire, and 'tis seldom we run into such errors. . . .

* * *

Locke and Hume were the giants among the British philosophers in their influence on later psychology. But their psychology was part and parcel of their larger philosophical systems and, despite Hume's great insights, they can hardly be said to have made any distinction between philosophical questions and problems of an empirical psychology. Such a distinction, however, soon begins to be noticeable, and it seems proper to assign Hartley, the Mills, and Bain to this next phase in the history of thought.

3

Early Associationism:
Philosophical Psychology

In mid-eighteenth century the mind still appeared to consist in large part of sensations and images formed from them. The way in which these ideas are strung together had been suggested but not yet worked out in detail. It was still vague as to how we progress from the raw data of sense impressions to the towering structures of thought of which man is capable. The first philosopher to take the law of association and turn it into a psychology of association was David Hartley in 1749.

Boring says of Hartley:

> He is important because he was the founder of associationism. He was not the originator; that was Aristotle, or Hobbes, or Locke, as one pleases. The principle had been used effectively and greatly developed by Berkeley and Hume. Hartley merely established it as a doctrine. He took Locke's little-used title for a chapter, "the association of ideas," made it the name of a fundamental law, reiterated it, wrote a psychology around it, and thus created a formal doctrine with a definite name, so that a school could repeat the phrase after him for a century and thus implicitly constitute him its founder.*

Perhaps part of Hartley's success in creating a school of psychology was due to his being a physician by trade rather than

---

* E. G. Boring, *A history of experimental psychology*, 2nd ed. New York: Appleton-Century-Crofts, 1950, pp. 193–194.

a philosopher. For the first time we are reading a work that does not have a theory of knowledge as its goal, but is aiming toward a theory of psychology such as we are familiar with today. True, it is still armchair theory, far from the laboratory, but there are some new emphases. One of the most important of these is Hartley's interest in physiology which led him not only to attempt a crude neurological basis for the psychological theory he was developing, but also to extend the laws of association to include muscular movements. Although information about neurology was too imprecise to make this part of his theory of any modern interest, the inclusion of motor phenomena in the theory enormously increased its power and scope; the law as stated in Proposition XX is a clear statement of the associative laws current a century and a half later.

Much of the characteristic temper of association theory as it was developed during the next century is represented in Hartley's writing. In Proposition XII, for example, the additive nature of complex ideas ("compound impression $A + B + C + D$") is boldly assumed. The simplicity of such an assumption was enormously appealing, but the notion of complex ideas being merely the linear sum of their component simple ideas was one of the most vulnerable positions of the theory. On the one hand the attacks concentrated on the theory's inability to handle the relational and unitary character of ideas and behavior; on the other hand, it seemed patently impossible that all the many complex and abstract concepts could be painstakingly constructed out of their relatively few constituents. From a modern point of view it seems that the many different associations to be acquired could not be fitted into a human lifetime.

Though not directly relevant to our topic we have included in the selections from Hartley a part of his account of early language learning as an example of the way in which he extended the laws of association to cover a wide variety of topics. These passages too could well have been written in the twentieth century.

David Hartley

The Doctrines of Vibrations and Association in General

My chief design in the following chapter is briefly to explain, establish, and apply the doctrines of *vibrations* and *association*. The first of these doctrines is taken from the hints concerning the performance of sensation and motion, which Sir Isaac Newton has given at the end of his Principia, and in the Questions annexed to his Optics; the last, from what Mr. Locke, and other ingenious persons since his time, have delivered concerning the influence of *association* over our opinions and affections, and its use in explaining those things in an accurate and precise way, which are commonly referred to the power of habit and custom, in a general and indeterminate one.

The doctrine of *vibrations* may appear at first sight to have no connexion with that of *association;* however, if these doctrines be found in fact to contain the laws of the bodily and mental powers respectively, they must be related to each other, since the body and mind are. One may expect, that *vibrations* should infer *association* as their effect, and *association* point to *vibrations* as its cause. I will endeavour, in the present chapter, to trace out this mutual relation.

The proper method of philosophizing seems to be, to discover and establish the general laws of action, affecting the subject under consideration, from certain select, well-defined, and well-attested phænomena, and then to explain and predict the other phænomena by these laws. This is the method of analysis and synthesis recommended and followed by Sir Isaac Newton.

D. Hartley, Observations on man, 6th ed. London: Tegg, 1834, pp. 1–5, 36–65 passim, 170–173. First edition: London, 1749.

I shall not be able to execute, with any accuracy, what the reader might expect of this kind, in respect of the doctrines of *vibrations* and *association,* and their general laws, on account of the great intricacy, extensiveness, and novelty of the subject. However, I will attempt a sketch in the best manner I can, for the service of future inquirers....

PROP. VIII: SENSATIONS, BY BEING OFTEN REPEATED, LEAVE CERTAIN VESTIGES, TYPES, OR IMAGES, OF THEMSELVES, WHICH MAY BE CALLED, SIMPLE IDEAS OF SENSATION. I took notice in the Introduction, that those ideas which resemble sensations were called ideas of sensation; and also that they might be called *simple* ideas, in respect of the intellectual ones which are formed from them, and of whose very essence it is to be *complex*. But the ideas of sensation are not entirely simple, since they must consist of parts both co-existent and successive, as the generating sensations themselves do.

Now, that the simple ideas of sensation are thus generated, agreeably to the proposition, appears, because the most vivid of these ideas are those where the corresponding sensations are most vigorously impressed, or most frequently renewed; whereas, if the sensation be faint, or uncommon, the generated idea is also faint in proportion, and, in extreme cases, evanescent and imperceptible. The exact observance of the order of place in visible ideas, and of the order of time in audible ones, may likewise serve to shew, that these ideas are copies and offsprings of the impressions made on the eye and ear, in which the same orders were observed respectively. And though it happens, that trains of visible and audible ideas are presented in sallies of the fancy, and in dreams, in which the order of time and place is different from that of any former impressions, yet the small component parts of these trains are copies of former impressions; and reasons may be given for the varieties of their compositions.

It is also to be observed, that this proposition bears a great resemblance to the third; and that, by this resemblance, they somewhat confirm and illustrate one another. According to the third proposition, sensations remain for a short time after the impression is removed; and these remaining sensations grow feebler and feebler, till they vanish. They are therefore, in some part of their declension, of about the same strength with ideas, and in their first state, are intermediate between sensations and ideas. And it seems reasonable to expect, that, if a single sensation can leave a perceptible effect, trace, or vestige, for a short time, a sufficient repetition of a sensation may leave a perceptible effect of the same kind, but of a more permanent nature, *i. e.* an idea, which shall recur occasionally, at long distances of time, from the impression of the corresponding sensation, and *vice versa*. As to the occasions and causes, which make ideas recur, they will be considered in the next proposition but one.

The method of reasoning used in the last paragraph is farther confirmed by the following circumstance; *viz.* that both the diminutive declining sensations, which remain for a short space after the impressions of the objects cease, and the ideas, which are the copies of such impressions, are far more distinct and vivid, in respect of visible and audible impressions, than of any others. To which it may be added, that, after travelling, hearing music, etc. trains of vivid ideas are very apt to recur, which correspond very exactly to the late impressions, and which are of an intermediate nature between the remaining sensations of the third proposition, in their greatest vigour, and the ideas mentioned in this.

The sensations of feeling, taste and smell, can scarce be said to leave ideas, unless very indistinct and obscure ones. However, as analogy leads one to suppose that these sensations may leave traces of the same kind, though not in the same degree, as those of sight and hearing; so the readiness with which we reconnoitre sensations of feeling, taste, and smell, that have been often impressed, is an evidence that they do so; and these generated traces or dispositions of mind may be called the ideas of feeling, taste, and smell. In sleep, when all our ideas are magnified, those of feeling, taste, and smell, are often sufficiently vivid and distinct; and the same thing happens in some few cases of vigilance. . . .

PROP. X: ANY SENSATIONS A, B, C, ETC. BY BEING ASSOCIATED WITH ONE ANOTHER A SUFFICIENT NUMBER OF TIMES, GET SUCH A POWER OVER THE CORRESPONDING IDEAS a, b, c, ETC. THAT ANY ONE OF THE SENSATIONS A, WHEN IMPRESSED ALONE, SHALL BE ABLE TO EXCITE

IN THE MIND, b, c, ETC. THE IDEAS OF THE REST. Sensations may be said to be associated together, when their impressions are either made precisely at the same instant of time, or in the contiguous successive instants. We may therefore distinguish association into two sorts, the synchronous, and the successive.

The influence of association over our ideas, opinions, and affections, is so great and obvious, as scarcely to have escaped the notice of any writer who has treated of these, though the word *association*, in the particular sense here affixed to it, was first brought into use by Mr. Locke. But all that has been delivered by the ancients and moderns, concerning the power of habit, custom, example, education, authority, party-prejudice, the manner of learning the manual and liberal arts, etc. goes upon this doctrine as its foundation, and may be considered as the detail of it, in various circumstances. I here begin with the simplest case, and shall proceed to more and more complex ones continually, till I have exhausted what has occurred to me upon this subject.

This proposition, or first and simplest case of association, is manifest from innumerable common observations. Thus, the names, smells, tastes, and tangible qualities of natural bodies, suggest their visible appearances to the fancy, *i. e.* excite their visible ideas; and, *vice versa*, their visible appearances impressed on the eye raise up those powers of reconnoitring their names, smells, tastes, and tangible qualities, which may not improperly be called their ideas, as above noted; and in some cases raise up ideas, which may be compared with visible ones, in respect of vividness. All which is plainly owing to the association of the several sensible qualities of bodies with their names, and with each other. It is remarkable, however, as being agreeable to the superior vividness of visible and audible ideas, before taken notice of, that the suggestion of the visible appearance from the name is the most ready of any other; and, next to this, that of the name from the visible appearance; in which last case, the reality of the audible idea, when not evident to the fancy, may be inferred from the ready pronunciation of the name. For it will be shewn hereafter, that the audible idea is most commonly a previous requisite to pronunciation. Other instances of the power of association may be taken from compound visible and audible impressions. Thus the sight of part of a large building suggests the idea of the rest instantaneously; and the sound of the words which begin a familiar sentence, brings the remaining part to our memories in order, the association of the parts being synchronous in the first case, and successive in the last.

It is to be observed, that, in successive associations, the power of raising the ideas is only exerted according to the order in which the association is made. Thus, if the impressions A, B, C, be always made in the order of the alphabet, B impressed alone will not raise a, but c only. Agreeably to which it is easy to repeat familiar sentences in the order in which they always occur, but impossible to do it readily in an inverted one. The reason of this is, that the compound idea, c, b, a, corresponds to the compound sensation C, B, A; and therefore requires the impression of C, B, A, in the same manner as a, b, c, does that of A, B, C. This will, however, be more evident, when we come to consider the associations of vibratory motions, in the next proposition.

It is also to be observed, that the power of association grows feebler, as the number either of synchronous or successive impressions is increased, and does not extend, with due force, to more than a small one, in the first and simplest cases. But, in complex cases, or the associations of associations, of which the memory, in its full extent, consists, the powers of the mind, deducible from this source, will be found much greater than any person, upon his first entrance on these inquiries, could well imagine.

PROP. XI: ANY VIBRATIONS, A, B, C, ETC. BY BEING ASSOCIATED TOGETHER A SUFFICIENT NUMBER OF TIMES, GET SUCH A POWER OVER a, b, c, ETC. THE CORRESPONDING MINIATURE VIBRATIONS, THAT ANY OF THE VIBRATIONS A, WHEN IMPRESSED ALONE, SHALL BE ABLE TO EXCITE b, c, ETC. THE MINIATURES OF THE REST. This proposition may be deduced from the foregoing, . . . [but] it seems also deducible from the nature of vibrations, and of an animal body. Let A and B be two vibrations, associated synchronically. Now, it is evident, that the vibration A (for I will, in this proposition, speak of A and B in the singular number, for the sake of greater clearness) will, by endeavouring to diffuse itself into those parts of the medullary substance which are affected primarily by the vibration

The Doctrines of Vibrations and Association in General 77

B, in some measure modify and change B, so as to make B a little different from what it would be, if impressed alone. For the same reasons the vibration A will be a little affected, even in its primary seat, by the endeavour of B to diffuse itself all over the medullary substance. Suppose now the vibrations A and B to be impressed at the same instant, for a thousand times; it follows, from the ninth proposition, that they will first overcome the disposition to the natural vibrations N, and then leave a tendency to themselves, which will now occupy the place of the original natural tendency to vibrations. When therefore the vibration A is impressed alone, it cannot be entirely such as the object would excite of itself, but must lean, even in its primary seat, to the modifications and changes induced by B, during their thousand joint impressions; and therefore much more, in receding from this primary seat, will it lean that way; and when it comes to the seat of B, it will excite B's miniature a little modified and changed by itself.

Or thus: When A is impressed alone, some vibration must take place in the primary seat of B, both on account of the heat and pulsation of the arteries, and because A will endeavour to diffuse itself over the whole medullary substance. This cannot be that part of the natural vibrations N, which belongs to this region, because it is supposed to be overruled already. It cannot be that which A impressed alone would have propagated into this region, because that has always hitherto been overruled, and converted into B; and therefore cannot have begotten a tendency to itself. It cannot be any full vivid vibration, such as B, C, D, etc. belonging to this region, because all full vibrations require the actual impression of an object upon the corresponding external organ. And of miniature vibrations belonging to this region, such as b, c, d, etc. it is evident, that b has the preference, since A leans to it a little, even in its own primary seat, more and more, in receding from this, and almost entirely, when it comes to the primary seat of B. For the same reasons B impressed alone will excite a; and, in general, if A, B, C, etc. be vibrations synchronically impressed on different regions of the medullary substance, A impressed alone will at last excite b, c, etc. according to the proposition.

If A and B be vibrations impressed successively, then will the latter part of A, *viz.* that part which, according to the third and fourth propositions, remains, after the impression of the object ceases, be modified and altered by B, at the same time that it will a little modify and alter it, till at last it be quite overpowered by it, and end in it. It follows therefore, by a like method of reasoning, that the successive impression of A and B, sufficiently repeated, will so alter the medullary substance, as that when A is impressed alone, its latter part shall not be such as the sole impression of A requires, but lean towards B, and end in b at last. But B will not excite a in a retrograde order; since, by supposition, the latter part of B was not modified and altered by A, but by some other vibration, such as C or D. And as B, by being followed by C, may at last raise c; so b, when raised by A, in the method here proposed, may be also sufficient to raise c; inasmuch as the miniature c being a feeble motion, not stronger, perhaps, than the natural vibrations N, requires only to have its kind, place, and line of direction, determined by association, the heat and arterial pulsation conveying to it the requisite degree of strength. And thus A impressed alone will raise b, c, etc. in successive associations, as well as in synchronous ones, according to the proposition.

It seems also, that the influence of A may, in some degree, reach through B to C; so that A of itself may have some effect to raise c, as well as by means of b. However, it is evident, that this chain must break off, at last, in long successions; and that sooner or later, according to the number and vigour of the repeated impressions. The power of miniature vibrations to raise other miniatures may, perhaps, be made clearer to mathematicians, by hinting, that the efficacy of any vibration to raise any other, is not in the simple ratio of its vividness, but as some power thereof less than unity; for thus b may raise c, a weaker vibration than b, c may raise d, etc. with more facility than if the efficacy was in the simple ratio of the vividness, and yet so that the series shall break off at last. . . .

[We] may prove this in somewhat a shorter and easier manner, as follows. Since the vibrations A and B are impressed together, they must, from the diffusion necessary to vibratory motions, run into one vibration; and consequently, after a number of impressions sufficiently repeated, will leave a trace, or miniature, of themselves, as one vibration, which will recur every now and then, from slight causes. Much rather, therefore, may the part b of the compound miniature $a + b$ recur, when the part A of the compound original vibration $A + B$ is impressed. . . .

[The] power of association is founded upon, and necessarily requires, the previous power of forming ideas, and miniature vibrations. For ideas, and miniature vibrations, must first be generated, . . . before they can be associated. . . . But then (which is very remarkable) this power of forming ideas, and their corresponding miniature vibrations, does equally presuppose the power of association. For since all sensations and vibrations are infinitely divisible, in respect of time and place, they could not leave any traces or images of themselves, *i. e.* any ideas, or miniature vibrations, unless their infinitesimal parts did cohere together through joint impression, *i. e.* association. Thus, to mention a gross instance, we could have no proper idea of a horse, unless the particular ideas of the head, neck, body, legs, and tail, peculiar to this animal, stuck to each other in the fancy, from frequent joint impression. And, therefore, in dreams, where complex associations are much weakened, and various parcels of visible ideas, not joined in nature, start up together in the fancy, contiguous to each other, we often see monsters, chimeras, and combinations, which have never been actually presented.

Association seems also necessary to dispose the medullary substance to this or that miniature vibration, in succession, after the miniatures of a large number of original vibrations have been generated.

Nor does there seem to be any precise limit which can be set to this mutual dependence of the powers of generating miniatures, and of association upon each other: however they may both take place together, as the heart and brain are supposed to do, or both depend upon one simple principle; for it seems impossible, that they should imply one another *ad infinitum.* There is no greater difficulty here than in many other cases of mutual indefinite implication, known and allowed by all. Nay, one may almost deduce some presumption in favour of the hypothesis here produced, from this mutual indefinite implication of its parts so agreeable to the tenor of nature in other things. And it is certainly a presumption in its favour, that a less power of generating miniatures will be a foundation for a larger of association, and *vice versa,* till, at last, the whole superstructure of ideas and associations observable in human life may, by proceeding upwards according to analysis, and downwards according to synthesis, be built upon as small a foundation as we please. . . . The least miniatures, with the feeblest cohesions of their parts, will, by degrees, run into larger, with stronger cohesions, from the same principles; nor are there any visible limits to the influence and extent of these powers, supposing the natural faculties of the being under consideration sufficiently extended.

Let me add, that the generation of sensible ideas from sensations, and the power of raising them from association, when considered as faculties of the mind, are evident and unquestionable. Since therefore sensations are conveyed to the mind, by the efficiency of corporeal causes of the medullary substance, as is acknowledged by all physiologists and physicians, it seems to me, that the powers of generating ideas, and raising them by association, must also arise from corporeal causes, and consequently admit of an explication from the subtle influences of the small parts of matter upon each other, as soon as these are sufficiently understood; which is farther evinced from the manifest influences of material causes upon our ideas and associations, taken notice of under the second proposition. And as a vibratory motion is more suitable to the nature of sensation than any other species of motion, so does it seem also more suitable to the powers of generating ideas, and raising them by association. However, these powers are evident independently, as just now observed; so that the doctrine of association may be laid down as a certain foundation, and a clew to direct our future inquiries, whatever becomes of that of vibrations.

PROP. XII: SIMPLE IDEAS WILL RUN INTO COMPLEX ONES, BY MEANS OF ASSOCIATION. In order to explain and prove this proposition, it will be requisite to give some previous account of the manner in which simple ideas of sensation may be associated together.

Case 1. Let the sensation A be often associated with each of the sensations B, C, D, etc. *i. e.* at certain times with B, at certain other times with C, etc. it is evident, from the tenth proposition, that A, impressed alone, will, at last, raise b, c, d, etc. all together,

The Doctrines of Vibrations and Association in General   81

i. e. associate them with one another, provided they belong to different regions of the medullary substance; for if any two, or more, belong to the same region, since they cannot exist together in their distinct forms, A will raise something intermediate between them.

Case 2. If the sensations A, B, C, D, etc. be associated together, according to various combinations of twos, or even threes, fours, etc. then will A raise b, c, d, etc. also B raise a, c, d, etc. as in case the first.

It may happen, indeed, in both cases, that A may raise a particular miniature, as b, preferably to any of the rest, from its being more associated with B, from the novelty of the impression of B, from a tendency in the medullary substance to favour b, etc. and in like manner, that b may raise c or d preferably to the rest. However, all this will be over-ruled, at last, by the recurrency of the associations; so that any one of the sensations will excite the ideas of the rest at the same instant, *i. e.* associate them together.

Case 3. Let A, B, C, D, etc. represent successive impressions, it follows from the tenth and eleventh propositions, that A will raise b, c, d, etc. B raise c, d, etc. And though the ideas do not, in this case, rise precisely at the same instant, yet they come nearer together than the sensations themselves did in their original impression; so that these ideas are associated almost synchronically at last, and successively from the first. The ideas come nearer to one another than the sensations, on account of their diminutive nature, by which all that appertains to them is contracted. And this seems to be as agreeable to observation as to theory.

Case 4. All compound impressions $A + B + C + D$, etc. after sufficient repetition leave compound miniatures $a + b + c + d$, etc. which recur every now and then from slight causes, as well such as depend on association, as some which are different from it. Now, in these recurrences of compound miniatures, the parts are farther associated, and approach perpetually nearer to each other, agreeably to what was just now observed; *i. e.* the association becomes perpetually more close and intimate.

Case 5. When the ideas a, b, c, d, etc. have been sufficiently associated in any one or more of the foregoing ways, if we suppose any single idea of these, a for instance, to be raised by the tendency of the medullary substance that way, by the association of A with a foreign sensation or idea X or x, etc. this idea a, thus raised, will frequently bring in all the rest, b, c, d, etc. and so associate all of them together still farther.

And upon the whole, it may appear to the reader, that the simple ideas of sensation must run into clusters and combinations, by association; and that each of these will, at last, coalesce into one complex idea, by the approach and commixture of the several compounding parts.

It appears also from observation, that many of our intellectual ideas, such as those that belong to the heads of beauty, honour, moral qualities, etc. are, in fact, thus composed of parts, which, by degrees, coalesce into one complex idea.

And as this coalescence of simple ideas into complex ones is thus evinced, both by the foregoing theory, and by observation, so it may be illustrated, and farther confirmed, by the similar coalescence of letters into syllables and words, in which association is likewise a chief instrument. I shall mention some of the most remarkable particulars, relating to this coalescence of simple ideas into complex ones, in the following corollaries.

Cor. I. If the number of simple ideas which compose the complex one be very great, it may happen, that the complex idea shall not appear to bear any relation to these its compounding parts, nor to the external senses upon which the original sensations, which gave birth to the compounding ideas, were impressed. The reason of this is, that each single idea is overpowered by the sum of all the rest, as soon as they are all intimately united together. Thus in very compound medicines the several tastes and flavours of the separate ingredients are lost and overpowered by the complex one of the whole mass: so that this has a taste and flavour of its own, which appears to be simple and original, and like that of a natural body. Thus also, white is vulgarly thought to be the simplest and most uncompounded of all colours, while yet it really arises from a certain proportion of the seven primary colours, with their several shades or degrees. And to resume the illustration above-mentioned, taken from language, it does not at all appear to persons ignorant of the arts of reading and writing, that the great variety of complex words of languages can be analysed up to a few simple sounds.

COR. II. One may hope, therefore, that, by pursuing and perfecting the doctrine of association, we may some time or other be enabled to analyse all that vast variety of complex ideas, which pass under the name of ideas of reflection, and intellectual ideas, into their simple compounding parts, *i. e.* into the simple ideas of sensation, of which they consist. This would be greatly analogous to the arts of writing, and resolving the colour of the sun's light, or natural bodies, into their primary constituent ones. The complex ideas which I here speak of, are generally excited by words, or visible objects; but they are also connected with other external impressions, and depend upon them, as upon symbols. In whatever way we consider them, the trains of them which are presented to the mind seem to depend upon the then present state of the body, the external impressions, and the remaining influence of prior impressions and associations taken together.

COR. III. It would afford great light and clearness to the art of logic, thus to determine the precise nature and composition of the ideas affixed to those words which have complex ideas, in a proper sense, *i. e.* which excite any combinations of simple ideas united intimately by association; also to explain, upon this foundation, the proper use of those words, which have no ideas. For there are many words which are mere substitutes for other words, and many which are only auxiliaries. Now it cannot be said, that either of these have ideas, properly so called. And though it may seem an infinite and impossible task, thus to analyse the significations and uses of words, yet, I suppose, this would not be more difficult, with the present philological and philosophical helps to such a work, than the first making of dictionaries and grammars, in the infancy of philology. Perhaps it may not be amiss just to hint, in this place, that the four following classes comprise all the possible kinds into which words can be distinguished, agreeably to the plan here proposed:

1. Words which have ideas, but no definitions.
2. Words which have both ideas and definitions.
3. Words which have definitions, but no ideas.
4. Words which have neither ideas nor definitions.

It is quite manifest, that words seen or heard, can raise no ideas in the mind, or vibrations in the brain, distinct from their visible and audible impressions, except as far as they get new powers from associations, either incidental ones or arising from express design, as in definitions; and therefore, that all other ways of considering words, besides what is here suggested, are either false or imperfect.

Cor. IV. As simple ideas run into complex ones by association, so complex ideas run into decomplex ones by the same. But here the varieties of the associations, which increase with the complexity, hinder particular ones from being so close and permanent, between the complex parts of decomplex ideas, as between the simple parts of complex ones: to which it is analogous, in languages, that the letters of words adhere closer together than the words of sentences, both in writing and speaking.

Cor. V. The simple ideas of sensation are not all equally and uniformly concerned in forming complex and decomplex ideas; *i. e.* these do not result from all the possible combinations of twos, threes, fours, etc. of all the simple ideas; but, on the contrary, some simple ideas occur in the complex and decomplex ones much oftener than others; and the same holds of particular combinations by twos, threes, etc. and innumerable combinations never occur at all in real life, and, consequently, are never associated into complex or decomplex ideas. All which corresponds to what happens in real languages; some letters, and combinations of letters, occur much more frequently than others, and some combinations never occur at all.

Cor. VI. As persons who speak the same language have, however, a different use and extent of words, so, though mankind, in all ages and nations, agree, in general, in their complex and decomplex ideas, yet there are many particular differences in them; and these differences are greater or less, according to the difference, or resemblance, in age, constitution, education, profession, country, age of the world, etc. *i. e.* in their impressions and associations.

Cor. VII. When a variety of ideas are associated together, the visible idea, being more glaring and distinct than the rest, performs the office of a symbol to all the rest, suggests them, and connects them together. In this it somewhat resembles the first letter of a word, or first word of a sentence, which are often made use of to bring all the rest to mind.

Cor. VIII. When objects and ideas, with their most common combinations, have been often presented to the mind, a train of them, of a considerable length, may, by once occurring, leave such a trace, as to recur in imagination, and in miniature, in nearly the same order and proportion as in this single occurrence. For, since each of the particular impressions and ideas is familiar, there will want little more for their recurrency, than a few connecting links; and even these may be, in some measure, supplied by former similar instances. These considerations, when duly unfolded, seem to me sufficient to explain the chief phænomena of memory; and it will be easily seen from them, that the memory of adults, and masters in any science, ought to be much more ready and certain than that of children and novices, as it is found to be in fact.

Cor. IX. When the pleasure or pain attending any sensations and ideas is great, all the associations belonging to them are much accelerated and strengthened. For the violent vibrations excited in such cases, soon overrule the natural vibrations, and leave in the brain a strong tendency to themselves, from a few impressions. The associations will therefore be cemented sooner and stronger than in common cases; which is found agreeable to the fact.

Cor. X. As many words have complex ideas annexed to them, so sentences, which are collections of words, have collections of complex ideas, *i. e.* have decomplex ideas. And it happens, in most cases, that the decomplex idea belonging to any sentence is not compounded merely of the complex ideas belonging to the words of it; but that there are also many variations, some oppositions, and numberless additions. Thus, propositions, in particular, excite, as soon as heard, assent or dissent, which assent and dissent consist chiefly of additional complex ideas, not included in the terms of the proposition. And it would be of the greatest use, both in the sciences and in common life, thoroughly to analyse the matter, to shew in what manner, and by what steps, *i. e.* by what impressions and associations, our assent and dissent, both in scientifical and moral subjects, is formed. . . .

PROP. XX: ALL THAT HAS BEEN DELIVERED ABOVE, CONCERNING THE DERIVATION OF IDEAL VIBRATIUNCLES FROM SENSORY VIBRATIONS, AND CONCERNING THEIR ASSOCIATIONS, MAY BE FITLY APPLIED TO MOTORY VIBRATIONS AND VIBRATIUNCLES. This proposition is the immediate consequence of admitting the doctrines of vibrations and association, in the manner in which they have been asserted in the foregoing propositions. It contains the theory of the voluntary and semi-voluntary motions; to facilitate the application of which theory in the next proposition, I shall deliver the principal cases of this, in the follow corollaries.

Cor. I. The motory vibrations . . . will generate a propensity to corresponding motory vibratiuncles.

Cor. II. These motory vibratiuncles will affect the brain, as well as the motory nerves along which they descend; and, indeed, their descent along the motory nerves will be principally owing to their being first excited in the brain. This is sufficiently evident in the motory vibratiuncles which are derived from the motory vibrations of the second and third classes. As to the motory vibrations of the other classes, it is evident, that the brain is strongly affected by the sensory vibrations which give birth to them, and consequently, that a proportional affection of the brain must take place in the motory vibratiuncles derived from them.

Cor. III. The motory vibratiuncles will cohere to one another, by associations both synchronous and successive. Hence the simple parts, of which complex and decomplex motions are compounded, may cohere closely, and succeed readily to each other.

Cor. IV. The motory vibratiuncles will also cohere to ideal ones by association. Common ideas may therefore excite motory vibratiuncles, and consequently be able to contract the muscles, provided the active powers lodged in their fibres and blood globules be sufficiently exalted for this purpose.

Cor. V. If we suppose the ideal vibratiuncles to be so much increased . . . as to be equal in strength to the usual sensory vibrations, the motory vibratiuncles connected with them by association must be supposed to be increased proportionably. Hence ideas may occasion muscular motions of the same strength with the automatic motions.

Cor. VI. The third and last connexion of the motory vibratiuncles is that with sensory vibrations, foreign to them, *i. e.* such as had no share in generating the motory vibratiuncles under consideration. Particular motions of the body may therefore by association be made to depend upon sensations, with which they have no natural and original connexion.

Cor. VII. As muscular motion has three connexions deducible from association, *viz.* those mentioned in the third, fourth, and sixth corollaries, so the sensations and ideas have the same three connexions. Hence the whole doctrine of association may be comprised in the following theorem, *viz.*

If any sensation A, *idea* B, *or muscular motion* C, *be associated for a sufficient number of times with any other sensation* D, *idea* E, *or muscular motion* F, *it will, at last, excite* d, *the simple idea belonging to the sensation* D, *the very idea* E, *or the very muscular motion* F.

The reader will observe, that association cannot excite the real sensation *D*, because the impression of the sensible object is necessary for this purpose. However, in certain morbid cases, the idea is magnified so as to equal, or even overpower, sensible impressions.

Words and the Ideas Associated with Them

PROP. LXXX: TO DESCRIBE THE MANNER IN WHICH IDEAS ARE ASSOCIATED WITH WORDS, BEGINNING FROM CHILDHOOD. This may be done by applying the doctrine of association, as laid down in the first chapter, to words. . . .

First, then, the association of the names of visible objects, with the impressions which these objects make upon the eye, seems to take place more early than any other, and to be effected in the following manner: the name of the visible object, the nurse, for instance, is pronounced and repeated by the attendants to the child, more frequently when his eye is fixed upon the nurse, than when upon other objects, and much more so than when upon any particular one. The word *nurse* is also sounded in an emphatical manner, when the child's eye is directed to the nurse with earnestness and desire. The association therefore of the sound *nurse,* with the picture of the nurse upon the *retina,* will be far stronger than that with any other visible impression, and thus overpower all the other accidental associations, which will also themselves contribute to the same end by opposing one another. And when the child has gained so much voluntary power over his motions, as to direct his head and eyes towards the nurse upon hearing her name, this process will go on with an accelerated velocity. And thus, at last, the word will excite the visible idea readily and certainly.

The same association of the picture of the nurse in the eye with the sound *nurse*, will, by degrees, overpower all the accidental associations of this picture with other words, and be so firmly cemented at last, that the picture will excite the audible idea of the word. But this is not to our present purpose. I mention it here as taking place at the same time with the foregoing process, and contributing to illustrate and confirm it. Both together afford a complete instance for the tenth and eleventh propositions, *i. e.* they shew, that when the impressions A and B are sufficiently associated, A impressed alone will excite b, B impressed alone will excite a.

Secondly, this association of words with visible appearances, being made under many particular circumstances, must affect the visible ideas with a like particularity. Thus the nurse's dress, and the situation of the fire in the child's nursery, make part of the child's ideas of his nurse and fire. But then as the nurse often changes her dress, and the child often sees a fire in a different place, and surrounded by different visible objects, these opposite associations must be less strong than the part which is common to them all; and consequently we may suppose, that while his idea of that part which is common, and which we may call essential, continues the same, that of the particularities, circumstances, and adjuncts, varies. For he cannot have any idea, but with some particularities in the non-essentials.

Thirdly, when the visible objects impress other vivid sensations besides those of sight, such as grateful or ungrateful tastes, smells, warmth, or coldness, with sufficient frequency, it follows from the foregoing theory that these sensations must leave traces, or ideas, which will be associated with the names of the objects, so as to depend upon them. Thus an idea, or nascent perception, of the sweetness of the nurse's milk will rise up in that part of the child's brain which corresponds to the nerves of taste, upon his hearing her name. And hence the whole idea belonging to the word *nurse* now begins to be complex, as consisting of a visible idea, and an idea of taste. And these two ideas will be associated together, not only because the word raises them both, but also because the original sensations are. The strongest may therefore assist in raising the weakest. Now, in common cases, the visible idea is strongest, or occurs most readily at least; but, in the present instance, it seems to be otherwise. We might proceed in like manner to shew the generation of ideas more and more complex, and the various ways by which their parts are cemented together, and all made to depend on the respective names of the visible objects. But what has been said may suffice to shew what ideas the names of visible objects, proper and appellative, raise in us.

Fourthly, we must, however, observe, in respect of appellatives, that sometimes the idea is the common compound result of all the sensible impressions received from the several objects comprised under the general appellation; sometimes the particular idea of some one of these, in great measure at least, *viz.* when the impressions arising from some one are more novel, frequent, and vivid, than those from the rest.

Fifthly, the words denoting sensible qualities, whether substantive or adjective, such as *whiteness, white,* etc. get their ideas in a manner which will be easily understood from what has been already delivered. Thus the word *white,* being associated with the visible appearance of milk, linen, paper, gets a stable power of exciting the idea of what is common to all, and a variable one, in respect of the particularities, circumstances, and adjuncts. And so of other sensible qualities.

Sixthly, the names of visible actions, as walking, striking, etc. raise the proper visible ideas by a like process. Other ideas may likewise adhere in certain cases, as in those of tasting, feeling, speaking, etc. Sensible perceptions, in which no visible action is concerned, as hearing, may also leave ideas dependent on words. However, some visible ideas generally intermix themselves here. These actions and perceptions are generally denoted by verbs, though sometimes by substantives.

And we may now see in what manner ideas are associated with nouns, proper and appellative, substantive and adjective, and with verbs, supposing that they denote sensible things only. Pronouns and particles remain to be considered. Now, in order to know their ideas and uses, we must observe.

Seventhly, that as children may learn to read words not only in an elementary way, *viz.* by learning the letters and syllables of which they are composed, but also in a summary one, *viz.* by associating the sound of entire words, with their pictures, in the eye; and must, in some cases, be taught in the last way, *i. e.* wheresoever the sound of the word deviates from that of its elements; so both children and adults learn the ideas belonging to whole sentences many times in a summary way, and not by adding together the ideas of the several words in the sentence. And wherever words occur, which, separately taken, have no proper ideas, their use can be learnt in no other way but this. Now pronouns and particles, and many other words, are of this kind. They answer, in some measure, to x, y, and z, or the unknown quantities in algebra, being determinable and decypherable, as one may say, only by means of the known words with which they are joined.

Thus *I walk* is associated at different times with the same visible impression as *nurse walks, brother walks,* etc. and therefore can suggest nothing permanently for a long time but the action of walking. However the pronoun *I*, in this and innumerable other short sentences, being always associated with the person speaking, as *thou* is with the person spoken to, and *he* with the person spoken of, the frequent recurrency of this teaches the child the use of the pronouns, *i. e.* teaches him what difference he is to expect in his sensible impressions according as this or that pronoun is used; the infinite number of instances, as one may say, making up for the infinitely small quantity of information, which each, singly taken, conveys.

In like manner, different particles, *i. e.* adverbs, conjunctions, and prepositions, being used in sentences, where the substantives, adjectives, and verbs, are the same, and the same particles, where these are different, in an endless recurrency, teach children the use of the particles in a gross general way. For it may be observed, that children are much at a loss for the true use of the pronouns and particles for some years, and that they often repeat the proper name of the person instead of the pronoun; which confirms the foregoing reasoning. Some of the inferior parts or particles of speech make scarce any alteration in the sense of the sentence, and therefore are called expletives. The several terminations of the Greek and Latin nouns and verbs are of the nature of pronouns and particles. . . .

* * *

A period of eighty years elapsed between Hartley's *Observations* and the publication of the major work of his intellectual successor, James Mill. Although no great advances were made in association theory during this time, its basic laws were being adopted by writers in widely varying fields, so that the apparent interregnum of almost a century was actually a time of consolidation of associationistic concepts into the intellectual life of the period. Economics, ethics, biology were all being influenced by this peculiar brand of empiricism, and even schools of psychology basically opposite in spirit, such as the faculty psychology flourishing in Scotland, were influenced by the laws of association. One representative of the Scottish school, Thomas Brown, attempted an amalgamation between the nativistic approach of faculty psychology and the empirical approach of British associationism. His work, published in 1820, influenced James Mill, but is of interest here primarily because of his discussion of a problem which was to plague any thoroughgoing associationism.[*]

As we shall see subsequently, it was going to be embarrassingly difficult to explain the perception and the use of relations within a strict associationist framework. How does the idea or image of "small a and large b" become transmuted into the idea of "greater than"? In one sense, Brown's answer is no answer at all, in that he says that this is merely one of the mind's capabilities, an innate capacity or sensibility to perceive relations. Nevertheless

[*] T. Brown, *Lectures on the philosophy of the human mind.* Edinburgh: Black, 1820.

he recognizes the importance of this mental process and that it is fundamentally different from the process of association:

> ... [The] feelings of relation are states of the mind essentially different from our simple perceptions, or conceptions of the objects that seem to us related, or from the combinations which we form of these, in the complex groupings of our fancy. . . . There is an original tendency or susceptibility of the mind, by which, on perceiving together different objects, we are instantly, without the intervention of any other mental process, sensible of their relation. . . .*

The admission of an extra-associational principle to his psychology allowed him a flexibility not to be found in the better-known system developed by James Mill and published in 1829.

Mill followed in Hartley's footsteps in making the concept of association the cornerstone of the mind's operations. From his basic analysis of the laws of association—a part of which is presented in the following selection—he proceeds to extend it to every facet of mental life: naming, language development, belief, reasoning, motivation, and the will. From Hartley's beginnings a complete system has emerged. In one sense, psychology has come into its own. There is an optimism about Mill's volumes: the mysteries of the mind have been pried open; in theory everything is available for study and analysis right down to its roots. Since all aspects of mental life have been built up from simple elements by means of a simple process, presumably nothing stands in the way of eventually analyzing the most complex processes of human thought. We have arrived at the height of the atomistic analysis of the conscious mind, which at this stage of psychology *is* mind. As can be seen in the last paragraph of his chapter on the association of ideas, the idea of "everything" is an enormous collection of the organism's past experience, which presumably could be laid bare by careful analysis. In turn, this past experience is in large part potentially recoverable since in memory we rapidly trace back each link in the chain.

But in exchange for this grand unifying principle, we must ac-

---

* T. Brown, *Lectures on the philosophy of the human mind,* 19th ed. Edinburgh: Black, 1851, p. 288.

cept vague generalities when it comes to the fine points. Thus Mill can analyze the process of reasoning or ratiocination in a total of three pages and conclude that it is, obviously, a complicated case of association. This brief chapter is appended to the more lengthy analysis of belief; what the problem of reasoning comes down to, then, is what makes us believe in the conclusion we draw from the premises of a syllogism.

Mill's famous son, John Stuart Mill, who edited and annotated his father's works, includes a footnote to the chapter on reasoning, in which he points out that reasoning does not *consist* of syllogisms; rather the latter are a means of checking the truth of conclusions drawn from a chain of reasoning—a point already made very clearly by Locke (see p. 44). This note is typical of the younger Mill's contribution to associationism. He takes the bare structure of his father's grand design and wherever possible makes the analysis both more sophisticated and more plausible. But in so doing, the nature of associationism is subtly changed. Take, for example, the following famous passage from the *Logic*:

. . . [The] laws of the phenomena of mind are sometimes analogous to mechanical, but sometimes also to chemical laws. When many impressions or ideas are operating in the mind together, there sometimes takes place a process, of a similar kind to chemical combination. When impressions have been so often experienced in conjunction, that each of them calls up readily and instantaneously the ideas of the whole group, those ideas sometimes melt and coalesce into one another, and appear not several ideas but one; in the same manner as, when the seven prismatic colours are presented to the eye in rapid succession, the sensation produced is that of white. But as in this last case it is correct to say that the seven colours when they rapidly follow one another *generate* white, but not that they actually *are* white; so it appears to me that the Complex Idea, formed by the blending together of several simpler ones, should, when it really appears simple (that is, when the separate elements are not consciously distinguishable in it), be said to *result from,* or *be generated by,* the simple ideas, not to *consist* of them.*

* J. S. Mill, *A system of logic,* 8th ed. New York: Harper, 1874, p. 592. First edition: 1843.

This view saves us from the difficulties of stating that the conscious idea of white consists of all the colors of the rainbow, an extension of the use of the term "consciousness" so extreme that it may be responsible in part for its ultimate rejection in the theory of thinking. At the same time the facts of psychology that only recently had seemed so clear and obvious suddenly became complicated again. For there is no reason to assume that the laws applying to a mental chemistry will be the same as those of a mental mechanics. Although the laws of association may account for the acquisition of simple ideas, we find a new principle in the way they form themselves into more complex ideas. Instead of simple addition of particles we are faced with—what? Multiplication? And higher order laws to go with it?

* * *

James Mill

The Association of Ideas

Thought succeeds thought; idea follows idea, incessantly. If our senses are awake, we are continually receiving sensations, of the eye, the ear, the touch, and so forth; but not sensations alone. After sensations, ideas are perpetually excited of sensations formerly received; after those ideas, other ideas: and during the whole of our lives, a series of those two states of consciousness, called sensations, and ideas, is constantly going on. I see a horse: that is a sensation. Immediately I think of his master: that is an

J. Mill, *Analysis of the phenomena of the human mind*, Vol. 1, 2nd ed. With notes illustrative and critical by Alexander Bain, Andrew Findlater, and George Grote. Edited with additional notes by John Stuart Mill. London: Longmans, Green, Reader, and Dyer, 1878, pp. 70–116. First edition: London, 1829.

idea. The idea of his master makes me think of his office; he is a minister of state: that is another idea. The idea of a minister of state makes me think of public affairs; and I am led into a train of political ideas; when I am summoned to dinner. This is a new sensation, followed by the idea of dinner, and of the company with whom I am to partake it. The sight of the company and of the food are other sensations; these suggest ideas without end; other sensations perpetually intervene, suggesting other ideas: and so the process goes on.

In contemplating this train of feelings, of which our lives consist, it first of all strikes the contemplator, as of importance to ascertain, whether they occur casually and irregularly, or according to a certain order.

With respect to the SENSATIONS, it is obvious enough that they occur, according to the order established among what we call the objects of nature, whatever those objects are; to ascertain more and more of which order is the business of physical philosophy in all its branches.

Of the order established among the objects of nature, by which we mean the objects of our senses, two remarkable cases are all which here we are called upon to notice; the SYNCHRONOUS ORDER and the SUCCESSIVE ORDER. The synchronous order, or order of simultaneous existence, is the order in space; the successive order, or order of antecedent and consequent existence, is the order in time. Thus the various objects in my room, the chairs, the tables, the books, have the synchronous order, or order in space. The falling of the spark, and the explosion of the gunpowder, have the successive order, or order in time.

According to this order, in the objects of sense, there is a synchronous, and a successive, order of our sensations. I have SYNCHRONICALLY, or at the same instant, the sight of a great variety of objects; touch of all the objects with which my body is in contact; hearing of all the sounds which are reaching my ears; smelling of all the smells which are reaching my nostrils; taste of the apple which I am eating; the sensation of resistance both from the apple which is in my mouth, and the ground on which I stand; with the sensation of motion from the act of walking. I have SUCCESSIVELY the sight of the flash from the mortar fired at a distance, the hearing of the report, the sight of the bomb, and of its motion in the air, the sight of its fall, the sight and hearing of its explosion, and lastly, the sight of all the effects of that explosion.

Among the objects which I have thus observed synchronically, or successively; that is, from which I have had synchronical or successive sensations; there are some which I have so observed frequently; others which I have so observed not frequently: in other words, of my sensations some have been frequently synchronical, others not frequently; some frequently successive, others not frequently. Thus, my sight of roast beef, and my taste of roast beef, have been frequently SYNCHRONICAL; my smell of a rose, and my sight and touch of a rose, have been frequently synchronical; my sight of a stone, and my sensations of its hardness, and weight, have been frequently synchronical. Others of my sensations have not been frequently synchronical: my sight of a lion, and the hearing of his roar; my sight of a knife, and its stabbing a man. My sight of the flash of lightning, and my hearing of the thunder, have been often SUCCESSIVE; the pain of cold, and the pleasure of heat, have been often successive; the sight of a trumpet, and the sound of a trumpet, have been often successive. On the other hand, my sight of hemlock, and my taste of hemlock, have not been often successive: and so on.

It so happens, that, of the objects from which we derive the greatest part of our sensations, most of those which are observed synchronically, are frequently observed synchronically; most of those which are observed successively, are frequently observed successively. In other words, most of our synchronical sensations, have been frequently synchronical; most of our successive sensations, have been frequently successive. Thus, most of our synchronical sensations are derived from the objects around us, the objects which we have the most frequent occasion to hear and see; the members of our family; the furniture of our houses; our food; the instruments of our occupations or amusements. In like manner, of those sensations which we have had in succession, we have had the greatest number repeatedly in succession; the sight of fire, and its warmth; the touch of snow, and its cold; the sight of food, and its taste.

Thus much with regard to the order of SENSATIONS; next with regard to the order of IDEAS.

As ideas are not derived from objects, we should not expect their order to be derived from the order of objects; but as they are derived from sensations, we might by analogy expect, that they would derive their order from that of the sensations; and this to a great extent is the case.

Our ideas spring up, or exist, in the order in which the sensations existed, of which they are the copies.

This is the general law of the "Association of Ideas"; by which term, let it be remembered, nothing is here meant to be expressed, but the order of occurrence.

In this law, the following things are to be carefully observed.
1 Of those sensations which occurred synchronically, the ideas also spring up synchronically. I have seen a violin, and heard the tones of the violin, synchronically. If I think of the tones of the violin, the visible appearance of the violin at the same time occurs to me. I have seen the sun, and the sky in which it is placed, synchronically. If I think of the one, I think of the other at the same time.

One of the cases of synchronical sensation, which deserves the most particular attention, is, that of the several sensations derived from one and the same object; a stone, for example, a flower, a table, a chair, a horse, a man.

From a stone I have had, synchronically, the sensation of colour, the sensation of hardness, the sensations of shape, and size, the sensation of weight. When the idea of one of these sensations occurs, the ideas of all of them occur. They exist in my mind synchronically; and their synchronical existence is called the idea of the stone; which, it is thus plain, is not a single idea, but a number of ideas in a particular state of combination.

Thus, again, I have smelt a rose, and looked at, and handled a rose, synchronically; accordingly the name rose suggests to me all those ideas synchronically; and this combination of those simple ideas is called my idea of the rose.

My idea of an animal is still more complex. The word thrush, for example, not only suggests an idea of a particular colour and shape, and size, but of song, and flight, and nestling, and eggs, and callow young, and others.

My idea of a man is the most complex of all; including not only colour, and shape, and voice, but the whole class of events in which I have observed him either the agent or the patient.

2 As the ideas of the sensations which occurred synchronically, rise synchronically, so the ideas of the sensations which occurred successively, rise successively.

Of this important case of association, or of the successive order of our ideas, many remarkable instances might be adduced. Of these none seems better adapted to the learner than the repetition of any passage, or words; the Lord's Prayer, for example, committed to memory. In learning the passage, we repeat it; that is, we pronounce the words, in successive order, from the beginning to the end. The order of the sensations is successive. When we proceed to repeat the passage, the ideas of the words also rise in succession, the preceding always suggesting the succeeding, and no other. *Our* suggests *Father, Father* suggests *which, which* suggests *art;* and so on, to the end. How remarkably this is the case, any one may convince himself, by trying to repeat backwards, even a passage with which he is as familiar as the Lord's Prayer. The case is the same with numbers. A man can go on with the numbers in the progressive order, one, two, three, etc. scarcely thinking of his act; and though it is possible for him to repeat them backward, because he is accustomed to subtraction of numbers, he cannot do so without an effort.

Of witnesses in courts of justice it has been remarked, that eye-witnesses, and ear-witnesses, always tell their story in the chronological order; in other words, the ideas occur to them in the order in which the sensations occurred; on the other hand, that witnesses, who are inventing, rarely adhere to the chronological order.

3 A far greater number of our sensations are received in the successive, than in the synchronical order. Of our ideas, also, the number is infinitely greater that rise in the successive than the synchronical order.

4 In the successive order of ideas, that which precedes, is sometimes called the suggesting, that which succeeds, the suggested idea; not that any power is supposed to reside in the antecedent over the consequent; suggesting, and suggested, mean only antecedent and consequent, with the additional idea, that such order is not casual, but, to a certain degree, permanent.

5 Of the antecedent and consequent feelings, or the suggesting, and suggested; the antecedent may be either sensations or ideas; the consequent are always ideas. An idea may be excited either by a sensation or an idea. The sight of the dog of my friend is a sensation, and it excites the idea of my friend. The idea of Professor Dugald Stewart delivering a lecture, recalls the idea of the delight with which I heard him; that, the idea of the studies in which it engaged me; that, the trains of thought which succeeded; and each epoch of my mental history, the succeeding one, till the present moment; in which I am endeavouring to present to others what appears to me valuable among the innumerable ideas of which this lengthened train has been composed.

6 As there are degrees in sensations, and degrees in ideas; for one sensation is more vivid than another sensation, one idea more vivid than another idea; so there are degrees in association. One association, we say, is stronger than another: first, when it is more permanent than another: secondly, when it is performed with more certainty: thirdly, when it is performed with more facility.

It is well known, that some associations are very transient, others very permanent. The case which we formerly mentioned, that of repeating words committed to memory, affords an apt illustration. In some cases, we can perform the repetition, when a few hours, or a few days have elapsed; but not after a longer period. In others, we can perform it after the lapse of many years. There are few children in whose minds some association has not been formed between darkness and ghosts. In some this association is soon dissolved; in some it continues for life.

In some cases the association takes place with less, in some with greater certainty. Thus, in repeating words, I am not sure that I shall not commit mistakes, if they are imperfectly got; and

I may at one trial repeat them right, at another wrong: I am sure of always repeating those correctly, which I have got perfectly. Thus, in my native language, the association between the name and the thing is certain; in a language with which I am imperfectly acquainted, not certain. In expressing myself in my own language, the idea of the thing suggests the idea of the name with certainty. In speaking a language with which I am imperfectly acquainted, the idea of the thing does not with certainty suggest the idea of the name; at one time it may, at another not.

That ideas are associated in some cases with more, in some with less facility, is strikingly illustrated by the same instance, of a language with which we are well, and a language with which we are imperfectly, acquainted. In speaking our own language, we are not conscious of any effort; the associations between the words and the ideas appear spontaneous. In endeavouring to speak a language with which we are imperfectly acquainted, we are sensible of a painful effort: the associations between the words and ideas being not ready, or immediate.

7 The causes of strength in association seem all to be resolvable into two; the vividness of the associated feelings; and the frequency of the association.

In general, we convey not a very precise meaning, when we speak of the vividness of sensations and ideas. We may be understood when we say that, generally speaking, the sensation is more vivid than the idea; or the primary, than the secondary feeling; though in dreams, and in delirium, ideas are mistaken for sensations. But when we say that one sensation is more vivid than another, there is much more uncertainty. We can distinguish those sensations which are pleasurable, and those which are painful, from such as are not so; and when we call the pleasurable and painful more vivid, than those which are not so, we speak intelligibly. We can also distinguish degrees of pleasure, and of pain; and when we call the sensation of the higher degree more vivid than the sensation of the lower degree, we may again be considered as expressing a meaning tolerably precise.

In calling one IDEA more vivid than another, if we confine the appellation to the ideas of such SENSATIONS as may with precision be called more or less vivid; the sensations of pleasure and pain, in their various degrees, compared with sensations which we do not call either pleasurable or painful; our language will still have a certain degree of precision. But what is the meaning which I annex to my words, when I say, that my idea of the taste of the pine-apple which I tasted yesterday is vivid; my idea of the taste of the foreign fruit which I never tasted but once in early life, is not vivid? If I mean that I can more certainly distinguish the more recent, than the more distant sensation, there is still some precision in my language; because it seems true of all my senses, that if I compare a distant sensation with the present, I am less sure of its being or not being a repetition of the same, than if I compare a recent sensation with a present one. Thus, if I yesterday had a smell of a very peculiar kind, and compare it with a present smell, I can judge more accurately of the agreement or disagreement of the two sensations, than if I compared the present with one much more remote. The same is the case with colours, with sounds, with feelings of touch, and of resistance. It is therefore sufficiently certain, that the idea of the more recent sensation affords the means of a more accurate comparison, generally, than the idea of the more remote sensation. And thus we have three cases of vividness, of which we can speak with some precision: the case of sensations, as compared with ideas; the case of pleasurable and painful sensations, and their ideas as compared with those which are not pleasurable or painful; and the case of the more recent, compared with the more remote.

That the association of two ideas, but for once, does, in some cases, give them a very strong connection, is within the sphere of every man's experience. The most remarkable cases are probably those of pain and pleasure. Some persons who have experienced a very painful surgical operation, can never afterwards bear the sight of the operator, however strong the gratitude which they may actually feel towards him. The meaning is, that the sight of the operator, by a strong association, calls up so vividly the idea of the pain of the operation, that it is itself a pain. The spot on which a tender maiden parted with her lover, when he embarked on the voyage from which he never returned, cannot afterwards be seen by her without an agony of grief.

These cases, also, furnish an apt illustration of the superiority which the sensation possesses over the idea, as an associating cause. Though the sight of the surgeon, the sight of the place, would awaken the ideas which we have described, the mere thought of them might be attended with no peculiar effect. Those persons who have the association of frightful objects with darkness, and who are transported with terrors when placed in the dark, can still think of darkness without any emotion.

The same cases furnish an illustration of the effect of recency on the strength of association. The sight, of the affecting spot by the maiden, of the surgeon by the patient, would certainly produce a more intense emotion, after a short, than after a long interval. With most persons, time would weaken, and at last dissolve, the association.

So much with regard to vividness, as a cause of strong associations. Next, we have to consider frequency or repetition; which is the most remarkable and important cause of the strength of our associations.

Of any two sensations, frequently perceived together, the ideas are associated. Thus, at least, in the minds of Englishmen, the idea of a soldier, and the idea of a red coat are associated; the idea of a clergyman, and the idea of a black coat; the idea of a quaker, and of a broad-brimmed hat; the idea of a woman and the idea of petticoats. A peculiar taste suggests the idea of an apple; a peculiar smell the idea of a rose. If I have heard a particular air frequently sung by a particular person, the hearing of the air suggests the idea of the person.

The most remarkable exemplification of the effect of degrees of frequency, in producing degrees of strength in the associations, is to be found in the cases in which the association is purposely and studiously contracted; the cases in which we learn something; the use of words, for example.

Every child learns the language which is spoken by those around him. He also learns it by degrees. He learns first the names of the most familiar objects; and among familiar objects, the names of those which he most frequently has occasion to name; himself, his nurse, his food, his playthings.

A sound heard once in conjunction with another sensation; the word mamma, for example, with the sight of a woman, would produce no greater effect on the child, than the conjunction of any other sensation, which once exists and is gone forever. But if the word mamma is frequently pronounced, in conjunction with the sight of a particular woman, the sound will by degrees become associated with the sight; and as the pronouncing of the name will call up the idea of the woman, so the sight of the woman will call up the idea of the name.

The process becomes very perceptible to us, when, at years of reflection, we proceed to learn a dead or foreign language. At the first lesson, we are told, or we see in the dictionary, the meaning of perhaps twenty words. But it is not joining the word and its meaning once, that will make the word suggest its meaning to us another time. We repeat the two in conjunction, till we think the meaning so well associated with the word, that whenever the word occurs to us, the meaning will occur along with it. We are often deceived in this anticipation; and finding that the meaning is not suggested by the word, we have to renew the process of repetition, and this, perhaps, again, and again. By force of repetition the meaning is associated, at last, with every word of the language, and so perfectly, that the one never occurs to us without the other.

Learning to play on a musical instrument is another remarkable illustration of the effect of repetition in strengthening associations, in rendering those sequences, which, at first, are slow, and difficult, afterwards, rapid, and easy. At first, the learner, after thinking of each successive note, as it stands in his book, has each time to look out with care for the key or the string which he is to touch, and the finger he is to touch it with, and is every moment committing mistakes. Repetition is well known to be the only means of overcoming these difficulties. As the repetition goes on, the sight of the note, or even the idea of the note, becomes associated with the place of the key or the string; and that of the key or the string with the proper finger. The association for a time is imperfect, but at last becomes so strong, that it is performed with the greatest rapidity, without an effort, and almost without consciousness.

In few cases is the strength of association, derived from repetition, more worthy of attention, than in performing arithmetic. All men, whose practice is not great, find the addition of a long column of numbers, tedious, and the accuracy of the operation, by no means certain. Till a man has had considerable practice, there are few acts of the mind more toilsome. The reason is, that the names of the numbers, which correspond to the different steps, do not readily occur; that is, are not strongly associated with the names which precede them. Thus, 7 added to 5, make 12; but the antecedent, 7 added to 5, is not strongly associated with the consequent 12, in the mind of the learner, and he has to wait and search till the name occurs. Thus, again, 12 and 7 make 19; 19 and 8 make 27, and so on to any amount; but if the practice of the performer has been small, the association in each instance is imperfect, and the process irksome and slow. Practice, however; that is, frequency of repetition; makes the association between each of these antecedents and its proper consequent so perfect, that no sooner is the one conceived than the other is conceived, and an expert arithmetician can tell the amount of a long column of figures, with a rapidity, which seems almost miraculous to the man whose faculty of numeration is of the ordinary standard.

8 Where two or more ideas have been often repeated together, and the association has become very strong, they sometimes spring up in such close combination as not to be distinguishable. Some cases of sensation are analogous. For example; when a wheel, on the seven parts of which the seven prismatic colours are respectively painted, is made to revolve rapidly, it appears not of seven colours, but of one uniform colour, white. By the rapidity of the succession, the several sensations cease to be distinguishable; they run, as it were, together, and a new sensation, compounded of all the seven, but apparently a simple one, is the result. Ideas, also, which have been so often conjoined, that whenever one exists in the mind, the others immediately exist along with it, seem to run into one another, to coalesce, as it were, and out of many to form one idea; which idea, however in reality complex, appears to be no less simple, than any one of those of which it is compounded.

The word gold, for example, or the word iron, appears to express as simple an idea, as the word colour, or the word sound. Yet it is immediately seen, that the idea of each of those metals is made up of the separate ideas of several sensations; colour, hardness, extension, weight. Those ideas, however, present themselves in such intimate union, that they are constantly spoken of as one, not many. We say, our idea of iron, our idea of gold; and it is only with an effort that reflecting men perform the decomposition.

The idea expressed by the term weight, appears so perfectly simple, that he is a good metaphysician, who can trace its composition. Yet it involves, of course, the idea of resistance, which we have shewn above to be compounded, and to involve the feeling attendant upon the contraction of muscles; and the feeling, or feelings, denominated Will; it involves the idea, not of resistance simply, but of resistance in a particular direction; the idea of direction, therefore, is included in it, and in that are involved the ideas of extension, and of place and motion, some of the most complicated phenomena of the human mind.

The ideas of hardness and extension have been so uniformly regarded as simple, that the greatest metaphysicians have set them down as the copies of simple sensations of touch. Hartley and Darwin, were, I believe, the first who thought of assigning to them a different origin.

We call a thing hard, because it resists compression, or separation of parts; that is, because to compress it, or separate it into parts, what we call muscular force is required. The idea, then, of muscular action, and of all the feelings which go to it, are involved in the idea of hardness.

The idea of extension is derived from the muscular feelings in what we call the motion of parts of our own bodies; as for example, the hands. I move my hand along a line; I have certain sensations; on account of these sensations, I call the line long, or extended. The idea of lines in the direction of length, breadth, and thickness, constitutes the general idea of extension. In the idea of extension, there are included three of the most complex of our ideas; motion; time, which is included in motion; and space, which is included in direction. We are not yet prepared to explain the simple ideas which compose the very complex ideas, of motion, space, and time; it is enough at present to have shewn, that in the idea of extension, which appears so very simple, a great number of ideas are nevertheless included; and that this is a case of that combination of ideas in the higher degrees of association, in which the simple ideas are so intimately blended, as to have the appearance, not of a complex, but of a simple idea.

It is to this great law of association, that we trace the formation of our ideas of what we call external objects; that is, the ideas of a certain number of sensations, received together so frequently that they coalesce as it were, and are spoken of under the idea of unity. Hence, what we call the idea of a tree, the idea of a stone, the idea of a horse, the idea of a man.

In using the names, tree, horse, man, the names of what I call objects, I am referring, and can be referring, only to my own sensations; in fact, therefore, only naming a certain number of sensations, regarded as in a particular state of combination; that is, concomitance. Particular sensations of sight, of touch, of the muscles, are the sensations, to the ideas of which, colour, extension, roughness, hardness, smoothness, taste, smell, so coalescing as to appear one idea, I give the name, idea of a tree.

To this case of high association, this blending together of many ideas, in so close a combination that they appear not many ideas, but one idea, we owe, as I shall afterwards more fully explain, the power of classification, and all the advantages of language. It is obviously, therefore, of the greatest moment, that this important phenomenon should be well understood.

9 Some ideas are by frequency and strength of association so closely combined, that they cannot be separated. If one exists, the others exist along with it, in spite of whatever effort we make to disjoin them.

For example; it is not in our power to think of colour, without thinking of extension; or of solidity, without figure. We have seen colour constantly in combination with extension, spread as it were, upon a surface. We have never seen it except in this connection. Colour and extension have been invariably conjoined. The idea of colour, therefore, uniformly comes into the mind, bringing that of extension along with it; and so close is the association, that it is not in our power to dissolve it. We cannot, if we will, think of colour, but in combination with extension. The one idea calls up the other, and retains it, so long as the other is retained.

This great law of our nature is illustrated in a manner equally striking, by the connection between the ideas of solidity and figure. We never have the sensations from which the idea of solidity is derived, but in conjunction with the sensations whence the idea of figure is derived. If we handle anything solid, it is always either round, square, or of some other form. The ideas correspond with the sensations. If the idea of solidity rises, that of figure rises along with it. The idea of figure which rises, is, of course, more obscure than that of extension; because, figures being innumerable, the general idea is exceedingly complex, and hence, of necessity, obscure. But, such as it is, the idea of figure is always present when that of solidity is present; nor can we, by any effort, think of the one without thinking of the other at the same time.

Of all the cases of this important law of association, there is none more extraordinary than what some philosophers have called, the acquired perceptions of sight.

When I lift my eyes from the paper on which I am writing, I see the chairs, and tables, and walls of my room, each of its proper shape, and at its proper distance. I see, from my window, trees, and meadows, and horses, and oxen, and distant hills. I see each of its proper size, of its proper form, and at its proper distance; and these particulars appear as immediate informations of the eye, as the colours which I see by means of it.

Yet, philosophy has ascertained, that we derive nothing from the eye whatever, but sensations of colour; that the idea of extension, in which size, and form, and distance are included, is derived from sensations, not in the eye, but in the muscular part of our frame. How, then, is it, that we receive accurate information, by the eye, of size, and shape, and distance? By association merely.

The colours upon a body are different, according to its figure, its distance, and its size. But the sensations of colour, and what we may here, for brevity, call the sensations of extension, of figure, of distance, have been so often united, felt in conjunction, that the sensation of the colour is never experienced without raising the ideas of the extension, the figure, the distance, in such intimate union with it, that they not only cannot be separated, but are actually supposed to be seen. The sight, as it is called, of figure, or distance, appearing, as it does, a simple sensation, is in reality a complex state of consciousness; a sequence, in which the antecedent, a sensation of colour, and the consequent, a number of ideas, are so closely combined by association, that they appear not one idea, but one sensation.

Some persons, by the folly of those about them, in early life, have formed associations between the sound of thunder, and danger to their lives. They are accordingly in a state of agitation during a thunder storm. The sound of the thunder calls up the idea of danger, and no effort they can make, no reasoning they can use with themselves, to show how small the chance that they will be harmed, empowers them to dissolve the spell, to break the association, and deliver themselves from the tormenting idea, while the sensation or the expectation of it remains.

Another very familiar illustration may be adduced. Some persons have what is called an antipathy to a spider, a toad, or a rat. These feelings generally originate in some early fright. The idea of danger has been on some occasion so intensely excited along with the touch or sight of the animal, and hence the association so strongly formed, that it cannot be dissolved. The sensation, in spite of them, excites the idea, and produces the uneasiness which the idea imports.

The following of one idea after another idea, or after a sensation, so certainly that we cannot prevent the combination, nor avoid having the *consequent feeling* as often as we have the *antecedent*, is a law of association, the operation of which we shall afterwards find to be extensive, and bearing a principal part in some of the most important phenomena of the human mind.

As there are some ideas so intimately blended by association, that it is not in our power to separate them; there seem to be others, which it is not in our power to combine. Dr. Brown, in exposing some errors of his predecessors, with respect to the acquired perceptions of sight, observes: "I cannot blend my notions of the two surfaces, a plane, and a convex, as one surface, both plane and convex, more than I can think of a whole which is less than a fraction of itself, or a square of which the sides are not equal." The case, here, appears to be, that a strong association excludes whatever is opposite to it. I cannot associate the two ideas of assafœtida, and the taste of sugar. Why? Because the idea of assafœtida is so strongly associated with the idea of another taste, that the idea of that other taste rises in combination with the idea of assafœtida, and of course the idea of sugar does not rise. I have one idea associated with the word pain. Why can I not associate pleasure with the word pain? Because another indissoluble association springs up, and excludes it. This is, therefore, only a case of indissoluble association; but one of much importance, as we shall find when we come to the exposition of some of the more complicated of our mental phenomena.

10 It not unfrequently happens in our associated feelings, that the antecedent is of no importance farther than it introduces the consequent. In these cases, the consequent absorbs all the attention, and the antecedent is instantly forgotten. Of this a very intelligible illustration is afforded by what happens in ordinary discourse. A friend arrives from a distant country, and brings me the first intelligence of the last illness, the last words, the last acts, and death of my son. The sound of the voice, the articulation of every word, makes its sensation in my ear; but it is to the ideas that my attention flies. It is my son that is before me, suffering, acting, speaking, dying. The words which have introduced the ideas, and kindled the affections, have been as little heeded, as the respiration which has been accelerated, while the ideas were received.

It is important in respect to this case of association to remark, that there are large classes of our sensations, such as many of those in the alimentary duct, and many in the nervous and vascular systems, which serve, as antecedents, to introduce ideas, as consequents; but as the consequents are far more interesting than themselves, and immediately absorb the attention, the antecedents are habitually overlooked; and though they exercise, by the trains which they introduce, a great influence on our happiness or misery, they themselves are generally wholly unknown.

That there are connections between our ideas and certain states of the internal organs, is proved by many familiar instances. Thus, anxiety, in most people, disorders the digestion. It is no wonder, then, that the internal feelings which accompany indigestion, should excite the ideas which prevail in a state of anxiety. Fear, in most people, accelerates, in a remarkable manner, the vermicular motion of the intestines. There is an association, therefore, between certain states of the intestines, and terrible ideas; and this is sufficiently confirmed by the horrible dreams to which men are subject from indigestion; and the hypochondria, more or less afflicting, which almost always accompanies certain morbid states of the digestive organs. The grateful food which excites pleasurable sensations in the mouth, continues them in the stomach; and, as pleasures excite ideas of their causes, and these of similar causes, and causes excite ideas of their effects, and so on, trains of pleasurable ideas take their origin from pleasurable sensations in the stomach. Uneasy sensations in the stomach, produce analogous effects. Disagreeable sensations are associated with disagreeable circumstances; a train is introduced, in which, one painful idea following another, combinations, to the last degree afflictive, are sometimes introduced, and the sufferer is altogether overwhelmed by dismal associations.

In illustration of the fact, that sensations and ideas, which are essential to some of the most important operations of our minds, serve only as antecedents to more important consequents, and are themselves so habitually overlooked, that their existence is unknown, we may recur to the remarkable case which we have just explained, of the ideas introduced by the sensations of sight. The minute gradations of colour, which accompany varieties of extension, figure, and distance, are insignificant. The figure, the size, the distance, themselves, on the other hand, are matters of the greatest importance. The first having introduced the last, their work is done. The consequents remain the sole objects of attention, the antecedents are forgotten; in the present instance, not completely; in other instances, so completely, that they cannot be recognized.

11 Mr. Hume, and after him other philosophers, have said that our ideas are associated according to three principles; Contiguity in time and place, Causation, and Resemblance. The Contiguity in time and place, must mean, that of the sensations; and so far it is affirmed, that the order of the ideas follows that of the sensations. Contiguity of two sensations in time, means the successive order. Contiguity of two sensations in place, means the synchronous order. We have explained the mode in which ideas are associated, in the synchronous, as well as the successive order, and have traced the principle of contiguity to its proper source.

Causation, the second of Mr. Hume's principles, is the same with contiguity in time, or the order of succession. Causation is only a name for the order established between an antecedent and a consequent; that is, the established or constant antecedence of the one, and consequence of the other. Resemblance only remains, as an alleged principle of association, and it is necessary to inquire whether it is included in the laws which have been above expounded. I believe it will be found that we are accustomed to see like things together. When we see a tree, we generally see more trees than one; when we see an ox, we generally see more oxen than one; a sheep, more sheep than one; a man, more men than one. From this observation, I think, we may refer resemblance to the law of frequency, of which it seems to form only a particular case.

Mr. Hume makes contrast a principle of association, but not a separate one, as he thinks it is compounded of Resemblance and Causation. It is not necessary for us to show that this is an unsatisfactory account of contrast. It is only necessary to observe, that, as a case of association, it is not distinct from those which we have above explained.

A dwarf suggests the idea of a giant. How? We call a dwarf a dwarf, because he departs from a certain standard. We call a giant a giant, because he departs from the same standard. This is a case, therefore, of resemblance, that is, of frequency.

Pain is said to make us think of pleasure; and this is considered a case of association by contrast. There is no doubt that pain makes us think of relief from it; because they have been conjoined, and the great vividness of the sensations makes the association strong. Relief from a pain is a species of pleasure; and one pleasure leads to think of another, from the resemblance. This is a compound case, therefore, of vividness and frequency. All other cases of contrast, I believe, may be expounded in a similar manner.

I have not thought it necessary to be tedious in expounding the observations which I have thus stated; for whether the reader supposes that resemblance is, or is not, an original principle of association, will not affect our future investigations.

12 Not only do simple ideas, by strong association, run together, and form complex ideas: but a complex idea, when the simple ideas which compose it have become so consolidated that it always appears as one, is capable of entering into combinations with other ideas, both simple and complex. Thus two complex ideas may be united together, by a strong association, and coalesce into one, in the same manner as two or more simple ideas coalesce into one. This union of two complex ideas into one, Dr. Hartley has called a duplex idea. Two also of these duplex, or doubly compounded ideas, may unite into one; and these again into other compounds, without end. It is hardly necessary to mention, that as two complex ideas unite to form a duplex one, not only two, but more than two may so unite; and what he calls a duplex idea may be compounded of two, three, four, or any number of complex ideas.

Some of the most familiar objects with which we are acquainted furnish instances of these unions of complex and duplex ideas.

Brick is one complex idea, mortar is another complex idea; these ideas, with ideas of position and quantity, compose my idea of a wall. My idea of a plank is a complex idea, my idea of a rafter is a complex idea, my idea of a nail is a complex idea.

These, united with the same ideas of position and quantity, compose my duplex idea of a floor. In the same manner my complex idea of glass, and wood, and others, compose my duplex idea of a window; and these duplex ideas, united together, compose my idea of a house, which is made up of various duplex ideas. How many complex, or duplex ideas, are all united in the idea of furniture? How many more in the idea of merchandise? How many more in the idea called Every Thing?

Ratiocination

Ratiocination is one of the most complicated of all the mental phenomena. And it is worthy of notice, that more was accomplished towards the analysis of it, at an early period in the history of intellectual improvement, than of any other of the complex cases of human consciousness.

It was fully explained by Aristotle, that the simplest case of Ratiocination consists of three propositions, which he called a syllogism. A piece of ratiocination may consist of one, or more syllogisms, to any extent; but every single step is a syllogism.

A ratiocination, then, or syllogism, is first resolved into three propositions. The following may be taken as one of the simplest of all examples. "All men are animals: kings are men: therefore kings are animals."

Next, the Proposition is resolved into its proximate elements. These are three; two Terms, one called the Subject, the other the Predicate, and the Copula. What is the particular nature of each of these elements we have already seen, and here, therefore, need not stay to inquire.

The ancient writers on Logic proceeded in their analysis, no farther than Terms. After this, they only endeavoured to enumerate and classify terms; to enumerate and classify propositions; to enumerate and classify syllogisms; and to give the rules for making correct syllogisms, and detecting incorrect ones. And this, as taught by them, constituted the whole science and art of Logic.

What, under this head, we propose to explain, is—the process of association involved in the syllogism, and in the belief which is part of it.

Mill, op. cit., Vol. 1, pp. 424–427.

That part of the process which is involved in the two antecedent propositions, called the premises, has been already explained. It is only, therefore, the third proposition, called the conclusion, which further requires exposition.

We have seen, that in the proposition, "All men are animals," Belief is merely the recognition that the meaning of the term, "all men," is included in that of the term "animals," and that the recognition is a case of association. In the proposition also, "kings are men," the belief is merely the recognition, that the individuals named "kings," are part of the many, of whom "men," is the common name. This has already been more than once explained. And now, therefore, remains only to be shewn what further is involved in the third proposition, or conclusion, "kings are animals."

In each of the two preceding propositions, two terms or names are compared. In the last proposition, a third name is compared with both the other two; immediately with the one, and, through that, with the other; the whole, obviously, a complicated case of association.

In the first proposition, "all men are animals," the term, "all men," is compared with the term animals; in other words, a certain association, already expounded, takes place. In the second proposition, "kings are men," the term "kings," is compared with the term "all men;" comparison here, again, being only a name for a particular case of association. In the third proposition, "kings are animals," the name "kings," is compared with the name "animals," but mediately through the name, "all men." Thus, "kings," is associated with "all men," "all men," with "animals;" "kings," therefore, with "animals," by a complicated, and, at the same time, a rapid, and almost imperceptible process. It would be easy to mark the steps of the association. But this would be tedious, and after so much practice, the reader will be at no loss to set them down for himself.[1]

---

[1] This chapter, which is of a very summary character, is a prolongation of the portion of the chapter on Belief, which examines the case of belief in the truth of a proposition; and must stand or fall with it. The question considered is, how, from belief in the truth of the two premises of a syllogism, we pass into belief in the conclusion. The exposition proceeds on the untenable theory of the import of propositions, on which I have so often had occasion to com-

The Will

We may ... reasonably be called upon to explain the power which the mind appears to possess over its associations. There is a distinction in the trains of the mind which is observed by every body. Some trains, as those in dreams, in delirium, in frenzy, are supposed to proceed according to the established laws of association without any direction from the mind. Other trains; a piece of reasoning, for example; any process of thought, directed to an end; are considered as wholly under the guidance of the mind. The guidance of the mind is but another name for the will.

Mill, op. cit., Vol. 2, 2nd ed., pp. 356–372.

---

ment. That theory, however, was not necessary to the author for shewing how two ideas may become inseparably associated through the inseparable association of each of them with a third idea: and inasmuch as an inseparable association between the subject and predicate, in the author's opinion, constitutes belief, an explanation of ratiocination conformable to that given of belief follows as a matter of course.

Although I am unable to admit that there is nothing in belief but an inseparable association, and although I maintain that there may be belief without an inseparable association, I can still accept this explanation of the formation of an association between the subject and predicate of the conclusion, which, when close and intense, has, as we have seen, a strong tendency to generate belief. But to shew what it is that gives the belief its validity, we must fall back on logical laws, the laws of evidence. And independently of the question of validity, we shall find in the reliance on those laws, so far as they are understood, the source and origin of all beliefs, whether well or ill-founded, which are not the almost mechanical or automatic products of a strong association—of the lively suggestion of an idea. We may therefore pass at once to the nature of Evidence, which is the subject of the next chapter.

I venture to refer, in passing, to those chapters in my System of Logic, in which I have maintained, contrary to what is laid down in this chapter, that Ratiocination does not *consist* of Syllogisms; that the Syllogism is not the analysis of what the mind does in reasoning, but merely a useful formula into which it can translate its reasonings, gaining thereby a great increase in the security for their correctness.—*Ed.* [J. S. Mill]

And thus it is inferred that the will is not association, but something which controuls association.

We now proceed to the solution of this difficulty. It can be supposed that the will controuls association, in only one of two ways; either, by calling up an Idea, independently of association; or, by making an Idea call up, not the Idea which would follow it spontaneously, but some other Idea.

The first supposition, that an Idea can be called up by the will, is relinquished by the common consent of philosophers.

We cannot will without willing something; and in willing we must have an Idea of the thing willed. If we will an Idea, therefore, we must have the Idea. The Idea does not remain to be called up. It is called up already. To say that we will to have an Idea, when we already have it, is a mere absurdity.

The second supposition is, that will can prevent an Idea from calling up one idea, make it call up another; prevent its calling up the Idea which would have followed it spontaneously, make it call up the Idea which the mind is in quest of.

The first question is, how the will, or the mind willing, can prevent an Idea from calling up another. We know that this is wholly impossible in all those cases in which the association is strong. We cannot think of colour without thinking of extension; we cannot think of the word bread without thinking of its meaning. It can be supposed that we have such power in those cases only in which an Idea has not an inseparable association with the idea in question, but only such an association with it as it has with many others. But how is it that we can hinder an idea which has those associations, from calling up any of the ideas with which it is associated? How can we foresee which of those ideas it will call up? And, if we do foresee that it will call up the idea which we desire to avoid, it follows that the Idea is already in our mind. There seems, therefore, the same incongruity in the supposition that the will can directly prevent, as that it can directly produce an idea.

If the mind, then, possesses any power over its trains, it seems to be confined to its power of making an idea call up other ideas than those which it would spontaneously excite. And if it possesses this power, it possesses that also of excluding ideas which would otherwise exist; since a new train of associations must take its origin from the state of consciousness thus produced. It is, therefore, in this, if in any thing, that the power of willing consists.

We are, however, immediately encountered by the question, If the mind cannot will an Idea, what power does it possess of introducing any idea into a train, but such as comes of its own accord? If it has the idea, it is in the train already. If it has it not, what can it do in order to obtain it? There is the existing train; but how can that be made any thing but what it is; or have any associations but those which are already established?

In cases where language is too imperfect to ensure the conveyance of definite ideas, there is an advantage in particular instances. There are two familiar processes, which are commonly adduced as examples of the power which the mind exercises over its trains. The one is, the endeavour to recollect something we do not remember. The other is, the process of attention.

When anything is remembered, the idea of the thing is always in the mind along with certain associations. In recollection, therefore, the object is attained by the excitement of this idea. Sometimes the effort which we make is successful; sometimes it is not. We are said to will to recollect; but this is obviously an improper expression. To recollect is to call up an Idea. But this, as we have seen already, is not within the province of will. When it is said that we will to recollect, the meaning only is, that we desire to recollect.

But it is also to be inquired, what here is the meaning of the word Desire. We have seen that it is a term applied to Pleasure, or the Cause of Pleasure. The idea, in this instance, which the mind is in quest of, is desired. But why desired? As Pleasure; or the Cause of Pleasure? As Cause, we may reply, in all instances. The idea is wanted for some purpose or end. In that End the pleasure is involved.

The End is thus a pleasurable, that is, an interesting, Idea. But it is in the character of interesting ideas, to dwell in the mind. The meaning is, that they are easily called up by other ideas; and, thus, that there is a perpetual recurrence of them. A young man in love, is said to be engrossed with the idea of his mistress. No sooner has her idea suggested another idea, that is, given place to it, than her idea is again suggested by another, and so on, continually. The man, who is to be executed to-morrow, can think of nothing but the terrible event which is approaching. It can be banished, hardly for an instant. Every thing serves to recall it; and along with it a rush of ideas of the most painful description. There is no law of association more remarkable than that of the rapidity with which pleasurable and painful ideas call up trains of great complexity, and the facility with which they themselves are excited by almost every idea which enters the mind.

When we endeavour, therefore, to recollect any thing, the pleasurable idea, the purpose or end, predominates in the mind, and gives birth to those associations, which are called the effort of recollection. The idea sought after, is sought as a means to this end. Till that idea is recalled, the Idea of the end, that is, an unsatisfied desire, exists, and calls up one circumstance after another, more or less connected with the Idea which is sought after. If these circumstances do not recall the idea; the feeling of unsatisfied desire still continues. The feeling of unsatisfied desire, accompanying successive cases of association, constitutes the feeling to which we give the name of effort of recollection. And the Idea of the End, perpetually calling up the idea of the absence of what is wanted, as the means to that end, and hence calling up in close association every circumstance connected with that unknown something, constitutes the feeling which we call casting about, for the unknown Idea. I believe that this is a full, though summary account of the mental process, or succession of ideas, which takes place when we endeavour to recall a forgotten idea.

The other process, through which the mind is supposed to influence its trains, is Attention. We seem to have the power of attending, or not attending to any object; by which is meant, that we can Will to attend to it, or not to attend. By attending to an object, we give it the opportunity of exciting all the ideas with which it is associated. By not attending to it we deprive it of more or less of that opportunity. And if the will has this power over every idea in a train, it has thence a power, which may be called unlimited, over the train.

What remains, therefore, to complete this inquiry, is, to point out the real process, on which the name ATTENTION is in this manner bestowed. The exposition has been substantially given by preceding writers. But it is desirable, if it be in our power, to set forth the several steps of the process a little more distinctly than has hitherto been done.

At first sight, the objects of attention seem to be infinite. When traced to their sources, however, it is found, that they are of two species only. We attend to Sensations; we attend to Ideas; and there is no other object of our attention.

For the present purpose, it is peculiarly necessary to bear in mind the important distinction we have already noticed, between the class of indifferent sensations, and the class of pleasurable or painful, which we may call, by one name, interesting, sensations. Uninteresting sensations are never, for their own sakes, an object of attention. If ever they become objects of attention, it is when they are considered as causes, or signs, of interesting sensations.

A painful or a pleasurable sensation is a peculiar state of mind. A man knows it, only by having it; and it is impossible that by words he can convey his feeling to others. The effort, however, to convey the idea of it, has given occasion to various forms of expression, all of which are greatly imperfect. The state of mind under a pleasurable or painful sensation is such, that we say, the sensation engrosses the mind; but this really means no more than that it is a painful or pleasurable sensation; and that such a sensation is a state of mind very different from an indifferent sensation. The phrase, engrossing the mind, is sometimes exchanged for the word Attention. A pleasurable or painful sensation is said to fix the Attention of the Mind. But if any man tries to satisfy himself what it is to have a painful sensation, and what it is to attend to it, he will find little means of distinguishing them. Having a pleasurable or painful sensation, and attending to it, seem not to be two things, but one and the same thing. The feeling a pain is attending to it; and attending to it is feeling it. The feeling is not one thing, the attention another; the feeling and the attention are the same thing.

An objector may appeal to certain cases, in which one sensation of the pleasurable or painful kind seems to be swallowed up, as it were, by another. Thus, in the agony of the gout, or toothache, the uneasiness of some local cutaneous inflammation is hardly perceived. The case here is that of two uneasy sensations, one slight, the other intense. According to the supposition, that attention is but a name given to the having of an interesting sensation, what ought to happen in this case is that precisely which does happen. The stronger sensation is, the stronger attention. And that the feebler sensation merges itself in the stronger, and is lost in it, is matter of common and obvious experience. Thus we are every instant, as long as we are awake, shutting and opening our eyelids. We are, therefore, alternately in light and darkness. But as the light is the stronger sensation of the two, we have the sensation of light without interruption. Thus, too, if a stick ignited at one end is rapidly turned round in a circle, though it is obvious that the ignited object is at only one part of the circle at a time, and all the other parts are in darkness, the circle, nevertheless, assumes the appearance of being wholly ignited. There is not a more striking exemplification of this law than what is exhibited by the comparison of our sleeping and waking thoughts. In dreams, when our trains are composed of Ideas, unmixed with sensations, the Ideas have so much vividness as to be taken for sensations. In our waking trains, sensations and ideas are mixed together; but as each sensation introduces many ideas, however numerous the sensations may be, the ideas are many times more numerous. Yet such is the effect of the more vivid to obscure the less vivid feeling, that our day does not appear a day of ideas but a day of sensations.

There are cases in which the effect which is thus produced by a stronger sensation with respect to a weaker, or by sensations with respect to ideas, is also produced by one idea with respect to another. Innumerable cases can be adduced to prove, and, indeed, it forms one of the great features of what we call the intellectual nature of man, that Ideas, by their accumulation, are capable of acquiring a power, superior to that of sensations, both as pleasure and as pain. The pleasures of Taste, the pleasures of Intellectual exertion, the pleasures of Virtue, acquire when duly cultivated, a power of controlling the solicitations of appetite, and are esteemed a more valuable constituent of happiness than all that sense can immediately bestow.

On the power of ideas, as the stronger feelings, to swallow up sensations, in the same manner as stronger sensations swallow up the weaker, some decisive experiments have been made. The wretches who, nearly a century ago, were made tools of in France, under the title of *convulsionnaires*, to carry on the purposes of Fanaticism, were so placed under the dominion of certain ideas, being persons of weak intellects and strong imagination, and operated upon by men skilled in the ways of perverting feeble understandings, that the ideas became feelings far more potent than the sensations; and when the bodies of the frenzied creatures were subjected to operations calculated to produce the most intense sufferings, they denied that they felt any thing, and by the whole of their demeanour confirmed, as far as it could confirm, the truth of their asseverations. That men in the ardour of battle receive wounds of a serious nature, without being aware of them, till after a considerable lapse of time, is testified upon unsuspicious evidence.

These instances, therefore, it is manifest, form no objection to our conclusion, that the attending to an interesting sensation, and the having the sensation, are but two names for the same thing.

We have now to consider, what it is, to attend to an indifferent sensation. The force of the word indifferent implies, that an indifferent sensation is not an object of attention on its own account. If it were an object of attention on its own account, it would not be indifferent. If it is regarded, however, as the cause, or the sign, of an interesting sensation, we are already acquainted with the process which takes place. The idea of the interesting sensation is immediately associated with it; the state of consciousness then is not an indifferent sensation merely; it is a sensation and an idea in union. The idea besides is an interesting idea, that of a pain or pleasure.

The union of an interesting idea, with an indifferent sensation, makes a compound state of consciousness which, as a whole, is interesting. As the having an interesting sensation, and the attending to it, are but two names for the same thing; the having a sensation rendered interesting by association, and the attending to it, cannot be regarded as two different things. In the first case, attention is merely a sensation of a particular kind; in the second, it is merely an association of a particular kind.

We have now to shew what takes place, when the attention, to use the common language, is not directed to Sensations but Ideas.

Ideas are, like sensations, of two kinds. They are either interesting, or not interesting. We need not repeat what has been so often said respecting the origin and composition of those two classes of Ideas, and the cause of the difference.

An indifferent idea, like an indifferent sensation, is, in itself, not an object of attention. If it were an object of attention, it would not be indifferent; in other words, it would be interesting. In fact, it is in the very import of the word attention, that the object of it is interesting. And if an object is interesting it must be so, either in itself, or by association.

As we found that the having an interesting sensation, and the attending to that sensation, were not two distinguishable states of consciousness, but one and the same state of consciousness, let us now observe, as carefully as we can, whether the having an interesting idea is a state of consciousness, which can be distinguished from attending to it, or whether they are not merely two names for the same thing. When the young man, in love, has the idea of the woman, who is the object of his affections, is not attention merely another word for the peculiar nature of the Idea? In like manner in the mind of the man, who is to be executed to-morrow, the idea of the terrible event before him, is an idea in the very essence of which attention is involved. Attention is but another name for the interesting character of the idea.

If there are any cases to which an objector's appeal can be made, they will be found, upon examination, to resemble those which we considered in the case of sensation, and which we found to be nothing more than instances of the prevalence of a stronger feeling over a weaker; stronger, either by its nature, or the peculiar circumstances of the moment. We shall not, therefore, stay to propound and explain them.

The Will   123

It only remains to expound the case in which an indifferent Idea becomes interesting by association. It cannot do so in any other way, than those in which it appeared that an indifferent sensation becomes interesting. It may be considered as the cause, or the sign, of some interesting state of consciousness. When that which is interesting becomes associated with that which is uninteresting, so as to form one compound state of consciousness, the whole is interesting. An idea, in itself indifferent, associated with interesting ideas, becomes part of a new compound which, as a whole, is interesting: and an interesting idea existing, and an interesting idea attended to, are only two names for the same thing.

In the case of Ideas, then, as in the case of sensations, attention to an interesting Idea, is merely having it; attention to an indifferent idea, is merely associating with it some idea that is interesting.

As far then, as ATTENTION gives us power over the trains of our ideas, it is not Will which gives it to us, but the occurrence of interesting sensations, or ideas.

There is not any of the phenomena, which are usually appealed to as the great manifestations of the power of the mind over its trains, which this mode of exposition does not satisfactorily account for. We may take as a sufficient exemplification of them all, the composition of a Discourse upon any important topic. The operation of the mind upon such an occasion seems to consist in a perpetual selection; that is, in the exercise of an uninterrupted power over the trains of association. There is no doubt that it consists of that peculiar class of associations, to which we give the names, of selection, and power.

In composing a Discourse, a man has some end in view. It is for the attainment of this end, that the Discourse is undertaken. If every thing in the discourse tends to the accomplishment of the end, the Discourse is said to be coherent, appropriate, consistent. If there are many things in it which have no tendency, or but little tendency, to the accomplishment of the end, the discourse is said to be rambling, and incoherent.

This is a case, the exposition of which corresponds very much with that which we have already explained; the endeavour to recollect a forgotten Idea. In that case, the existence of an interesting idea calls up a variety of circumstances, that is, a variety of ideas; and it very often happens, that the idea which is sought for, is called up among them.

In this case, what the seeker has occasion for, is a single Idea; a single idea accomplishes the end he has in view. In the case of the composer of a discourse a great many ideas are wanted. His end cannot be attained by one or a few. But his proceeding is precisely of the same kind in regard to his many Ideas, as that of the man who desires to recollect in regard to his single Idea. He knows there are a number of ideas, connected with the end he has in view, which he can employ for his purpose, provided he can call them up. How they are called up, after the practice we have had in those solutions, requires but little explanation. The end in view is an interesting Idea. It is, at the time, the prevalent Idea. It is that by which the man is stimulated to action. This idea calls up by association many ideas and trains of Ideas. Of these a large proportion pass, and are not made use of. Others are detained and employed. This detaining and employing is all that needs to be explained. It is the same sort of result as the recognition of the forgotten Idea, in the case of recollection.

The forgotten Idea is an Idea associated, as cause, with the end to be obtained by it, as its effect. The same is the case with the ideas which the composer of a discourse selects out of the multitudes, which the continual suggestions of the interesting Idea by which he is actuated, that of his end, bring before him. The greater number are not associated with the idea of his end as cause and effect. Some among them are. These immediately suggest the use to be made of them; and thence, by the regular chains of association, the operations take place.

It is from these explanations, also, easy to see what constitutes the difference between the man who composes a coherent, and the man who composes a rambling discourse. In the man who composes the coherent discourse, the main Idea, that of the end in view, predominates, and controls the association, in every part of the process. It is not only the grand suggesting principle, which sets trains of the ideas connected with itself in motion; but it is the grand selecting principle. As ideas rise in the train, this interesting and predominating idea stands ready to be associated as effect with every idea in the train which can operate as cause; it so associates itself with no other; and therefore no wrong selection is made. If, however, it does not thus predominate in the mind of the composer of the discourse, as his exclusive end; if it gives way at every turn to some other end; as the idea of applause from some lively jest, from some gaudy description, from some florid thought, the selection is made so far upon other principles, and the object of the discourse is forgotten.

* * *

With James Mill—and his son's embellishments—we have reached the zenith of British associationism. What followed was mostly elaboration and problem statement. Psychology was about to break loose from philosophy; observation and verification were to replace the contemplative mode. But the period closed with a flourish. Alexander Bain undertook to subsume all of human mental life under the principles of association and in 1855, in his book *The Senses and the Intellect,* he ranged from simple problems of sensation to artistic creation, from the association of ideas to the explanation of scientific creativity. Bain writes with a disarming sense of comprehension; the world is laid wide open and if one only applies the principles properly all can be easily understood.

In the following passage he takes up the problem of directed thinking which has plagued the doctrine of association from the beginning. Why—with all the possible associations available—is one more likely than another? We have seen Mill struggle with the problem and Bain succinctly states what has been suggested by many others. His statement was to remain the major description of direction in thought, and some sixty years later Bain was credited with the invention of the constellation theory by G. E. Müller, who developed it to its highest state.

Alexander Bain

Compound Association

Hitherto we have restricted our attention to single threads or indivisible links of association, whether of Contiguity or Similarity. It remains for us to consider the case where several threads, or a Plurality of links or bonds of connexion, unite in reviving some previous thought or mental state. No new principle is introduced here; we have merely to note, what seems an almost unavoidable effect of the combined action, that the re-instatement is thereby made more easy and certain. Associations that are individually too weak, to operate the revival of a past idea, may succeed by acting together; and there is thus opened up to our view a means of aiding our recollection, or invention, when the one thread in hand is too feeble to effect a desired recall. It happens, in fact, that, in a very large number of our mental transitions, there is present a multiple bond of association.

The combinations may be made up of Contiguities alone, of Similarities alone, or of Contiguity and Similarity mixed. Moreover, we shall find that in Emotion and in Volition there are influences either assisting or obstructing the proper intellectual forces. In the reviving of a past image or idea, it is never unimportant, that the revival gratifies a favourite emotion, or is strongly willed in the pursuit of an end. We must endeavour to appreciate, as far as we are able, the influence of these extra-intellectual energies within the sphere of intellect; but, as they would rarely suffice for the reproduction of thought, if acting apart and alone,

A. Bain, *The senses and the intellect*, 3rd ed. London: Longmans, Green, 1868, pp. 544–545, 560–562. First edition: London, 1855.

we are led to look at them chiefly as modifying the effects of the strictly intellectual forces, or as combining elements in the composition of associations.

The general law may be stated as follows: *Past actions, sensations, thoughts, or emotions, are recalled more easily, when associated either through contiguity or through similarity, with* more than one *present object or impression.*

The Singling Out of One among Many Trains

If I look at a mountain, there are many trains that I may be led into, by taking this as a point to start from. By contiguity, I may pass to the other mountains of the chain, to the plains and the villages beyond, to the mineral composition of the mass, to the botany, to the geological structure, to the historical events happening there. By similarity, I may be led away to mountains that I have seen in other lands, or in the representations of the painter and the poet, to the analogous geometrical forms, to equivalent artistic effects. All these vents may be open to me, but it will happen that I go on some one track by preference, and there will be a motive for the preference. Perhaps one of the associations may have come by repetition to have greater force than any other; I may have been so accustomed to associate together the mountain and the neighbouring village, that I am led at once upon this one special transition. Another cause may be the presence of a second associating bond. If I see the adjoining mountain, I am then liable to be led along the chain; if I catch the glancings of the cascades, there is a double link of contiguity, tending to carry my mind to the river flowing from the sides of the mountain. If historical events have been recently in my mind, the events referable to this locality are suggested. If botany or geology is my study, a bent corresponding to these is impressed on the current of thought; if geometry, the forms suggested by preference are the figures of geometry; if I am an artist, the forms of art spring up instead.

The position supposed almost demands an additional and a specializing bond to set the mind in motion at all. We could imagine an intellectual situation so equally balanced, that no revival took place in any direction, just as in a conflict of equal volitions. Some *inequality* of restorative power in the various trains, or some second association coming in aid of one to give that one a preponderance, is the condition of our reviving anything. The case of an intellectual standstill between opposing suggestions is neither chimerical nor unexampled.

I will suppose another instance. A violent storm has flooded the rivers, blown down trees and buildings, and inspired general terror. The trains of thought suggested by such an incident are extremely various, and will depend on the mental condition of the observer in other respects, or on the special ideas that concur with the aspect common to all. The sailor's wife thinks of her husband at sea. The merchant and underwriter have their thoughts on the same element. The farmer calculates the loss to his fields. The millowner sees a prospect of abundant water power. The meteorologist studies the direction, duration, and force of the hurricane, and compares it with previous cases. The poet sees grand and imposing effects. The religious man has his mind carried upwards to the Deity.

These instances imply some *habitual attitude* of the mind, or an emotion, occupation, or pursuit, ever ready as a starting-point to the intellectual movement, and combining itself with every casual impetus given to the mental trains, so as to constitute an element of the composite effect. The principle is exactly the same in cases where the second association is present merely by accident.

We have more than once adverted to the mental aggregates, formed by the cluster of properties attaching to natural objects, especially as viewed by the scientific mind. Thus the idea of the mineral quartz is a vast assemblage of facts, properties, and influences, all which are liable to come before the view, when the mineral is seen or named. So even a naked circle is rich in associations to the geometrical mind. It does not therefore follow that, every time a mineralogist looks upon a piece of quartz, all its many qualities shall rise and pass before his view; or that every circle shall hurry the mind of a geometer all through the Third Book of Euclid. The associating links in both cases are good and sound; but some motive additional to the force of the acquired adhesions is needed actually to recover the train. Not only must the mind be disengaged from other trains, there must also be a positive stimulus, a second starting point, to individualize and determine the bent of the suggesting power to one or other of the many associated ideas. If I am handling a piece of quartz and trying a knife edge upon it, the degree of hardness of the mineral is the quality suggested; if an acid is at hand, the chemical action of quartz is brought up to the view, and so on. When one of the many properties of the circle strung together in the mind of a mathematician is resuscitated by preference, it is by the agency of some specializing notion pointing to that individual. The most opulent mind has moments of quiescence, and yet how numerous the possible outlets of thought at every moment!

* * *

James Mill and Alexander Bain were probably the most influential and most widely read of the British associationists in Germany where the ferment of the new psychology was brewing. They most certainly appear to be the most quoted and, at least bibliographically, they provide us with the link from British to German associationism, from the armchair doctrine of association to its elaboration in the laboratory. But before taking the leap across the Channel, let us take stock of the associationist theory of the higher mental processes.

First of all, from the standpoint of one interested in the "higher" aspects of mental processes, in the heights of creative and productive thought, the associationists barely got off the ground. One of the most obvious reasons for this earthbound failure lies in the incredible complexities to be found in the rarified atmosphere of creative thinking. But other reasons, perhaps of more interest historically, lie in the contemplative nature of the associationist's attack on these problems. The object of his studies was his own mind; the scientist was using himself as his own laboratory with all its attendant limitations and confusions. The limitations depend upon what can be observed by this method. For one thing, the scientist is almost certainly restricted to the observation of conscious processes. Even if he is so sophisticated as to be able to observe gaps in his thought processes, or is forced to deduce the presence of lacunae by the bare fact of not being able to follow a line of thought, there is not much he can do or say about these unobservables. Furthermore, the confusions involved in the scientist's using himself as subject are numerous. When working within the manifold of one's own consciousness, is it possible to tell the relevant from the irrelevant, the plain fact from the fact varnished by the theoretical brush of the scientist-observer? These are difficult problems under the best of observational conditions in a laboratory and well nigh impossible to solve without one.

One of the results of the limitation of the study of thought to the conscious mind was the emphasis placed upon sensations and images, as should be abundantly apparent from the preceding selections. It is difficult to attack the so-called regulative aspects of thinking—set, motivation, *Aufgabe*—from a point of view unaware of or unwilling to admit unconscious activities. And without these aspects, emphasis tends to be placed wholly on the units of thought themselves—the idea or the image. The static and atomistic analysis of thought that resulted was rather like a giant Humpty Dumpty deliberately and carefully pushed off the wall, with all the king's philosophers trying to put him together again. It cannot be said they met with much more success than the soldiers of the nursery rhyme. Once the pieces were broken apart, it was impossible to fit them together in any semblance of a human thought. Once the mechanical laws devised by James Mill to fit units together were found wanting by the younger Mill, it became apparent that some glue was badly needed.

Every now and then these shortcomings became painfully obvious. Reasoning was relegated to the status of a faculty and thus put beyond the pale of explanation, or the will was invoked (or rejected), or all creative, productive processes were relegated (for example by Bain) to the operation of trial and error plus a little bit of luck.

Retrospectively, we can see that the time was obviously ripe for the introduction of organizing and directing forces that might not be available to introspection. It would take another fifty years before this advance was achieved, but Wundt first had to open up the possibility of an experimental psychology.

4

Thinking and the New Psychology: Imageless Thought

Although the birthdate of an experimental psychology can be argued, Wilhelm Wundt's assumption of paternity cannot. It was Wundt in 1874 who marked out the "new domain of science" and who made the break with self-observation by insisting that "all accurate observation implies . . . that the observed object is independent of the observer."* The psychical processes had to be properly controlled in order to make objective observation possible. But the transition of psychology to the laboratory also brought with it some Wundt-imposed restrictions on the subject matter of experimental psychology.

In the first place all analytic work in psychology was to be based on the notion that "there is only *one* kind of causal explanation in psychology, and that is the derivation of more complex psychical processes from simpler ones."† Second, experimental study was possible only when external manipulation of conditions was possible, that is, it was restricted to relations between stimulus and consciousness in the simplest sense. Mental products—including complex thought—"are of too variable a character to be the sub-

---

* W. Wundt, *Principles of physiological psychology*, 5th ed., transl. by E. B. Titchener. New York: Macmillan, 1904. Originally published as *Grundzüge der physiologischen Psychologie*. Leipzig: Engelmann, 1874.

† W. Wundt, *Outlines of psychology*, transl. by C. H. Judd. Leipzig: Engelmann, 1897. Originally published as *Grundriss der Psychologie*. Leipzig: Engelmann, 1896.

jects of objective observation . . . [and] gain the necessary degree of constancy only when they become collective." Their study is thus part of social psychology. "[The] experimental method [serves] the analysis of the simpler psychical processes, and the observation of general mental products [serves] the investigation of the higher psychical processes and developments."*

The nineteenth century thus passed without any significant experimental work being undertaken on these "higher psychical processes."

The slack created by Wundt's dicta was taken up with a vengeance at the University of Würzburg. Karl Marbe and Oswald Külpe triggered one of the most active periods in the investigation of human thought; the former provided much of the experimental and conceptual impetus, the latter—though credited with the leadership of the Würzburg school—was more concerned with philosophical questions and generally encouraged the direction of the laboratory investigations.

The first paper to come out of this new school was by Mayer and Orth in 1901. They, like the other members of the Würzburg group, assumed much of the associationist theory which preceded them, but in the course of a study of qualitative aspects of the associational process—initiated by Marbe—they stumbled across an unexpected finding. While examining the thought processes intervening between a stimulus word and the subject's reaction, they found that subjects frequently reported a kind of conscious experience that was neither an image nor an awareness of an act of will or choice. They also noted that sometimes associations were made to the stimulus word without any conscious processes whatsoever, and although this finding might seem to be troublesome for a theory of thinking based on the association of images, this aspect of the problem seemed not to bother them. They were struck, however, by those conscious processes that seemed to be completely imageless. Since their subjects could not describe these processes beyond saying that they had them, Mayer and Orth were in turn helpless to say anything about them. As a solution, they

---

* W. Wundt, *Outlines of psychology*, transl. by C. H. Judd. Leipzig: Engelmann, 1897.

coined a phrase, dispositions of consciousness (*Bewusstseinslagen*), took note of the occurrence of these states, called them states of consciousness inaccessible to further analysis, and let it go at that.*

This seemingly negative finding was an extremely important one. First of all, it was an entering wedge into the closed ranks of association theory. For if thinking consists of associations between images—asserted since Aristotle's time—how can there be thought with no images present? What mediates the obviously meaningful response to the stimulus word? Perhaps even more important, however, was that Mayer and Orth were forced to invent, albeit reluctantly, a new theoretical term. In the face of their subjects being unable to describe what was going on, they were forced to remove themselves from the subjects' theorizing and to invent a term of their own. This is not to say that theoretical terms were alien to psychologists or that they were invented by the Würzburgers. Rather, this was the major step toward letting the subjects' *behavior* dictate the necessity for inventing such a term. Just as in other fields of psychology, the theory of thinking was forced to invent theoretical concepts to bridge an introspective void.

---

* Alfred Binet, working in France at the same time as the Würzburgers in Germany, came to the same conclusion with regard to imageless thought (*L'étude expérimentale de l'intelligence*, Paris, 1903). He stated his position even more strongly, saying that elaborate images such as found in daydreaming were incompatible with the rapid processes of thought. He once illustrated the inadequacy of the image theory by remarking that with a million dollar thought one only has a nickel's worth of images.

A. Mayer and J. Orth

The Qualitative Investigation of Associations

Marbe and Orth have previously pointed out that all the usual categorizations of associations suffer to some degree from the error that the bases for these categories have been derived from logical points of view, rather than from the nature of the associations. The reasonable demand to base the categorization of associations on their qualities and not on other considerations suggests a more thorough examination of the qualitative differences among associations.

At the same time it must be made quite clear that many different experiences are subsumed under the concept of association and that facts and categories that are derived from one group of associations cannot be simply transferred to others. Qualitative investigations and new attempts at the categorization of associations must at first be limited to a certain class of associative processes, and only later can the question be asked whether the same facts can be found within other classes and whether the same categories make sense there.

On the basis of such considerations, Dr. Marbe has set us the task of examining the associations that arise when the subject reacts with a spoken word to a word called out to him, and to attempt to find a useful categorization of these associations.

Such an examination can only be fruitful if we assume that we

---

A. Mayer and J. Orth, Zur qualitativen Untersuchung der Association. Z. f. Psychol., 1901, **26**, 1–13. Transl. by George and Jean M. Mandler.

can become acquainted, as precisely as possible, with those processes which the observer experiences during the experiment.

Since it seemed likely that the qualitative differences among the associations to be examined would be reflected in their association [reaction] times, we incorporated appropriate time measurements into our experiment. In particular, our experiments pursued the following sequence:

After having attracted the observer's attention with a "ready" signal, the experimenter called out the stimulus word and activated a stop watch at the same time. As soon as the subject had begun to pronounce the response word, the watch was stopped. The observer then reported all his conscious processes which had taken place from the moment of the presentation of the stimulus word up to the end of his reaction. These reports were recorded by the experimenter. The association time, obtained from the stop watch, was then also noted in the protocol. [There follows an apology and justification for using a clock with divisions no finer than a fifth of a second.] . . . During the entire experimental period the observer closed his eyes in order to avoid disturbing or influencing the associative process through visual perceptions. [There follows a description of the primarily monosyllabic nouns that were used as stimulus words as well as a description of the number and identity of experimenters and subjects ($N = 4$).] . . .

An examination of the results showed, first, that for a number of associations the stimulus word acted directly to elicit the response, i.e., without any conscious processes mediating the link between stimulus and response word. We shall designate these responses as responses without intervening conscious processes in contrast to those where psychic events are interposed between stimulus and response word.

We next set ourselves the task of determining the relative frequency and duration of these associations. [There follows some description of the method of determining mean latency values and of the tables that contain the relative frequency and duration of these two types of associative processes.] . . .

The first table seems to show that associations with intervening conscious processes generally appear more frequently than those without intervening conscious processes [by ratios from 13:1 to 3:1]. Despite large individual differences, it is quite clear that associations with intervening conscious processes show relatively longer durations than those without intervening conscious processes.... [The same results were obtained in a second series which also showed that], despite obvious individual differences, the associations with intervening conscious processes are more frequent and take place more slowly than those without intervening conscious processes.

The next tables are concerned with a more detailed classification of the associations with intervening conscious processes. Internal psychic events—that is, conscious processes exclusive of perceptions—are divided into images, which may be more or less complex and more or less characterized by feeling tone, and acts of will, which also may be more or less complex and more or less accompanied by feeling tone. For the time being, we do not want to take any position on the question whether acts of will can be derived from images and feelings, much less would we want to answer this question in the negative. Apart from these two classes of conscious processes, we must introduce a third group of conscious events which has not been adequately stressed by contemporary psychology and to the recognition of which we were—in the course of our experiment—forcibly directed. The subjects very frequently reported that they experienced certain conscious processes which they could describe neither as definite images nor as acts of the will. Mayer, serving as a subject, made the observation that following the stimulus word "meter" there occurred a peculiar conscious process, not further definable, which was followed by the spoken word "trochee." In other cases, the subject was able to describe these psychic events more clearly. For example, Orth observed that the stimulus word "mustard" released just such a peculiar conscious process, which he thought might be characterized as "a memory of an idiomatic expression." This was followed by the response "grain." In all such cases, however, the subject was unable to find in his consciousness the slightest trace of the presence of those images which he used in his report of the psychic events. Despite their obviously quite different qualities we include all of those conscious processes under the name of "*Bewusstseinslagen*" [dispositions of consciousness].* The reports of the observers show that these dispositions were sometimes accompanied by feeling tone, but also sometimes without any feeling tone whatever.

Our data indicated that frequently only one psychic event intervenes between stimulus and response word. For example, one subject reported that the stimulus word "crayon" ["*Stift*"—which has a variety of different meanings] was followed by a very clear visual image of a friend of that name, whereupon the response "student" followed. The protocols also show that two conscious processes may intervene between stimulus and response. For example, for one subject the stimulus word "lead" evoked a clear visual image of a flat, light gray piece of lead; this was followed by the acoustic-motoric word image "heavy," which on its part produced the response "heavy." Finally, our results showed that even three and more conscious processes may intervene between stimulus and response word.

[There follow tables showing the relative frequency with which one, two, three, and more intervening conscious events were reported by subjects, as well as the respective reaction times.]

These results show certain differences in the response mode of individual observers in that for three subjects one intervening conscious process was most frequent, while two, three, or more such processes occurred less frequently. For the fourth observer, one psychic event was relatively infrequent while two psychic events most frequently intervened between stimulus and response. Despite all individual differences, the results quite clearly produce the law that the average association time increases with the number of intervening conscious processes.

As our next task, we decided to investigate in greater detail those responses where only one conscious process intervened between stimulus and response.

Our results show that this one psychic event is not infrequently a word image. For example, for one subject, the stimulus word

---

* Translators' note: Titchener first translated "*Bewusstseinslagen*" as "conscious attitudes." The changed modern usage of the word "attitudes" suggests, among other considerations, the choice of "dispositions."

The Qualitative Investigation of Associations   139

"soul" evoked the acoustic-motoric word image "body" which then produced the association "spirit." The one intervening conscious process was also frequently the image of an object. For example, one subject reported that following the stimulus word "chimney" the visual image of a chimney-sweep was evoked, which was followed by the response "chimney-sweep." Some of our previous examples also show that a general disposition of consciousness may form the only mental process that occurs between stimulus and response words. Finally, the subjects often described this one intervening conscious event as an act of will. One subject reported that the stimulus word "luster" occasioned a search for a connection, whereupon the response "sun" was evoked. We then asked ourselves the question: Which was the most frequent intervening event between stimulus and response: a word image, an object image, a disposition of consciousness, or an activation of will? At the same time, we sought to solve the problem whether one or the other type of intervening conscious events slows down or speeds up the response process. Despite intensive investigation of our material, we found very little lawfulness in this direction. What was shown was the already fairly obvious fact that images intervene more frequently than dispositions of consciousness or activations of the will, as well as the rather valuable result that acts of the will slow down the associative sequence.

[There follow two tables that show that for all subjects the mean reaction time for responses with intervening conscious processes involving an activation of will is longer than for those responses where no activation of the will was observed.]

These tables show quite clearly that processes involving the will slow down the associative sequence.

Our material also indicated that the conscious processes intervening between stimulus and response may either be accompanied by feeling tone or not. One subject observed, for example, that for him the stimulus word "forest" evoked a visual image of a forest accompanied by positive feeling, which was then followed by the response "green."

[There follow two tables showing the frequency of those associations that are and those that are not accompanied by feeling tone, as well as their average reaction times.]

Despite obvious individual differences, these tables show clearly that the intervening experiences are in most cases without any feeling tone; beyond that, however, we observed that the average duration of associations with intervening conscious processes accompanied by feeling tone is considerably longer than the duration of all the others.

We now asked ourselves whether the direction of the feelings that accompany the associative processes influence the associative duration.

[There follow two tables that show the frequency of responses with pleasurable mediating links as against those with unpleasurable mediating links, as well as their respective reaction times.]

These tables show clearly that the negative feeling tone of intervening conscious processes decreases the associative speed.

Finally, we found during the perusal of our protocols that conscious processes (including feelings) may be observed not only parallel to the stimulus word but also parallel to the response word. For one subject, the response "worm" that immediately followed the stimulus word "tape" was accompanied by the visual image of a tapeworm. For another observer, hearing the stimulus word "chorale" evoked a pleasurable feeling, whereupon the response "sing" followed. The small number of cases falling into this category, however, does not permit us to draw any important generally valid conclusions. Therefore, we must leave for later investigations the solution to such questions as whether parallel psychic processes accompany the stimulus or the response word more frequently, whether any one particular group of psychic processes plays this parallel role more frequently than others, and in what direction these parallel events influence the association time. We can only say that accompanying experiences (including feelings) may occur parallel with either the stimulus or the response word. Despite the fact that our results do not directly support it, we may assume that even within an associative process various experiences may accompany the stimulus as well as the response word.

In the following we summarize the most important results of our study:

When a subject is given the task of responding to a spoken word with another spoken word, different conscious processes may oc-

The Qualitative Investigation of Associations 141

cur. First, the response word may immediately follow the stimulus word; second, one or more conscious processes may intervene between stimulus word and response word.

It then appears that responses without intervening conscious processes take place more quickly than those with intervening conscious events, and responses with one intervening conscious process take place more quickly than those where several psychic events intervene between stimulus and response word.

Responses with intervening conscious processes occur in general more frequently than those without intervening conscious events.

Whenever activations of the will are found among the intervening conscious processes, the reaction process is slowed down.

The conscious processes following the stimulus words are only in a few cases accompanied by feeling tone. In most cases there is no accompanying feeling tone. The feeling tone of the intervening conscious events slows down the associative process; negative feeling tones delay it more than positive ones.

If one now were to attempt a categorization of the associations that occur between spoken stimulus and response words, and if such a categorization is to be based on qualitative differences among associations, it would look approximately as follows:

The associations are divided either into:

(a) Those without intervening conscious processes, and

(b) Those with intervening conscious processes which may further be subdivided according to their number, type and feeling tone,

or

(a) Those without accompanying conscious processes,

(b) Those where conscious processes accompany the stimulus word,

(c) Those where the response words are accompanied by conscious processes, and,

(d) Those where both stimulus and response words are accompanied by other experiences.

Extensive further observations would show that even this second categorization is subject to further subdivision.

[There follows a paragraph thanking Marbe for his valuable advice as well as two subjects for their support of the study.]

* * *

It was an uneasy transition in the history of thought. Neither Mayer and Orth, nor Marbe, with whom they were working, were able to do much with this new phenomenon, but Marbe was startled to find a similar problem in his studies of judgment.

Marbe had set himself the task of determining, with the help of the new experimental method of controlled introspection, what conscious processes were involved in the act of judgment. The judgment was considered to be the most basic unit of rational thought; it had been studied intensively by logicians for centuries, and thus it was clear that a great deal was known about it. But exactly what? No distinction had yet been made between the judgment as a human act, and judgment or proposition as a statement of fact. The intertwining of logic and psychology in the history of thought frequently led to facile interpretations of reasoning and judging, such as we noted earlier in James Mill's treatment of the problem. But Marbe set for himself a genuinely psychological problem when he asked: What goes on in consciousness during the act of making a judgment?

The psychological importance of Marbe's monograph on judgment, published in 1901, lies in the fact that it was the first unified study of complex thought processes. Although it has also been credited with introducing the concept of *Bewusstseinslagen* [dispositions of consciousness], Marbe makes little of his use of that category. Having ventured into the area of judgment, he finds it necessary to justify his method in an introduction and repeats the, by then, traditional complaints against the armchair psychologists. His results he finds astounding; his subjects fail to discover any state of consciousness that is coordinated with the judgmental act. Again and again he stresses this negative finding, for example, "The present data are quite sufficient to draw the conclusion that no psychological conditions of judgments exist. . . . Even . . . the observers concerned . . . were extremely surprised to note the paucity of experiences that were connected with the judgmental process." *

In the following selection we have translated part of his introduction and his major theoretical conclusion. The latter produces a theory that permits the deduction that judgments could not have any conscious correlates since they are based on knowledge. Like practically all his predecessors, Marbe too had difficulties with the problem of knowledge. To know something implies that we can judge the correctness of a judgment, but the judgment of correctness depends on knowledge which Marbe then relegates to a psychological disposition, a faculty. Knowledge is built into the subject; he either has it or not. As we shall see, the next major attack on knowing was to be undertaken by Ach who introduced the notion of *Bewusstheit*, an awareness of knowledge without palpable content.

* K. Marbe, *Experimentell-psychologische Untersuchungen über das Urteil*. Leipzig: Engelmann, 1901, p. 43.

* * *

Karl Marbe

The Psychology of Judgments

Current scholarly views about the psychological nature of judgment vary widely. According to Brentano the nature of judgment consists of recognition or denial, while according to the so-called psychology of association the judgment is a special associative process. On the other hand, other scholars assume that judgment

K. Marbe, *Experimentell-psychologische Untersuchungen über das Urteil*. Leipzig: Engelmann, 1901. Pp. 13–14 and 91–92 transl. by George and Jean M. Mandler.

goes far beyond the simple associative process. For example, according to Wundt it consists of dissecting a complex image into its parts, a segmentation of a thought into its component elements, whereby the content of the judgment, though in an uncertain form, is given as a whole before it dissolves into its parts. At the same time Wundt assumes that the differentiation that takes place in judging cannot be associatively explained, but rather that it has its basis in the so-called apperception. Sigwart's notion of the psychological process of judgment is just the opposite. According to him, judging consists not of a taking apart but of a coagulation of images. Sigwart teaches that analysis into parts is one of the conditions of judging, but the judgment unifies the partial elements.

This great diversity of scholarly views about the psychological facts of judgments, which could easily be further documented with a mass of other examples, is obviously tied to the method that these scholars use in their research upon the problem in question. The psychology of judgment has not yet gone beyond unmethodical, natural, internal perceptions [introspection] and unsystematic experiments. Those who talk about judgments base their views upon conscious processes taking place within themselves during the act of judging—processes that either have developed haphazardly or have been produced by the observer in some experimental fashion, using experiment in the widest sense of the word. These researchers report nothing about the systematic use of a larger number of internal perceptions. Even the use of additional observers is not common; each scholar restricts himself to internal perceptions which he himself has experienced. Since the psychologist may be subject to serious errors even with relatively easy investigations that he conducts solely on himself, he is even more likely to be subject to such errors when he is dealing with difficult investigations such as those about judgment. One must, therefore, demand that whoever works on judgment should base his views on a larger series of internal perceptions which have been obtained, at least in part, from subjects other than himself.

My goal in the experiments to follow was to fulfill this requirement. At the same time I have tried to raise them to the level of experiments in the narrower sense. The internal perceptions about judgment to be reported on have been, as the reader will note, undertaken under familiar conditions that were artificially varied. . . .

THE THEORY OF THE COMPREHENSION AND INTERPRETATION OF JUDGMENTS. Since not all judgments that have been perceived or read are also understood and since comprehension is not related to psychologically determinable facts derived from the perceived and read judgments, comprehension must be related to other, psychologically indeterminate, presuppositions.

What are these presuppositions; when do we understand perceived or read judgments? If somebody tries to reproduce a tone that he has heard at some previous time, then [another] person, listening to this reproduction, can understand such a judgment only if he knows that it was the intention of the singer to have his tone correspond to some other tone. If somebody is asked: "How much are two and three?" and replies by stretching out the five fingers of his right hand or by saying the word "five," then [another] person who has heard only the replies but not the question cannot understand these judgments. In order to understand them he must know the judging person's intended meaning. Finally, when somebody hears a judgmental proposition in a foreign language he can only understand it when he knows to what objects the words of the sentence are intended to refer. To understand a judgment requires some knowledge; we understand a judgment when we know to what object its meaning corresponds in the intention of the experiencing person. . . .

We can thus easily see that the comprehension of a judgment, dependent as it is upon knowledge, cannot possibly be shown to exist in consciousness. What does it mean to say we know something? What does it mean to say that we know the first ten digits of π, that we know Kant's birthdate, or what he has written? These assertions can only mean that we are able to make *correct* judgments about the objects concerned. Thus to have reached the conclusion that to understand a judgment means to know what objects are, in the intention of the judge, supposed to coincide with the judgment, i.e., its meaning, implies simply: to understand a judgment says the same as being able to experience certain other judgments. This ability [to make correct judgments] is going to depend, just as musical ability, on certain psychological dispositions. But this ability will not be noticeable in consciousness, any more than the ability to sing on pitch and so forth, until it is translated into certain actions.

Just as we understand judgments only when we know to what object they refer, so can we judge their correctness or falsity only when we know whether or not they in fact correspond to the objects to which they or their meaning make reference. When this correspondence occurs, we judge them as correct, when it is missing, we call them false. Since the ability to evaluate a perceived or read judgment and the end result of this evaluation both depend upon some knowledge, it is understandable why our experimental investigations of those abilities and end results of the judgments could not yield any positive results. At the same time it cannot be denied that the ability to compare a judgment and its object may at times be related to feelings of unpleasure.

* * *

Comprehensible or not, the dispositions, or *Bsl*'s as they were soon called, were here to stay. In fact, an interesting thing soon happened to them. Subjects and experimenters being pretty much interchangeable in the Würzburg laboratories, the term *Bsl* found its way from the theoretical language into the protocol language of the introspecting subject.

The infestation of the language of the subject with the theoretical concepts of the psychologist is beautifully illustrated in the following few examples from the 1906 article by Messer. In these examples, the occurrence of the abbreviation *Bsl* is directly reproduced from Messer's protocols. It refers to the fact that his subjects, who were also his colleagues working on problems of thinking, actually used the word *"Bewusstseinslagen"* [dispositions of consciousness] in reporting the effects of a particular stimulus.

Thinking and the New Psychology: Imageless Thought 147

The general nature of Messer's experiments was typical of the Würzburger school. The subject is given a task [*Aufgabe*] and then a series of stimulus words. The task may be to give the first word the subject can think of, or to give a coordinated concept for the stimulus word, or to make a judgment about a sentence, and so forth. After a description of some of the quantitative (reaction time) results, some of the images evoked by the reactions, and a long section on the psychology of judgment, Messer discusses the *Bewusstseinslagen*. Imbedded in the protocols of that section, we find examples of the following order:

Subject 4: "*Bsl*, containing two thoughts: 1. You have to wait, 2. The coordinated object will come to you."—"*Bsl*, for which I can give the thought: that's easy."—"*Bsl:* There is a subordinate concept somewhere, but you can't formulate it very easily."

Subject 6: "*Bsl:* don't say that."—"*Bsl*, my father always used to mispronounce that name."—"*Bsl:* you could say that at any time."

Subject 4: "*Bsl:* Can't I think of anything? Is that a coordinated whole? Then I remembered the word 'anvil.' Then for a time being an emptiness of consciousness and then a further *Bsl* which went in the direction of the questions: What are you supposed to do now: Are you supposed to test or to search?"

Subject 2: "*Bsl:* Let's take the other meaning!"

Subject 3: "*Bsl:* Why not think about something else!"

Messer bravely attempted to classify or order this endless array of *Bsl* and came to the conclusion that what he was dealing with was not a peculiar type of conscious experience occurring now and again during the thinking process but rather was thought itself. Thus his task of classification became no less than to put order into the entire range of thought.

One of the prominent aspects of his classification is the emphasis on relations. The experiencing of relations had always posed difficulties for classical associationism. How are relations among images perceived? A consistent associationist, such as Ebbinghaus, had to say that in perceiving two tones, for example, we perceive their equality just as directly and in exactly the same way as we perceive the tones and their various qualities themselves. The difficulty of this position had been frequently criticized, perhaps most succinctly by William James, who, in the *Principles of Psychology*, pointed out that the perception of A followed by the perception of B is not the same thing as the perception of B following A. With the advent of imageless thought it was at least possible to tackle this problem, although a satisfactory solution was not to be reached until Selz, and later the Gestalt school, addressed themselves to these questions.

Messer seems to be groping to the conclusion that much of the thinking process goes on below the conscious level, with conscious processes attending it with varying degrees of clarity. Consciousness is beginning to take shape as the visible portion of an iceberg, with much of the work of the thinking process going on below the surface.

The following selection shows Messer trying to bring order into the world of *Bsl* and his conclusion that the term might as well be abandoned. His footnote on page 151 suggests a solution that Binet had previously advocated and that Bühler was to adopt in the following year.

* * *

August Messer

Experimental-Psychological Investigations on Thinking

DISPOSITIONS OF CONSCIOUSNESS [BEWUSSTSEINSLAGEN]. Our subjects either knew or were actually quite familiar with the concept of "dispositions of consciousness" introduced by Marbe and characterized as "states of consciousness, the contents of which either completely elude a closer characterization or at least make it difficult." Thus we find this term used quite frequently in our subjects' responses. . . . [From our previous encounter with this concept in our investigation of comprehension and judgment] we

A. Messer, Experimentell-psychologische Untersuchungen über das Denken. Arch. f. d. ges. Psychol., 1906, **8**, 1–224. Pp. 175–188 transl. by George and Jean M. Mandler.

obtain the *first group of dispositions of consciousness:* those which immediately follow word images and which represent the meaning (the concept or sense) of the word in consciousness. Into this group belong dispositions of comprehension (with its various nuances and graduations), dispositions of various degrees of ambiguity, and of synonymity....

These dispositions of consciousness can be said to represent a middle region between two other relevant groups of states of consciousness.

If we use the degree of unfolding in consciousness as our ordering principle, then the bottom level consists of the usual forms of meaningful speech in which meaning and word are inextricably fused in consciousness. At the upper end, however, we come into the region of cases where consciousness of meaning is represented by objective images of the optical or other sensory type, or by further word images.

Thus, these three forms of consciousness can be brought into a single dimension, though obviously one with continuous transitional states. We can assume the same for the concrete processes which we have, metaphorically, postulated as the "carriers" of these states of consciousness.

Just as these dispositions of meaning can, so to speak, appear as appendices or tails of word images, so can they also appear without words.

We now come to the *second main group of dispositions of consciousness.* Here meaning (concepts) are present but the words are missing. One might be looking for the words but even before they are found one knows what is meant—what one wants to say. Here, too, there is no dearth of transitory forms: word fragments may be found or one knows how the missing word sounds.

Both groups of dispositions of consciousness can be extended without any difficulty from the individual word, that is, from the individual word meanings, to propositions and judgmental contents.

These cases where the meaning of a proposition is not immediately present upon reading, but appears lightning-like as a separate experience, belong to the first group. To the second group belong those cases where a judgment or a thought is present which could only be adequately formulated in a sentence but where still no words can be found in consciousness. We need only suggest that here, too, there are many transitional forms.

[There follows a series of examples and a further subclassification of these two groups, ending up in some thirty-odd different types of dispositions of consciousness.]

The dispositions of consciousness with which we have dealt here may be concrete or more abstract, they may be reproducible in a word or in one or several sentences, and they may be purely intellectual or affective in type. All these manifold types of dispositions are included within the region of experiences which B. Erdmann has described as "unformulated" (or "intuitive") thinking.

Obviously, in our actual thought processes, it is not possible to differentiate strictly between formulated and unformulated thinking. Not only must we recognize manifold subcategories in both classes, but also continuous intermediary stages and various transitions from one to the other. We can consider as borderline cases on the one side thinking and completely formulated propositions with a clear consciousness of meaning, on the other a lightning-like reflection and recognition which is bare of any trace of a word. The difference between the two is probably greater than that between the slow and correct writing of a child who has just learned to write, and the hasty symbols of a practiced stenographer.

This should not lead us to think of the relationship in the following fashion: that fully formulated thinking in the child is the original type which in the adult is eventually abridged and condensed. Rather, we will have to assume . . . a preverbal, hypological thinking in the child which needs verbal shaping in order to gain certainty, in order to become communicable and reliably reproducible.

In order to explain these varied dispositions of consciousness, however, we will have to adopt a hypothesis that the concrete psychic processes which underlie completely formulated thinking occur in shortened forms of great variety, interlaced with one another, using more or less of the available psychophysical energy.

The dispositions of consciousness have thus become somewhat comprehensible in their *intellectual* aspects. In their *affective* aspects, however, they offer nothing that is either new or particularly obscure. The term *"Bewusstseinslagen"* has done its duty as a temporary collective name, and it seems advisable to replace it with the familiar expression *"Gedanken"* [thoughts].[1] . . .

[1] It would probably fit language usage best if we were to restrict "thoughts" to those *Bsl*'s whose content can only be formulated in one or more sentences, while the *Bsl*'s concerned with the meaning of single words or phrases should be designated as "concepts."

* * *

Messer only mentioned the unconscious aspects of thought *en passant* but Narziss Ach had already treated the problem in 1905, the previous year. Ach worked out both an ambitious experimental program and a comprehensive theory. He proclaimed the heuristic and scientific value of "systematic self-observation," which was his phrase for the experimental technique used in the Würzburg laboratory. His theory, which depends a good deal on unconscious mechanisms of thought, we will deal with in greater detail later on, but for the present we shall concentrate on his development of the concept of the *Bsl*. For Ach, the *Bsl* was one type of imageless thought, fitting into his larger schema of *Bewusstheit,* or awareness. The *Bewusstheiten* were described as the imageless knowing that something is the case. Although in themselves they were unanalyzable experiences, they served the purpose of bringing the elementary experience of knowing, or knowing the meaning of something, into consciousness; they are what the familiar "Uh-huh" of daily recognition is about. Around these knowings or awarenesses, Ach wove a somewhat vague physiological theory to explain when images will arise to consciousness and what degree of intensity they will attain. The general level of this theoretical framework is illustrated in the following selection.

Ach used a wide variety of reaction experiments. The subject might be instructed to flex his right index finger when a white card was presented, or to give a motor response only to a certain class of stimuli, or to name the stimulus (one of several cards of different colors) when it was presented. In more complex situations the response might be conditional, that is, the motor response was required only when a red card was presented to the left of a white card, or a discrimination was required in which the subject reacted to one color with the right thumb, to another with the left thumb. In addition, there were purely verbal tasks, such as free associations or judgments, or tasks that required the subject to give the name of the river on which a given town was situated. The introspections collected after the completion of the task dealt primarily with the main period, that is, the interval between the perception of the stimulus and the completion of the response.

* * *

Narziss Ach

Awareness

Analyses of the contents of consciousness obtained by means of systematic experimental self-observation have shown a variety of experiences in which all of a complex content is simultaneously present in the form of a "knowledge." This knowledge exists in an imageless form, that is, no phenomenological components are demonstrable—neither visual, acoustic, nor kinesthetic sensations, nor their memory images—which would qualitatively define the content of this knowledge. We encountered such experiences in every subject in these experiments. *It is the presence of such imageless knowledge which we designate as awareness.*

N. Ach, *Über die Willenstätigkeit und das Denken*. Göttingen: Vandenhoeck and Ruprecht, 1905. This selection translated by D. Rapaport, and reprinted from D. Rapaport, *Organization and pathology of thought*. New York: Columbia University Press, 1951, pp. 24–38. By permission of the publisher.

The content of such knowledge is given unequivocally and definitively, even though the manner in which it is given is not amenable to analysis. Immediately after the experience of this knowledge, the subject can state what he was aware of concerning it. Such awareness, therefore, is characterized by the knowledge it implies. In our experiments, such experiences were most obvious in the content of expectation at the end of the preparatory period, and in the perseverating contents of consciousness in the period following the experiment. Because we can direct our attention to this perseverating content as though it were a perceptual content, we can use it to obtain self-observations. In these, the process just experienced is present all at once—*in nuce*, as it were—without details or images. For example, in a none-too-habituated state of expectation, one of the following complex contents is often simultaneously present as awareness: (a) The stimulus with its spatial determination; that is, the subject knows that an unequivocally determined change (the appearance of a white card) will occur at the spot he fixates on. (b) The subject is aware that this must be followed by a known and unequivocally determined change on his part (the reaction-movement). Also, a relationship between these two unequivocally determined changes is given, in the awareness that as soon as the stimulus appears the reaction-movement must follow. (c) The awareness has a temporal component, in the knowledge that the stimulus will appear within a certain known time-span. . . . Besides these directly given contents of the expectation, and the visual percept (in our case, the screen of the card-changer), the usual phenomena accompanying sensory attention are also present—such as tension-experiences in the upper half of the body and in the optical sense-organ. Occasionally some of these elements of the awareness-complex may appear in the form of images, particularly at the beginning of the preparatory period or in the first experiments of a day. In this respect there are great individual differences, which are rooted in individual endowment. Yet in the majority of the experiments the whole expectation-content, excepting the accompanying phenomena, is present only as imageless knowledge, which we call awareness.

Should such experiences occur frequently, the simultaneously given constituents of the awareness-content usually begin to fade:

the intensity of awareness abates. The knowledge-content remains clear and unequivocal, but it is no longer experienced in its original intensity. This process may also be characterized as the decrease of attention-concentration. Besides these changes in the intensity of a total awareness, there are also intensity differences in the awareness of the various simultaneously given part-contents; in other words, attention is directed more to some than to other constituents of the simultaneously experienced complex content. Meanwhile, the entire content is present as awareness. Thus, for instance, in states of expectancy it frequently happens that the awareness of the reaction to be made—described under (b) above —recedes, relative to that of an unequivocally defined change— described under (a) above.... With some subjects—for example, Subject L.—this was more the rule than the exception, in the beginning. L. was unable to maintain simultaneously an equally great intensity of the two part-contents.... With much experience, the intensity of awareness—of the whole or part-content— may so recede that its presence as awareness is no longer demonstrable. This was the case with Subject J.: when fixating on the screen, besides weak intentional sensations in the reactor organ, there was only a vague awareness that he must react. We designate this recession of the content of awareness as the *automatization* of the process. In contrast to this, in other instances an increase in the intensity of awareness is demonstrable. Such intensification may occur, for instance, because of repeated internal utterances and continuous concentration of attention. Therefore, we are justified in distinguishing degrees of intensity of awareness in simultaneously given complex contents, as well as in consecutive experiences. . . .

When a content is only an imageless knowledge, immediately preceding or simultaneous with the meaning-awareness, there exists in consciousness a visual, acoustic, or kinesthetic sensation (tension-sensation), or a memory image of the content. These sensations are image-representations in consciousness of the imageless knowledge. They are indicators of the meaning-content. The sensations may, of course, come without such meaning-content, as pure sensory qualities. Thus it happened repeatedly in our experiments that, after the appearance of a colored card, the sensation "yellow" was present solely in its optical quality. Only afterwards did the knowledge arise, "This is yellow," as an independent thought. It could be said that only this thought identified the sensation as the familiar yellow color. Somehow a link to *previous experience* became effective and found expression in this knowledge. This is the process known as *apperception,* which always implies the presence or appearance of the knowledge of a meaning. When a complex content, the part-contents of which show varying degrees of awareness-intensity, is present simultaneously, then that part of the conscious complex which is momentarily in the foreground of awareness may be designated as the apperceived part. It is, as Wundt puts it, in the focus of consciousness. Because of their continuous change of intensity, it is often difficult to judge the degree of awareness of simultaneously given part-contents. As systematic experimental self-observation plainly indicates, attention may be evenly distributed and the simultaneously present part-contents may momentarily show no differences of awareness intensity; therefore, the here-described appearance of the meaning-content must be considered the crucial characteristic of apperception. Herbart gave most careful attention to this phenomenon. These considerations are supported by my previous demonstration that, when a stimulus is apperceived, from the moment of its appearance maximal attention is directed toward a single conscious content (on the basis of a previous *Einstellung*). Thus, the developing stimulus-impression is in the focus of consciousness; yet in this phase we cannot speak of [complete] apperception. Rather, what takes place is the development of the stimulus-apperception; the apprehension of the stimulus-impression in accordance with the preceding *Einstellung* takes time. Thus a content may be in the focus of consciousness, in the center of attention, without having been apperceived.

In analyzing their experience, subjects often find it difficult to describe an imageless awareness-content. Part of the experience is at times indicated phenomenologically: by internal utterances such as "must come," or "edge, edge," or word fragments like "add," "before," "after." Such kinesthetic or acoustic-kinesthetic images may well be the basis for the widespread assumption that our thinking occurs always by means of internal speech or adequate visual, acoustic, and other memory images. It must be pointed out, however, that there are very complex contents of which only part-contents and their mutual relationships are present in consciousness, whereas the contents themselves are not or even cannot be represented by adequate verbal designation or by anything like it. When a phenomenological constituent [of such a complex content] is present, it refers only to a corresponding [partial] meaning-content; for instance, "edge" refers to the expectation of the upper edge of the card. At the same time, other simultaneous expectation-contents do not have such phenomenological representation, and are present within the total tension-state only as awareness. Furthermore, it happens at times that complex contents, the verbal expression of which would take several sentences, appear momentarily, like a flash of lightning. Therefore, in their brief existence they could not be given in internal speech. Their meaning-content is unequivocal, and their memory clear and definite, though we cannot demonstrate the presence of any sensory qualities. Thus, for instance, in the preparatory period of an experiment with optical reactions of twofold coordination, Subject C. had a visual memory picture of "O," and with it a lightning thought that it would be most practical to be prepared only for "O"; beside this, there was the awareness that perhaps there would be only "E." . . . In view of the clear and unequivocal content of such awareness, it seems incorrect to assume that these are "obscure sensations" or memory images, too weak to be demonstrable as single contents, but which when taken together result in a realization of the meaning-content.

Experiences such as the following speak against such an assumption: when an awareness without demonstrable imagery is in the focus of consciousness, together with it a reproduced sensation—for example, a white card—appears as a part-content, with a lesser degree of awareness intensity. . . . Often we first observe the presence of an image representation of a meaning-content (for instance, in the form of internal speech, "as fast as possible"), and only then the corresponding meaning-content as an awareness without phenomenological representation. There are, however, instances in which awareness is followed by an image. Thus, in an experiment with numbers, after the intention "subsequent," the number 9 was presented ... first came the awareness, "I know it," and only then the visual image of zero.

Even though the experience we call awareness was demonstrable in all subjects, there were great individual differences. Many people are given to immediate visual or acoustic-kinesthetic imaging of meaning-contents. The author himself, having neither strong motor nor visual bent, has a definite inclination to think in awarenesses; this circumstance may well have contributed to his interest in the analysis of imageless thinking. One area where imageless conceptual thinking is most obvious is the quick and understanding reading of a text. When, for instance, the written sign of the word "bell" is before me, I apperceive the sign and know what it means. The awareness of the meaning is then present in me. According to the *theory of awareness*, it is not necessary that presentations—apperceiving presentation-masses—arise to assimilate the impression, for example, the sound or visual image of a bell. According to this theory, the realization of the meaning-content occurs in a different fashion. It is well-known that every presentation in consciousness—for example, the stimulus-impression "bell"—puts many associated presentations into readiness. This readiness of presentations—that is, their reproduction tendencies—suffices for a conscious representation of what we call their meaning, without their having to enter consciousness. The reproduction is not yet complete, it has only been initiated by, we might say, a stimulation of reproduction tendencies. This stimulation suffices to create an unequivocal relationship in the direction of the "stimulated" reproduction tendencies. These unequivocal relationships are experienced as knowledge, that is, meaning. . . . One of the reproduction tendencies corresponding to it may then become over-valent; that is to say, one of the associated presentations enters consciousness and appears as the conceptual sign of that knowledge. . . .

According to the laws of association and of reproduction of ideas, the more often the associated ideas have been in consciousness (other factors remaining constant), the stronger the reproduction tendency. If the meaningful word "bell" is given, ideas most frequently associated with this sign will be put into the highest degree of readiness. Thus, the stronger the reproduction-tendencies, the greater the state of excitation. On the basis of our previous discussion, we are entitled to speak about differences in awareness-intensity within a simultaneously given complex. Nothing seems to be in the way of assuming that the greater the excitation of readied presentations, and the greater the intensity of reproduction-tendencies, the more intensive the awareness. Therefore, we may describe awareness as an increasing function of excitations of reproduction-tendencies. It follows that of all the reproduction-tendencies stimulated by the word "bell," the awareness of those most frequently experienced will be most intensive. In contrast to these, the other readied presentations, being only occasional and incidental, are of a lesser awareness-intensity. The meaning-content of a given word implies a knowledge in which regularly recurring associative connections have far greater awareness-intensity than those occasionally and incidentally formed. The latter will be neglected and not become effective as awarenesses. Here we encounter an experience-determined process of *associative abstraction,* in that only those presentations become consciously effective in a given meaning-content which have recurred regularly as its constituents. This abstraction process, through the continuous assimilation of presentations in their varying connections, occurs entirely automatically.

Since associated presentations which recur regularly represent the constant characteristics of a given concept, associative abstraction determines *the kind of awareness in which a concept is psychologically present in an individual.* This shows that there is no general psychological representation of a concept which is valid for all individuals. Awareness of a concept depends on the association of ideas corresponding to experiences, which again greatly vary with people. Even in the same individual, awareness of a concept does not remain constant. The factors determining the intensity of reproduction-tendencies, that is, of the readiness of a presentation, are also decisive for awareness-intensity. (Such factors are: the frequency of the attention-deployment which brought about the association; the feeling-tone; the time lapse since the association was formed; the generative, effectual, and retroactive inhibitions; the perseverating reproduction-tendencies; the determining tendencies.) For example, if one of these factors reinforces the excitation of one of the readied presentations, the conceptual awareness changes. The mental constellation is subject to constant change, and so is awareness. Herein lies the developmental potentiality of mental processes. As apperceptive masses are progressively replaced through new associations of ideas, there is a constant change of conceptual awareness; at the same time the excitation of now one, now another, readied presentation is increased by a previous determination. Therefore, even identical stimulations, following each other at brief intervals, may result in differing conceptual awarenesses. The psychological representation of a concept by an awareness is thus not identical with the logical characteristics in its definition. This incongruity of the logical and the psychological contents of concepts is most obvious in children. On the one hand, they lack the broad experience and varied associative connections necessary for the process of associative abstraction, that is, for the differentiation of the regular from the incidental; on the other hand, their attention often turns to striking but not regular contents of consciousness. Therefore, often the child does not differentiate between essential and unessential characteristics. For him, any incidental accompanying phenomenon may appear the major characteristic of a concept. A child's drawings offer a very instructive opportunity to observe his thinking. They express what he knows about an object rather than what he has perceived of it: the drawing is objectified awareness.

These considerations suggest that presentations are abstract, or rather, that all conscious content given as awareness is abstract. The reason is that the incidental associations which are the overtones of every awareness do not attain appreciable conscious influence as compared with the regular associations.

The discussion of the concept of awareness has bearing on the role of determining tendencies. We have seen that these tendencies determine the course of mental happening so as to accord with the goal-presentation. In the preparatory period of the experiment, when the intention is formed, reproduction-tendencies corresponding to the meaning of the goal-presentation achieve a high degree of excitation, by means of the heightened concentration of attention and the perseverance of the goal-presentation in consciousness. These reproduction-tendencies, accompanied by meaning-awareness, are brought simultaneously into relationship with the referent-presentation, influencing it in accordance with the goal-presentation. Such relationships between goal-presentations and referent-presentations we call intentions. In contrast to the referent-presentation implied in the intention-awareness, the one on which the determination actually takes effect we call "concrete referent-presentation" (for example, when the intention is to calculate, the number 2 that appears as stimulus is the "concrete referent-presentation"). If the intention is accompanied by a good concentration of attention, it also implies a reference to the future in that it is directed toward a concrete referent-presentation to appear subsequently.

The influence of determining tendencies appears in simplest form in the varieties of apperceptive fusion. To this category belong even those forms of apperception in which the meaning-content may be considered an after-effect of a preceding "Einstellung"; for example, the recognition-reaction in which a yellow or red card is apperceived as colored, in accord with the instructions, or the apperception of its color with the awareness of consent or affirmation, "Yes, this is red." These forms of apperception, therefore, may be designated as *determined apperceptions.* Such is the case also when a white or colored card is apperceived as "something to react to," since this apperception complies with a preceding determination. There is an apperceptive fusion here between the stimulus-impression and the readied reproduction-tendencies, so that comprehension is directly connected with the corresponding meaning....

In contrast to this, in those experiments in which *Einstellung* is poor, the insufficient determination is noticeable already in the apperception. In cases where the preparation has been insufficient, we observe a state of disorientation upon the appearance of the stimulus: the subject does not know what to do.

Besides these described forms, determination may manifest itself in what is known as *specific apperceptive fusion.* Such are particularly frequent and various in reactions without coordination of activity. For example, in the preparatory period Subject B. had a visual image of the plus-sign, representing the intention to "add"; when the stimulus appeared, an apperceptive fusion took place in that the appearing numbers fell into the prepared scheme. The determined presentation followed associatively from this apperceptive fusion. Subject C. experienced a spatial displacement of the two numbers which corresponded to the intention: in adding they pulled together, in subtracting the smaller figure sidled to the larger. . . .

A middle position between special apperceptive fusion and determined apperceptions is occupied by the cases where the apperception of the concrete referent-presentation (for example, of a number) is followed by an imageless meaning-awareness, and where, after that apperception but before the appearance of the result (that is, the determined presentation), knowledge of what will appear is present.

Another form of apperceptive fusion is *apperceptive substitution,* in which a preceding *Einstellung* comes to expression. In the simplest cases, a presentation is given as a part-content of the intention of the preparatory period. This is the case, for example, in our rhyming experiments: the letter "b" appears [as a part content of the intention] and replaces the initial letter of the concrete referent-presentation (stimulus-syllable). The determined presentation may be considered the product of an apperceptive substitution, effected by the determination. . . .

The list, apperceptive fusion, determined apperception, specific apperceptive fusion, apperceptive substitution, does not exhaust the varieties of the effects of determining tendencies. Some of these are transitions to those forms in which determination finds its most striking expression. In these cases, the determined presentation, the end-product of the determination, appears in consciousness immediately in conjunction with the concrete referent-presentation; and neither the goal-presentation itself, from which the determination arises, nor any part-content of it is demonstrable in consciousness after the appearance of the concrete referent-presentation. The selfsame concrete referent-presentation, once given, may be followed by a variety of determined presentations, selected by the determining tendencies. It is characteristic that even though the appearance of the determined presentation is precipitated by the concrete referent-presentation, its quality depends on the goal-presentation, though the latter is not demonstrable in consciousness. The qualitative characteristics of the determined presentation are beyond doubt due to unconscious (meaning simply not conscious) effects. Thus we define determining tendencies as *unconsciously acting* Einstellungen *which arise from the meaning of the goal-presentation and, directed toward the coming referent-presentation, result in the spontaneous appearance of the determined presentation.* . . .

* * *

In the preceding selection it is clear that Ach is attempting to explain and utilize in his theory what were to him clear facts derived from his experimental findings: meaning, or recognition, may sometimes be carried by visual images, but at other times it occurs without their presence or before any images have crystalized. Yet his "facts" and those of Marbe and Messer were soon to be bitterly disputed.

Wundt for one was not the man to admit the appearance of an experimental psychology of thinking that he had declared as impossible just ten years previously. And in 1907 Karl Bühler published the *nec plus ultra* of the Würzburger method in a study which did not fail to point out Wundt's previous misgivings.*

Bühler's investigation was much more ambitious than those of his colleagues. His stimulus materials were complex questions requiring extensive thought processes that terminated in "yes" or "no" judgments; the subjects then gave a retrospective account of the processes intervening between stimulus and response. Bühler concluded from these protocols that there were basic unanalyzable units in the thinking process, which should simply be called "thoughts." These units could, however, be classified into types, three of the most important being: first, consciousness of a rule [*Regelbewusstsein*], a knowing that one can solve a

---

* K. Bühler, *Tatsachen und Probleme zu einer Psychologie der Denkvorgänge. I. Über Gedanken*, Würzburger Habilitationsschrift, 1907.

problem and how it is done, without actually having the steps in mind; second, consciousness of knowing the meaning of something, "intending" it [*Intentionen*], without having the meaning-content clearly in mind; and third, consciousness of relations [*Beziehungsbewusstsein*], an awareness similar to Ach's conception.

The following passage illustrates Bühler's conception of these "thoughts" and also presages the concern with the unit of thought that was to reach full flowering in the next decade.

What really is the consciousness of a rule? It is a thought in which something, that from a logical point of view we call a rule, comes to consciousness. But this does not quite unequivocally determine the concept. I could simply designate a rule just as I designate any other object. But consciousness of rule is not such thinking *of* a rule, rather it is thinking *a* rule or thinking according to a rule. The object of the consciousness of a rule is not the rule, but rather the state of affairs, the object, that the rule describes, on which it is used, from which it might possibly be derived. Using a distinction of Husserl's, we might say: Consciousness of a rule is a thought with which we can adequately think certain objects that the logician calls laws. There are at least two ways, . . . and not just one, in which objects can be adequately represented in consciousness, in perception. Perception is image; the other self-sufficient (adequate) object-consciousness is the consciousness of a rule. . . . One thing seems to me to be certain, that consciousness of a rule is a very frequent experience in scientific thinking. . . .*

There is a greater emphasis in this analysis of thinking on processes than on contents, and it illustrates the influence of "act psychology" on Külpe and thus on others of the Würzburg school. In their eager attempts at classification of imageless contents, some of the Würzburgers at times had ignored the obvious active processes occurring in their thinking subjects, and seemed to be harking back to the static classificatory schemes of the early associationists.

---

* K. Bühler, Tatsachen und Probleme zu einer Psychologie der Denkvorgänge. I. Über Gedanken. *Arch. f.d. ges. Psychol.*, 1907, **9,** 297–365. Pp. 339–340. See also Bühler's companion articles: II. Über Gedankenzusammenhänge. *Arch. f.d. ges. Psychol.*, 1908, **12,** 1–23; III. Über Gedankenerinnerungen. *Arch. f.d. ges. Psychol.*, 1908, **12,** 24–92.

Unfortunately for Bühler, his retrospective technique of introspection, plus some incautious remarks on the necessity of sympathetic interaction between the subject and experimenter, brought swift retribution. That same year Wundt thundered from on high. He defended his earlier position, criticized the Würzburger methods, questioned their data and rejected their conclusions. After some fifty pages of detailed analysis he concludes:

1. The inquiry experiments are not real experiments, but rather self-observations with handicaps. Not a single one of the requirements set for psychological experiments is met by them, on the contrary they realize the opposite of each of these requirements.
2. They represent the most inadequate of the older forms of self-observation; they occupy the attention of the observer with an unexpected, more or less difficult, intellectual problem and demand of him in addition that he observe the behavior of his own consciousness.
3. The method of inquiry must be rejected in both of the forms in which it has been used. As an inquiry prior to the experiment it subjects self-observation to the unfavorable influence of examination pressure; as an inquiry after the experiment it opens wide the door to the interfering influence of suggestion. In both forms the method vitiates self-observation most severely in that the subject who is to observe himself is at the same time subjected to observation by others.
4. The representatives of the method of inquiry ignore the well tried rule that in order to solve complex problems one must first master the simpler ones which the former presuppose. As a result they confuse attention with consciousness and fall victim to a popular error in believing that everything that occurs in consciousness may easily be pursued in self-observation. This last error alone would be sufficient to explain the lack of results obtained by the inquiry experiments.*

Perhaps the success of the Würzburger attack can be measured by the virulence of the reply. In any case, a more dispassionate examination of their results was soon mounted by Edward Bradford Titchener.

In 1909 Titchener gave a series of lectures, printed in book form as *Lectures on the Experimental Psychology of the Thought-Processes,* in which he summarizes and analyzes the work of the Würzburg school in detail and includes his own forceful objections to some of their conclusions. Primarily he disputes that there are

---

* W. Wundt, Über Ausfrageexperimente und über die Methoden zur Psychologie des Denkens. *Psychol. Studien,* 1907, **3**, 301–360. P. 358.

such things as imageless thoughts. The quarrel is a curious one. It rests on two distinct yet related problems. The first problem is to be found in the nature of introspection itself, and the second in the nature of theories of mind or thinking that would be acceptable to the two schools.

If one carefully observes his own thought processes, does he find imageless thinking or not? At first glance, this seems to be a factual question. And yet we have already noticed how the Würzburg subjects, as they became practiced in their techniques and familiar with the theoretical notions abroad in their laboratory, gradually began to use the term "imageless thought" to describe their mental processes, whereas originally the term was invented in order to define an unexpressable experience. The *Bsl* became more and more common and eventually came to pepper the protocols. That is not to say that there was no such experience (the term *was* invented to fill a gap in the common language), but rather to point out the vulnerability of introspection to the theoretical language in vogue. It is quite possible that Marbe and Ach experienced the *Bsl* and that Titchener did not. Perhaps it should not be said that Titchener did not believe in imageless thought because he could not observe any such process in himself, but rather that he could not observe any such process because he did not believe there was such a thing.

What is probably more important, however, is the disagreement as to the kinds of statements that are to be acceptable, not only in the theoretical language of psychology, but in its protocol language as well.

For Titchener, as for the Würzburgers, the essence of the psychological experiment was controlled introspection. But he carried this principle to its ultimate conclusion and, as frequently happens to principles stretched to the breaking point, it led him into absurdities. If our experimental technique is introspection and if this is all the material we have to work with, then psychology must remain the analysis of the conscious mind. Other, unconscious processes may be taking place within the organism, but strictly speaking they are not psychological; they fall rather within the realm of physiology. What does this imply for the protocol language, the language the subjects use? First of all, Titchener, rather than implicitly suggesting, *directed* his subjects as to the language they must use. They were explicitly trained to reduce their experience to the most basic terms possible, and these terms were prescribed: sensations and affections. The goal was "to describe the contents of consciousness not as they mean but as they are." Thus meanings, that is, objects, relations, recognitions, and so forth, are not to be admitted to the protocol language (this would be committing the "stimulus error"), but are to be built up by the experimenter-theoretician out of the raw sensations as given to him by the subject. The difficulties inherent in carrying out this edict are enormous. To learn to describe our familiar three-dimensional meaningful world in terms of patches of colors and vague kinesthetic images is not only difficult to the point of impossibility, but it also introduces some degree of distortion of the basic data. The Würzburgers before Titchener and the Gestaltists after him were at great pains to show that such sensations are not the raw data of psychology, but theoretical abstractions of a high order.

Indeed, when the sensationalist position is carried to its extreme, it seems literally impossible to commit the "stimulus error." As Humphrey states in his careful analysis of Titchener's position:

[The] sensationist position endeavours in effect to analyze all experience (save affect) into pure sense datum. But such sense datum can, of itself, give no indication concerning its occasion (stimulus, as Titchener uses the word). To take a single example: Nobody experiencing simply "blue visual image . . . vague kinaesthetic image," etc., would be in the position to commit the stimulus-error of maintaining that he thought about a woman coming in secretly. [This refers to a previously given protocol.] How does he know to what these "pure" images refer unless there is something present in consciousness to tell him, and something which is of necessity of a non-sensory nature, since a complete inventory of sensory process has already been made? The *reductio ad absurdum* of the sensationist position is surely given in the following quotation from Titchener: "I was not at all astonished to observe that the recognition of a gray might consist of a quiver in the stomach." What is there *in this particular "quiver"* to indicate that it is a recognition "quiver," or even to allow the stimulus error to be made from it? The sensationist hypothesis is in the position of precluding the error with which it taxes its opponent.*

---

* G. Humphrey, *Thinking*. London: Methuen, 1951, pp. 126–127.

It might be added that the difficulty cannot be removed by allowing meaning to be handled by the psychologist by deducing it from the protocol, since it is impossible to discover such meaning without the subject lapsing into the stimulus error.

In the following selections Titchener presents his views on imagery and discusses some of the then current notions about thinking.

* * *

Edward Bradford Titchener

Imagery and Sensationalism

My visual imagery voluntarily aroused as for Galton's breakfast-table test, is extremely vivid, though it seems bodiless and papery when compared with direct perception. I have never, so far as I am aware, experienced a visual hallucination; I have no number-form; I know nothing of coloured hearing. On the other hand, my mind, in its ordinary operations, is a fairly complete picture gallery—not of finished paintings, but of impressionist notes. Whenever I read or hear that somebody has done something modestly, or gravely, or proudly, or humbly, or courteously, I see a visual hint of the modesty or gravity or pride or humility or courtesy. The stately heroine gives me a flash of a tall figure, the only clear part of which is a hand holding up a steely grey skirt; the humble suitor gives me a flash of a bent figure, the only clear part of which is the bowed back, though at times there are hands held deprecatingly before the absent face. A great many of these sketches are irrelevant and accessory; but they

E. B. Titchener, *Lectures on the experimental psychology of the thought-processes.* New York: Macmillan, 1909. Pp. 13–27, 30–34, 170–183 reprinted by permission.

often are, and they always may be, the vehicles of a logical meaning. The stately form that steps through the French window to the lawn may be clothed in all the colours of the rainbow; but its stateliness is the hand on the grey skirt. I shall not multiply instances. All this description must be either self-evident or as unreal as a fairy-tale.

It leads us, however, to a very important question—the old question of the possibility of abstract or general ideas. You will recall the main heads of the controversy. Locke had maintained that it is possible to form the general idea, say, of a triangle which is "neither oblique nor rectangle, neither equilateral, equicrural, nor scalenon; but all and none of these at once." Berkeley replied that "if any man has the faculty of framing in his mind such an idea of a triangle, as is here described, it is in vain to pretend to dispute him out of it, nor would I go about it. . . . For myself, I find indeed I have a faculty of imagining, or representing to myself, the ideas of those particular things I have perceived, and of variously compounding and dividing them, . . . [but] I cannot by any effort of thought conceive the abstract idea described above. . . . The idea of man that I frame to myself must be either of a white, or a black, or a tawny, a straight, or a crooked, a tall, or a low, or a middle-sized man." The dispute has lasted down to our own day. Hamilton calls the Lockean doctrine a "revolting absurdity." Huxley finds it entirely acceptable. "An anatomist who occupies himself intently with the examination of several specimens of some new kind of animal, in course of time acquires so vivid a conception of its form and structure, that the idea may take visible shape and become a sort of waking dream. But the figure which thus presents itself is generic, not specific. It is no copy of any one specimen, but, more or less, a mean of the series"—a composite photograph of the whole group.

All through this discussion there runs, unfortunately, the confusion of logic and psychology that is characteristic of the English school. It is no more correct to speak, in psychology, of an abstract idea, or a general idea, than it would be to speak of an abstract sensation or a general sensation. What is abstract and general is not the idea, the process in consciousness, but the logical meaning of which that process is the vehicle. All that we can say of the idea is that it comprises such and such qualities; shows these and these temporal and spatial characters; has a certain degree of vividness as focal or marginal, clear or obscure; has the vague haziness of distant sounds and faint lights or the clean-cut definiteness of objects to which the sense-organ is accommodated; is arranged on a particular pattern. Locke and Huxley, now, believed that abstract meaning is represented in consciousness by abstract or composite imagery; Berkeley and the other Nominalists believed that imagery is always individual and concrete, and that abstract meaning is accordingly represented by the abstract term, the general name. But here is no alternative for psychology. Imagery might be strictly reproductive in form, and yet—for a certain type of mental constitution—be the psychological equivalent of an abstract meaning; and, again, imagery might be vague and indefinite, and yet be the psychological equivalent of an individual, particular meaning. The issue, in its psychological formulation, is an issue of fact. Is wordless imagery, under any circumstances, the mental representative of meaning? And if it is, do we find a correlation of vague imagery with abstract and of definite imagery with particular meaning?

The first of these questions I have already answered, for my own case, in the affirmative. In large measure I think, that is, I mean and I understand, in visual pictures. The second question I cannot answer in the affirmative. I doubt whether particularity or abstractness of meaning has anything essentially to do with the degree of definiteness of my images. The mental vision of the incoming tide, which I described at the beginning of this Lecture, is no more definite when it recalls an afternoon's ramble than when it means the progress of science. We must, above all things, distinguish between attentional clearness and intrinsic clearness of definition—sharpness, precision, cognitive clearness. A process may be transversing the very centre of consciousness, and therefore from the point of view of a psychology of attention may be maximally clear: yet it may be so weak, so brief, so instable, that its whole character is vague and indefinite. In my own experience, attentional clearness seems to be the one thing needful to qualify a process for meaning. Whether the picture as picture is sharply outlined and highly coloured is a matter of indifference.

Come back now to the authorities: to Locke's triangle and Huxley's composite animal. My own picture of the triangle, the image that means triangle to me, is usually a fairly definite outline of the little triangular figure that stands for the word "triangle" in the geometries. But I can quite well get Locke's picture, the triangle that is no triangle and all triangles at one and the same time. It is a flashy thing, come and gone from moment to moment: it hints two or three red angles, with the red lines deepening into black, seen on a dark green ground. It is not there long enough for me to say whether the angles join to form the complete figure, or even whether all three of the necessary angles are given. Nevertheless, it means triangle; it is Locke's general idea of triangle; it is Hamilton's palpable absurdity made real. And the composite animal? Well, the composite animal strikes me as somewhat too even, too nicely balanced. No doubt, the idea in Huxley's mind was of that kind; he, as an anatomist, was interested to mark all the parts and proportions of the creatures before him. But my own ideas of animals are sketchier and more selective: horse is, to me, a double curve and a rampant posture with a touch of mane about it; cow is a longish rectangle with a certain facial expression, a sort of exaggerated pout. Again, however, these things mean horse and cow, are the psychological vehicles of those logical meanings.

And what holds of triangle and horse and cow holds of all the "unpicturable notions of intelligence. No one of them is unpicturable, if you do but have the imaginal mind. "It is impossible," remarks a recent writer, "to ideate a meaning; one can only know it." Impossible? But I have been ideating meanings all my life. And not only meanings, but meaning also. Meaning in general is represented in my consciousness by another of these impressionist pictures. I see meaning as the blue-grey tip of a kind of scoop, which has a bit of yellow above it (probably a part of the handle), and which is just digging into a dark mass of what appears to be plastic material. I was educated on classical lines; and it is conceivable that this picture is an echo of the oft-repeated admonition to "dig out the meaning" of some passage of Greek or Latin. I do not know; but I am sure of the image. And I am sure that others have similar images. I put the question not long since to the members of my graduate seminary, and two of the twelve students present at once gave an affirmative answer. The one reported the mental unrolling of a white scroll: what he actually saw was a whitish lump or mass, flattened and flattening towards the right. The other reported a horizontal line, with two short verticals at a little distance from the two ends. The suggestion in these two cases is plain enough: meaning is something that you find by straightening things out, or it is something that is included or contained in things. There was, however, no such suggestion in the minds of my informants: for them, as for me, the mental representation of meaning is a simple datum, natural and ultimate.

I have dwelt at some length upon this visualisation of meanings because the point in dispute is of great importance, historically and systematically, and because visual imagery offers, so to say, the most substantial materials for its discussion. Let me repeat, however, that my mind, the mind which I am trying to describe to you, is by no means exclusively, is not even predominantly, of the visual type. I have, as I have said, a great deal of auditory imagery; I have also a great deal of kinæsthetic imagery. The former needs no further discussion, since it plays no active part in my thinking; but I must speak briefly of kinæsthesis.

As recently as 1904 I was not sure whether or not I possessed free kinæsthetic images. I could not decide whether my kinæsthetic memories were imaginal, or whether they involved an actual reinstatement, in weaker form, of the original sensations. I had no criterion by which to distinguish the sensation from the image. However, as so often happens, I had hardly recorded my difficulty when the criterion was found: a ground of distinction so simple, that one wonders why there should have been any difficulty at all. It may be roughly phrased in the statement that actual movement always brings into play more muscles than are necessary, while ideal movement is confined to the precise group of muscles concerned. You will notice the difference at once—provided that you have kinæsthetic images—if you compare an actual nod of the head with the mental nod that signifies assent to an argument, or the actual frown and wrinkling of the forehead with the mental frown that signifies perplexity. The sensed nod and frown are coarse and rough in outline; the imaged nod and frown are cleanly and delicately traced. I do not say, of course, that this is the sole difference between the two modes of experience. On the contrary, now that it has become clear, I seem to find that the kinæsthetic image and the kinæsthetic sensation differ in all essential respects precisely as visual image differs from visual sensation. But I think it is a dependable difference, and one that offers a good starting point for further analysis.

We shall recur to this kinæsthetic imagery in a later Lecture. All that I have to remark now is that the various visual images, which I have referred to as possible vehicles of logical meaning, oftentimes share their task with kinæsthesis. Not only do I see gravity and modesty and pride and courtesy and stateliness, but I feel or act them in the mind's muscles. This is, I suppose, a simple case of empathy, if we may coin that term as a rendering of *Einfühlung;* there is nothing curious or idiosyncratic about it; but it is a fact that must be mentioned. And further: just as the visual image may mean of itself, without kinæsthetic accompaniment, so may the kinæsthetic image occur and mean of itself, without assistance from vision. I represent the meaning of affirmation, for instance, by the image of a little nick felt at the back of the neck—an experience which, in sensation, is complicated by pressures and pulls from the scalp and throat. . . .

Sensationalism is succinctly defined, in Baldwin's *Dictionary,* as "the theory that all knowledge originates in sensations; that all cognitions, even reflective ideas and so-called intuitions, can be traced back to elementary sensations." It is thus, primarily, a theory of the origin of knowledge, not a theory of the genesis of thought. "Historically," the *Dictionary* continues, "it is generally combined with Associationalism." Turning to Associationism, in the same work, we find the following definition: "The theory which, starting with certain simple and ultimate constituents of consciousness, makes mental development consist solely or mainly in the combination of these elements according to certain laws of association. According to this theory, rigidly carried out, all genesis of new products is due to the combination of pre-existing elements." Here is psychological formulation. But it would be a great mistake, though it is a mistake not seldom made, to confuse the sensationalism of experimental psychology with the doctrine of associationism. Let us see wherein the two kinds of sensationalism differ.

In the first place, the associationists did not distinguish the theory of knowledge from the theory of thought. "The British thinkers of the past"—I am quoting from a British thinker of the present—"were far from keeping their psychology unadulterated. ... They gave us, in general, psychology and philosophy inextricably intermingled." "Their work often shows a crossing of interests and of points of view. Questions of logic and theory of knowledge were mixed up with the more properly psychological inquiry." In fact, the associationists dealt, on principle, with logical meanings; not with sensations, but with sensations-of; not with ideas, but with ideas-of; it is only incidentally that they leave the plane of meaning for the plane of existence. The experimentalists, on the other hand, aim to describe the contents of consciousness not as they mean but as they are. . . .

Locke's ideas, then, and James Mill's ideas, were meanings, thought-tokens, bits of knowledge; the sensations and ideas of modern psychology are *Erlebnisse*, data of immediate experience. And the change of standpoint brings with it a second principal difference between the older and the newer sensationalism. Meanings are stable, and may be discussed without reference to time; so that a psychology whose elements are meanings is an atomistic psychology; the elements join, like blocks of mosaic, to give static formations, or connect, like the links of a chain, to give discrete series. But experience is continuous and a function of time; so that a psychology whose elements are sensations, in the modern sense of the term, is a process-psychology, innocent both of mosaic and of concatenation. This is a point which Wundt, the father of experimental psychology, never tires of emphasizing. In a well-known passage, in which he is appraising the value of the experimental method for his own psychological development, he says: "I learned from it that the 'idea' must be regarded as a process, no less variable and transitory than a feeling or a volition; and I saw that, for that reason, the old doctrine of association is no longer tenable." And again, in protesting against the hypostatisation of ideas, he writes: "The ideas themselves are not objects, as by confusion with their objects they are supposed to be, but they are occurrences, *Ereignisse,* that grow and decay and during their brief passage are in constant change." . . .

But we must return for a moment to associationism. I said that the psychology of meanings left us with mosaic arrangements or with discrete series. You may reply that this characterisation is unfair. James Mill speaks, for instance, of the coalescence of ideas: "where two or more ideas have been repeated together, and the association has become very strong, they sometimes spring up in such close combination as not to be distinguishable"; the idea of weight—to take a single illustration—involves the ideas of resistance and direction and the "feeling or feelings denominated Will," and resistance and direction are themselves compounded of simpler ideas. And John Mill writes, in the same spirit: "When impressions have been so often experienced in conjunction that each of them calls up readily and instantaneously the ideas of the whole group, those ideas sometimes melt and coalesce into one another, and appear not several ideas, but one, in the same manner as, when the seven prismatic colours are presented to the eye in rapid succession, the sensation produced is that of white. . . . These therefore are cases of mental chemistry, in which it is proper to say that the simple ideas generate, rather than that they compose, the complex ones." That is from the *Logic.* There is a similar passage in the *Examination of Sir William Hamilton's Philosophy:* "If anything similar to this [that is, to colour mixture] obtains in our consciousness generally (and that it obtains in many cases of consciousness there can be no doubt) it will follow that whenever the organic modifications of our nervous fibres succeed one another at an interval shorter than the duration of the sensations or other feelings corresponding to them, those sensations or feelings will, so to speak, overlap one another, and becoming simultaneous instead of successive, will blend into a state of feeling, probably as unlike the elements out of which it is engendered as the colour of white is unlike the prismatic colours." It seems to me, however, that associationism has here fallen out of the frying-pan into the fire. The principle of association, which was to be in the world of mind what the principle of gravitation is in the world of matter—"Here is a kind of attraction," said Hume, "which in the mental world will be found to have as extraordinary effects as in the natural, and to show itself in as many and as various forms,"—this principle has broken down, and composition has been supplemented by generation, mechanical mixture by chemical combination. I see no gain; I see rather an equal misunderstanding of chemistry and of psychology. It is, however, a misunderstanding which has been fruitful of bad consequences, and of which we are not yet wholly free. I believe, nevertheless, that experimental psychology has, in the main, transcended the doctrine of mental chemistry. Colour mixture—the illustration chosen by the two Mills and before them by Hartley— is, as we all know, not a mixture of visual sensations, but the sensory resultant of the interplay of excitatory processes in the retina. That is a minor matter. But, in general, we have better means than a false chemical analogy for explaining what cannot be explained in terms of a straightforward associationism. We have learned, for instance, to make allowance for complication of conditions; we do not expect, if two sensations are put together, to obtain a simple concurrence of their two qualities; we expect that the synergy of the underlying physiological processes will, in some way, become manifest in consciousness. We may speak of general attributes of sensation, as Ebbinghaus does; or we may speak of *Gestaltqualität*, form of combination, funded character; or we may speak of the organisation of elements in the state of attention. Different systems deal with the facts in different ways, and one psychologist entertains possibilities that another rejects; but at all events there is no need of a mental chemistry. We have learned, again, that physiological conditions may produce their effect not within but upon consciousness; that nervous sets and tendencies may direct the course of conscious processes without setting up new and special processes of their own. We have learned, also, that such formations as perception and action can be understood only in the light of their history and development; the life of mind is, throughout, subject to a law of growth and decay, of gradual expansion and gradual reduction; what is now, so to say, a mere tag or label upon a dominant formation may, a little while ago, have been itself a focal complex, and the formation to which it attaches may, a little while hence, sink to the parasitic level. We have all this knowledge, and much more, to supplement what we know of the mechanics of reproduction, the modern substitute for the laws of association; and there is, surely, good hope that we may work out a psychology of thought without taking any such leap in the dark as John Mill took when he added generation to composition.

I have mentioned two principal differences between the older and the newer sensationalism. The experimental psychologist deals with existences, and not with meanings; and his elements are processes, whose temporal course is of their very nature, and not substances, solid and resistant to the lapse of time. These differences illustrate, as they follow from, the more fundamental difference of general attitude. Current sensationalism is a result to which we are led by empirical analysis, and its sensations are simple processes abstracted from conscious experience, last terms in the psychological study of mind. The associationism of the English school is a preconceived theory, and its sensations are, accordingly, productive and generative elements, first terms in a logical construction of mind. Associationism, in other words, puts sensations together, as physical atoms or chemical molecules, while modern psychology finds sensations together in the given mental process. . . .

The Psychology of Thought

What shall be adopted . . . as the criterion of a mental element? I regard as a mental element any process that proves to be irreducible, unanalysable, throughout the whole course of individual experience. Consider, for instance, the processes of sensation and affection. They have certain salient characteristics in common; they suggest the biological analogy of two species of the same genus; I have felt justified in deriving them from a single hypothetical mental ancestor. Nevertheless, I can trace no passage from the one to the other in the individual mind; they seem to be separate and distinct, so soon as nervous organisation is complete; and they must, therefore, I believe, be regarded by analytical psychology as separate elements. Consider, on the other hand, the attitudes and awarenesses of which we have said so much. If we can trace an attitude back, within the same mind, to an imaginal source; if it thus appears not as original endowment but as residuum, not as primule but as vestige, then I should protest against its ranking as a mental element. Even if there are certain minds in which the derivation is impossible, in which the attitude can neither be identified with sensation and image nor referred with certainty to precedent sensory and imaginal experience, I should still hesitate—so long as there are other minds in which the derivation is possible—to adopt the purely phenomenological standpoint, and to class it outright as elementary; I should prefer to term it a secondary element, or a derived element, and so to distinguish it from the elements proper, as defined a moment ago. Classification is, of course, always a matter of expediency, and I have no quarrel with those who differ from me on this particular point. But it seems to me inexpedient to give the rank of element to anything that is not a matter of original and general human endowment.

You see, then, the place that I allow to genetic consideration. The misunderstanding to which I have referred arises, I imagine, from a confusion of two points of view, which may be distinguished as the analytical and the integrative. The analytical psychologist, even when he is occupied with mind in its development, is always trying to analyse. He may, and he does, protest that it never occurs to him to consider sensation, for instance, the sensation of the adult human consciousness, as a genetic unit. Nevertheless, what he finds by his genetic consideration must, of necessity, be sensation over again, in some less differentiated form; his problem is analysis, and his results are conditioned by the problem. The integrative psychologist, eager to preserve that continuity of mind which the analyst purposely destroys, and working from below upwards instead of from above downwards, reaches results that, in strictness, are incomparable with the results of analysis: as incomparable, let us say as "seasonal dimorphism" and "unstriped muscle." Incomparables, of course, are not incompatibles; but the attempt to compare them, to bring them under a common rubric as "facts of psychological observation" or what not, must inevitably lead to misunderstanding.

I have only to add the caution that we must not expect a genetic inquiry to reveal, in every case, a complete series of nicely graded transitional forms. If I may trust some observations of my own, the path that leads, for example, from full imagery to *Bewusstseinslage* is more likely to be broken than continuous consciousness seems to drop, at a single step, from a higher to a lower level; the progress is effected by substitutions and short cuts, rather than by a gradual course of transformation. This, however, is a matter of descriptive detail, and does not affect the principle which is laid down in the maxim.

I assume, thirdly, that consciousness may be guided and controlled by extra-conscious, physiological factors, by cortical sets and dispositions; and I agree with Ach that this extra-conscious determination may lead to novel conscious connections, which would not have been effected by the mere play of reproductive tendencies, though I do not agree with Messer that the disposition as such is represented in consciousness by a specific experience. In a paper which is intended to form the basis for a theory of thought, a paper entitled "On the Nature of Certain Brain States connected with the Psychical Processes," von Kries, in 1895, worked out a theory of *cerebrale Einstellung*, cerebral set or adjustment, with the main features of which I am in entire accord. He distinguishes two types of adjustment, the connective and the dispositional: the former illustrated, in simple terms, by the reading of a musical score in a particular key, the latter by our understanding of abstract words like "red," "triangle." It is needless to point out that a theory of this sort serves admirably to explain the experimental results of Watt and Ach; indeed, Ach's determining tendencies and subexcited reproductive tendencies are merely specialised types of von Kries' connective and dispositional adjustments. And the idea of determination is now so familiar to us that I need not further discuss it here, or devote further time to my third and last regulative maxim. I pass on to the problems themselves; and I take up first of all the problem of meaning.

The Problem of Meaning

Some time ago we met with the objection that it is nonsense to call a psychical fact or occurrence the meaning of another psychical fact or occurrence; two ideas are and must remain two ideas, and cannot be an idea and its meaning. I said, in reply, that in my belief two ideas do, under certain circumstances, make a meaning. What are the circumstances?

I hold that, from the psychological or existential point of view, meaning—so far as it finds representation in consciousness at all—is always context. An idea means another idea, is psychologically the meaning of that other idea, if it is that idea's context. And I understand by context simply the mental process or complex of mental processes which accrues to the original idea through the situation[1] in which the organism finds itself—primitively, the natural situation; later, either the natural or the mental. In another connection, I have argued that the earliest form of attention is a definitely determined reaction, sensory and motor both, upon some dominant stimulus; and that as mind developed, and image presently supervened upon sensation, this gross total response was differentiated into three typical attitudes, the receptive, the elaborative and the executive, which we may illustrate by sensible discrimination, reflective thought, and voluntary action. Now it seems to me that meaning, context, has extended and developed in the same way. Meaning is, originally, kinæsthesis;

---

[1] The term "situation" seems to me to bring out more clearly than any nearer equivalent of *Aufgabe* the part played in determination by the organism itself. Externally regarded, a situation is a collocation of stimuli; but it becomes a situation only if the organism is prepared for selective reaction upon that collocation. An *Aufgabe*, on the other hand, a task or problem, may be set to any organism, prepared or unprepared. I have no wish to press the word: but I here mean by "situation" any form of *Aufgabe* that is normal to the particular organism.

the organism faces the situation by some bodily attitude, and the characteristic sensations which the attitude involves give meaning to the process that stands at the conscious focus, are psychologically the meaning of that process. Afterwards, when differentiation has taken place, context may be mainly a matter of sensations of the special senses, or of images, or of kinæsthetic and other organic sensations, as the situation demands. The particular form that meaning assumes is then a question to be answered by descriptive psychology.

Of all the possible forms, however—and I think they are legion—two appear to be of especial importance: kinæsthesis and verbal images. We are animals, locomotor organisms; the motor attitude, the executive type of attention, is therefore of constant occurrence in our experience; and, as it is much older than the elaborative, so it is the more ingrained. There would be nothing surprising in the discovery that, for minds of a certain constitution, all non-verbal conscious meaning is carried by kinæsthetic sensation or kinæsthetic image. And words themselves, let us remember, were at first motor attitudes, gestures, kinæsthetic contexts: complicated, of course, by sound, and therefore, fitted to assist the other types of attention, the receptive and the elaborative; but still essentially akin to the gross attitudes of primitive attention. The fact that words are thus originally contextual, and the fact that they nevertheless as sound, and later as sight, possess and acquire a content-character, these facts render language preeminently available for thought; it is at once idea and context of idea, idea and meaning; and as the store of free images increases, and the elaborative attitude grows more and more natural, the context-use of words or word-aspects becomes habitual. The meaning of the printed page may now consist in the auditory-kinæsthetic accompaniment of internal speech; the word is the word's own meaning; or some verbal representation, visual or auditory-kinæsthetic or visual-kinæsthetic or what not, may give meaning to a non-verbal complex of sensations or images. There would, again, be nothing surprising—we should simply be in presence of a limiting case—in the discovery that, for minds of a certain constitution, all conscious meaning is carried either by total kinæsthetic attitude or by words.

As a matter of fact, meaning is carried by all sorts of sensational and imaginal processes. Mental constitution is widely varied, and the meaning-response of a mind of a certain constitution varies widely under varying circumstances. A descriptive psychology is primarily concerned with types and uniformities; but if we were to make serious work of a differential psychology of meaning, we should probably find that, in the multitudinous variety of situations and contexts, any mental process may possibly be the meaning of any other.

But I go farther. I doubt if meaning need necessarily be conscious at all—if it may not be "carried" in purely physiological terms. In rapid reading, the skimming of pages in quick succession; in the rendering of a musical composition in a particular key; in shifting from one language to another as you turn to your right or left hand neighbour at a dinner table: in these and similar cases I doubt if meaning necessarily has any kind of conscious representation. It very well may; but I doubt if it necessarily does. There must be an *Aufgabe*, truly, but then the *Aufgabe*, as we have seen, need not either come to consciousness. I was greatly astonished to observe, some years ago, that the recognition of shades of grey might be effected, so far as my introspection went, in this purely physiological way. I am keenly alive to the importance of organic sensations and, as I shall show in a moment, to that of reduced or schematic kinæsthetic attitudes. I was not at all astonished to observe that the recognition of a grey might consist in a quiver of the stomach. But there were instances in which the grey was "recognised" without words; without organic sensations, kinæsthetic or other; without the arousal of a mood; without anything of an appreciably conscious sort. I found not the faintest trace of an image-less apprehension, if that apprehension is supposed to be something conscious over and above the grey itself. I cannot further describe the experience: it was simply a "recognition" without consciousness.

Nevertheless, you may say, there must have been something there; you would have had a different experience had the grey not been recognised. So a word that you understand is experienced otherwise than a nonsense word or a word of some unknown foreign language. Certainly! But my contention is that the *plus* of consciousness, in these comparisons, lies on the side of the unrecognised, the unknown, and not on the side of the recognised and known. There was plenty of consciousness, in the experiments to which I am referring, when a grey was not recognised: the point is that there was sometimes none at all when there was recognition. But let me repeat that this statement is made tentatively, and subject to correction; I believe it to be true of myself, but it requires confirmation from others.

What, then, of the imageless thoughts, the awarenesses, the *Bewusstseinslagen* of meaning and the rest? I have, as you may suppose, been keeping my eyes open for their appearance; and we have several investigations now in progress that aim, more or less directly, at their examination. What I have personally found does not, so far, shake my faith in sensationalism. I have become keenly alive, for instance, to the variety of organic attitude and its kinæsthetic representation. I am sure that when I sit down to the typewriter to think out a lecture, and again to work off the daily batch of professional correspondence, and again to write an intimate and characteristic letter to a near friend—I am sure that in these three cases I sit down differently. The different *Aufgaben* come to consciousness, in part, as different feels of the whole body; I am somehow a different organism, and a consciously different organism. Description in the rough is not difficult: there are different visceral pressures, different distributions of tonicity in the muscles of back and legs, differences in the sensed play of facial expression, differences in the movements of arms and hands in the intervals between striking the keys, rather obvious differences in respiration, and marked differences of local or general involuntary movement. It is clear that these differences, or many of them, could be recorded by the instruments which we employ for the method of expression, and could thus be made a matter of objective record. But I have, at any rate, no doubt of their subjective reality; and I believe that, under experimental conditions, description would be possible in detail. I find, moreover, that these attitudinal feels are touched off in all sorts of ways: by an author's choice and arrangement of words, by the intonation of a speaking voice, by the nature of my physical and social environment at large. They shade off gradually into those em-

The Problem of Meaning 183

pathic experiences which I mentioned in the first Lecture, the experiences in which I not only see gravity and modesty and pride and courtesy and stateliness in the mind's eye, but also feel or act them in the mind's muscles. And I should add that they may be of all degrees of definiteness, from the relatively coarse and heavy outlines of the typewriting illustration, down to the merest flicker of imagery which lies, I suppose, on the border of an unconscious disposition.

I do not for a moment profess to have made an exhaustive exploration of my own mind, in the search for *Bewusstseinslagen*. But if there were any frequent form of experience, different in kind from the kinæsthetic backgrounds that I have just described, I think that I am sufficiently versed in introspection, and sufficiently objective in purpose, to have come upon its track. I have turned round, time and time again, upon consciousnesses like doubt, hesitation, belief, assent, trying to remember, having a thing on my tongue's tip, and I have not been able to discover the imageless processes. No doubt, the analysis has been rough and uncontrolled; but it has been attempted at the suggestion of the imageless psychologists, and with the reports of their introspections echoing in my mind. Bühler's thought-elements I frankly disbelieve in. The unanalysable and irreducible *Bewusstseinslagen* of other investigators may, I conceive, prove to be analysable when they are scrutinised directly and under favourable experimental conditions. If they still resist analysis, they may perhaps be considered as consciousnesses of the same general sort as my attitudinal feels, but as consciousnesses that are travelling toward the unconscious by another road. It is conceivable, in other words, that while, in my mind, the attitudes thin out, tail off, lose in bulk, so to say, as they become mechanised, in minds of a different type they retain their original area, their extension, and simply become uniform and featureless, as a variegated visual surface becomes uniform under adaptation. If that hypothesis is worth consideration, then the first problem for experiment is, as I have earlier suggested, to trace this course of degeneration within the same mind. Whether the featureless fringes or backgrounds shall be classified as a secondary kind of mental element—in any event, as we have seen, a question of expediency—would then depend upon the success or failure of the search for intermediaries that should link them to imagery.

*   *   *

What exactly did Titchener and his subjects find when they introspected on the same thought processes which the Würzburgers had investigated? What was the manner of the squabble going back and forth across an ocean, via the psychological journals? Interestingly enough, in spite of the quarrel about the allowable language in the protocol statements and about permissible conclusions to be drawn from these protocols, the actual descriptions elicited by subjects are highly similar and the *practical* conclusion drawn is almost identical: there is "a paucity of conscious contents in much of our thinking." The *theoretical* conclusion is of course entirely different, but the protocols themselves, drawn from Marbe, Messer, and Ach on the one hand, or from Jacobson, Okabe, Clarke, and other students of Titchener on the other, could be interchanged with little noticeable difference. To take just one example from Jacobson's study in 1911 in which he visually presented words and sentences to subjects who were instructed to report everything that occurred in consciousness, Jacobson found that at least in some instances subjects reported that the sentences were meaningful to them while the visual and auditory sensations from reading the stimulus were the only conscious contents they had. He adds a footnote about his own experiences in this regard:

> The writer finds that he can converse or think in words or in incipient verbal articulations, with the meaning present, while for considerable periods of time he can discern no vestige of sensations or images other than those from the words themselves. There are, in the background, sensations due to bodily position and to general set; but while it is introspectively clear that these play an important part in the whole experience, they do not seem to vary correspondingly with the verbal meanings, as the conversation proceeds or the thought goes on.*

* E. Jacobson, On meaning and understanding. *Amer. J. Psychol.*, 1911, **22**, 553–577. P. 572.

This statement is adduced as evidence for the purely sensory content of consciousness, yet it could equally well be used as a perfect illustration of imageless thought. In either case the paucity of consciousness involved in understanding a sentence is manifest.

Faced with this scarcity, Titchener seems on occasion to drop his context theory of meaning and relegate meaning to the unconscious or the physiological substratum. But once there, meaning is out of Titchener's experimental psychology and the experimental study of thinking has reached a dead end. Indeed, the backwater in which Titchener soon found himself seems not so much due to a return to atomistic associationist principles per se, as to the restriction of psychological research to the realm of consciousness and the restrictions on the theoretical language.

At this point let us return to Würzburg and meet the next problem to be faced there, that of *Aufgabe*, or more generally, of motive and purpose, a problem that places us squarely into the realm of the unconscious.

5

The New Psychology: Directed Thinking

In the last chapter we saw how the new tradition attacked one of the stumbling blocks of the British associationists—the problem of elements, the atomistic conception of complex thinking being made up of simple ideas, and the dependence on the Aristotelian dogma of "no image—no thought." In modern terms the resolution might have been to call the thinking processes theoretical and therefore not necessarily accessible to observation.

However, there was still left another associationist heritage—the problem of direction. Why does one train of thought rather than any other occur? What determines the direction of thinking?

There was no a priori reason why an associationistic psychology should ignore problems of motivation or purpose in thinking. In fact, these topics occur occasionally throughout our selections in Chapters 2 and 3. But the mention tends to be casual, as in Hobbes' *Leviathan,* for example, and even when James Mill introduces such concepts as desire or end in order to deal with directed thinking, the notion is nonetheless given a subsidiary and secondary role. For a long time it seemed that the associative play of sensory elements would be sufficient, that no directive or motivational concept would be needed to explain the flow of thought. Even when directive notions were considered, they were couched in associationistic terms, as when James Mill speaks of a pleasurable idea of the future being associated with the means to that end.

Nevertheless, by the end of the nineteenth century various extraassociational principles to account for the directional aspects of thought and action began to appear. In 1889 Müller and Schumann published a paper on motor set,* in 1900 Müller and Pilzecker talked about perseverative tendencies,† and in 1893 Külpe, in his *Grundriss der Psychologie*,‡ mentioned the importance of the subject's preparation in determining reactions to various stimuli.

The major credit for introducing a directional concept to the psychology of thought goes to Henry J. Watt who wrote his doctoral dissertation at Würzburg in 1904 on this topic. He experimentally investigated the effects of the task (*Aufgabe*) and demonstrated its vital importance to the course of the associations which took place in his reaction experiments. His work, and that of Ach on the similar concept of determining tendencies which was done at about the same time, created a true milestone in the history of thought. As Titchener put it, their work made it impossible for any future psychologist to write a theory in the language of content alone.

The beginnings were modest enough. Watt gave his subjects specific tasks to perform. When they saw the stimulus word they were either to name an example of the class to which it belonged, or to name a whole, or a part of it, or some similar simple problem. Not surprisingly he found that these tasks were at least as important as any associations or reproductive tendencies in determining the subject's response to the stimulus word.

At first, then, as the name "task" implies, the directive concept was an external or situational one. It might be conceived of as an independent variable, controlled by the experimenter and presented in the form of instructions in the same way as other stimuli were presented. Sophistication quickly set in, however. One of the first things Watt noticed was that, whereas in the beginning of an experiment the subject was completely conscious of the task, it

---

* G. E. Müller and F. Schumann, Über die psychologischen Grundlagen der Vergleichung gehobener Gewichte. *Arch. f.d. ges. Physiol.*, 1889, **45**, 37–112.

† G. E. Müller and A. Pilzecker, Experimentelle Beiträge zur Lehre vom Gedächtniss. *Z.f. Psychol.*, Ergzgsbd. 1, 1900, 300 pp.

‡ O. Külpe, *Grundriss der Psychologie*. Leipzig: Engelmann, 1893. Published in English: *Outlines of psychology*, transl. by E. B. Titchener. London: Swan Sonnenschein, 1895.

gradually seemed to drop out of consciousness, at the same time losing none of its effectiveness in determining the course of the reactions. Here then was another glimpse of the submerged portion of the iceberg; not only were large parts of the content of thought to be found outside of consciousness, but a vital controlling factor was found to be outside of consciousness as well. Watt was unwilling to commit himself on the status of this factor, stating firmly in the last page of the following selection that the ideas he has propounded in his thesis do not imply "notions like the unconscious"; in fact he implies that the concept of unconscious operations is unnecessary. Rather the *Aufgaben* seem to hold the same status as the reproductive tendencies (associative bonds); they are extraconscious rather than unconscious. The one concept provides the material of thought and the other a kind of steering or guiding mechanism.

A certain theoretical confusion is evident here, wherein *Aufgaben* can move from consciousness and the protocol language, out of consciousness and into the theoretical language. Such slippage from one universe to another, common in many psychological treatises of the time, was to be criticized with growing sophistication by Koffka (see p. 236) and later writers. Whatever the exact status of the *Aufgaben*, however, their introduction provided much needed flexibility for an associationistic theory of thought.

Henry J. Watt

Experimental Contribution to a Theory of Thinking[1]

For this thesis a long series of experiments was carried out. *Several hundred nouns* of common occurrence were printed in big type on cards and were shown to the observing subject one at a time by means of an automatic *card-changer* (Dr. Ach's). A metal plate, which covered the card, sprang up, when a string was pulled, and by so doing closed an electric current, which flowed through a Hipp *chronoscope* and a *speaking tube* (Cattell's). The chronoscope therefore marked the time which passed from the appearance of the printed word until the first vibrations from the subject's

---

H. J. Watt, Experimental contribution to a theory of thinking. *J. Anat. Physiol.*, 1905–1906, **40**, 257–266.

[1] This paper, which is to be regarded as an abstract of a thesis entitled, "Experimentelle Beiträge zu einer Theorie des Denkens" (Doctor Dissertation, Würzburg, 1904, *Archiv. für die gesamte Psychologie*, vol. iv. Leipzig: Engelmann, 1904. Pp. 154), was accompanied by a letter from the author addressed to Professor M'Kendrick, of which the following is a paragraph:

"I have made no attempt to sketch a physiological theory which would give a basis for the psychological factors I distinguish in my thesis. It is only just to those who know the possibilities of such physiological theories better than I do, to allow a clear account of psychological analysis to tempt *them* to any such undertaking. In several points, besides, as will be evident to you, my work goes rather to strengthen the hands of those who, for the present, want to work out their physiological material directly without any conclusions from psychological theory. The most we psychologists can hope meanwhile is, that some analysis of ours may suggest a new idea to some physiologist which he might try and investigate directly on physiological material. That would be something to be proud of! It will also be good if the impression gains ground that experimental psychology is an intelligible and exact science and not a mere play with dreams."

voice broke the current in the speaking tube. This constituted the measure of the duration of the reaction and formed, with a full account of all the reproducible experiences of the observing subject, which were at once written down in full, and any other remarks he had to make, the experimental data of the thesis.

In contrast to previous experiments on association definite *tasks* (*Aufgaben*) were given, which the subject had to accomplish in the reaction. These referred to what the printed word on the card signified, and were as follows: to classify it, to name an example of it, to name a whole to which it belonged, to name a part, to name another of the same class or another part of the same whole. Each subject performed the experiments separately, and every care was taken, both in regard to technical details and to the way the experiments were carried out, that no disturbing factors should be present. The most of the work was done by four practised observers, and over three thousand experiments were made in all.

The following are *the results*. In almost every case the subject is able to accomplish his task correctly. His description of his experiences shows that there are in the main *three kinds of complexes of experiences*. Most frequently the subject follows one line right through the experiment, which then leads to the spoken word. In the other cases, he may seek a word which he does not find, and which he even afterwards cannot name, or he may have intended to say a certain word, but for some reason or other, wittingly or unwittingly, have said another. In general the first class, the *simple reproductions*, take place in a good deal less time than the other two classes, the *complex reproductions*, of which two the second named usually and naturally last longer.

Within each of these classes there are *three groups*. In the *first* of these the spoken word follows directly on the given optical stimulus, sometimes after a pause which can be described in no particularly definite way, sometimes with the assurance of the subject that between the stimulus and the reaction nothing whatever has been experienced. Such a reaction lasts in general a very short time, and in the second form a shorter time than any other kind of association reaction. In a *second* and very large class, a *visual representation* follows the stimulus. Directly after that, or after a short pause or a so-called search, comes the spoken word. These are a good deal longer than the first set, and sometimes longer, sometimes shorter, among themselves according to the detail and vividness of the representation and the frequency of occurrence of such reactions containing visual representations for the particular subject. *Last* of all come those reactions in which a *word-representation,* or some experience which could only be described in conceptual terms and not analytically according to its psychological content—call it a thought—appeared between the presentation of the word and the spoken reaction. These were often shorter than those containing visual representations and sometimes longer. It is not, however, contended in this classification that the reaction could take no other course. On the contrary, it is easy to see that we could have tone, smell, taste, touch and other such representations playing a part in the reaction, provided the conditions of experiment produced them. None of these were clearly present among these experiments.

But what are these *conditions of experiment?* How does any one particular reaction come about and not another? The *first influence* at work on the subject is the given *task*. This he hears spoken by the experimenter, and generally repeats to himself in words, *e.g.* "find a part!" "name an example!" or he may exemplify the experiment to himself, *e.g.* "animal—dog," and so on. The scanty description of the preparation for the experiment given in the subject's account of it does not help us to form a very clear idea of what the process itself is. It was found, however, as a series of detailed curves show, that of all the simple reproductions the percentage of occurrence of each of the three above-named classes changes regularly and similarly with each subject from one task to another. This leads to the assertion that the task has a regular influence on the *nature* of the experiences of each subject, which becomes particularly evident between the two larger groups of simple reproductions, those containing visual representations and those containing nothing at all. The change of task has a most decisive influence on the percentage of these classes, and a subject who has hardly a single visual representation when the task "classify" is given, may have them in 50 per cent of the cases when the task "find a part" is given. Alongside this, a subject with 50 per cent visual representations in the first case, may have 90–100 per cent in the second. Moreover it is found that the *duration* of the reaction in each of these classes is also on the average dependent on the nature of the task. So too is the duration of the complex reproductions, but the percentage occurrence of these, out of all experiments made, is, curiously enough, quite *independent* of the nature of the task, as curves show. The attempt is made to explain this by a fairly probable consideration. The number of tendencies to reproduction which diverge from any one stimulus, must depend on the number of ideas with which the stimulus is associated. It is impossible to conceive how the task should change these, as an association must be presupposed before the task working with the stimulus could produce any reaction. The occurrence of a complex reproduction would depend then on the nature of the stimulus-word given and not on that of the task. The influence of the *task* has therefore to be carefully differentiated from that of the *stimulus*.

An analysis of the experiments worked with the fifth and sixth tasks shows that an experience which plays an *important* part in producing or leading to a reaction makes the reaction longer than when the experience only comes along with the stimulus or the reaction-word, that is, when it is only side-play, as it were.

States of consciousness *tend to persist* and to return more easily once they have been experienced. It is found that they come *more rapidly* after the first time. It is found, besides, that the task also tends to persist, for it also often comes to consciousness, in the form of a word-presentation or the like, during the course of the experiment. In the great majority of cases this occurs only where some disturbing factor has been present, while the normal reproduction runs its course smoothly from beginning to end, as soon as the regular preparation for the experiment, *i.e.* the given task, has worked on the stimulus without any repetition during the experiment. The *repetition of the task* is therefore, we suppose, made necessary as soon as the task ceases to operate sufficiently well. This shows the exchange which goes on between representations and the task in operation. A suitable representation may introduce the task, which then, when it has ceased to operate effectually, may come to consciousness in similar representations. By means

Experimental Contribution to a Theory of Thinking 193

of such exchange it is possible to modify, strengthen, restrain, or check the task which is operating.

It has already been shown in experimental work on memory that the *rapidity of a reproduction* is dependent on the number of times the reproduction has occurred. In accordance with this it is found that the rapidity of such reproductions as those here described is dependent to a very large degree on the number of subjects who make any particular reproduction. The dependence is, of course, not supposed to be direct, but the co-ordination and the result presupposes that the number of subjects who make any given reproduction is a fair sign of the frequency of its repetition.

The result is very distinct and the exceptions can, as a rule, be explained by the record the subject gave of his experiences or by other experimental data. Further, if the average duration of each grade of frequency is co-ordinated with the change in the task for each subject, the *influence of the task* on the duration of the reaction *in each grade of frequency* is seen to be surprisingly similar to its influence in the previous cases. This means that the influence of the task is *independent* of the rapidity of the tendency to reproduction in itself, so that the influence of the stimulus-word is for the second time differentiated from that of the task. It is, then, probable that the rapidity of a tendency to reproduction from one point to another in the stream of succeeding ideas is something by itself, independent of the influence of the task operating at the moment. Whether the latter be to the increase of the former in every case remains to be settled.

It has often been asserted that over and above more or less mechanical reproductions, which are often to be found in our mental experience, there is a large number of cases in which the decision is not uniformly and completely determined by regular laws, but in which a greater or less amount of scope is allowed for the usually indefinite activity called choice or selection by the attention and the like. But a thorough examination of the complex reproductions, in which no particular description was given of the second tendency to reproduction, produces a large mass of evidence, partly from the record of the subject and partly from manifold combinations of the various experimental data, much too detailed to be described, in favour of the reproduction which actually took place. This shows that, if other conditions remain the same, it is the individual strength or *rapidity* of the tendency to reproduction *which determines the reproduction,* and not anything else. In other words, the influence of the task is the same for all the reproductions it makes possible. It is not meant, of course, that our everyday conception of choice has no meaning, but only that the influences which determine every event in our mental experience fall into two large groups, the operating task and the individual strength of the reproductions which come thereby in question. On the one hand, the task may find no reproductions, in which case no reaction can occur; and, on the other hand, the strength of the tendency to reproduction may be too great for the task to operate, in which case it forces its way out in spite of the task, or before any reproduction which the task favours has had time to become actual: in other words, a wrong reaction takes place. Otherwise, more or less suitable reactions occur. This is thought to be *valid for the whole of our mental experience,* because the very few cases which offered no explanation, contained no indication of any other determining factors, and are therefore to be placed alongside the others with the remark that in these cases the record of the subject or the experimental data were probably deficient, as can always occur in such experiments.

A detailed examination shows further that the general content, the vividness, and the frequency of our *visual representations* is dependent on the nature of the *task* in question. It is therefore probable that rather hasty generalisations have been made of the possible *types of mental imagery.* It could very well be, according to this result, that a subject who showed an entire absence of visual representation with the kind of task which has hitherto been given to determine the types of mental imagery, would with other tasks show quite a lively and detailed visual imagination. An example of almost such a case occurred among the subjects used for these experiments. It is probable, however, that one who has fewer and less vivid imagery than another with one task, will with another task again have less vivid and detailed imagery than the other.

The attempt to establish an *association by contrast* or by *similarity* is then discussed, on the basis of the experiments, and is rejected, because it is found to be impossible to show that similarity as such could determine an association. Apparent determinations of reproductions by similarity are found to dissolve into more detailed reproductions, which are themselves determined by the factors already discovered. There is no reason to expect that the subject in his record should be able to give the reason for any reaction, or even always the previous mental experience by which the reproduction in question under the operation of the task was determined.

A detailed examination of the experiments with each task by themselves, leads to interesting results which tend to separate the task as a psychological factor still more from the tendency to reproduction in itself and from other factors. Interesting connections are shown between the logical relations contained in the tasks given and the psychological processes found in the experiments, in which the psychological simplicity and rapidity of happening are shown to be sometimes on the side of the logical simplicity and sometimes not.

In a lengthy *summary* the results are brought together under various points of view and several *theories* formulated.

After a short summary of *individual differences*, a *criticism of the distinction between motor and sensory reaction* is given. First of all, the facts are brought together to show that this distinction is a fairly good description of some differences between the subjects. The first basis of the distinction was the usual arithmetical mean, but of late it has been thought that the *curve of distribution* of the reaction-times gives a better foundation. This curve is formed by making a time equal to the probable error of all time-observations of the series the unit in the horizontal, and by setting the number of cases which occur at each such unit on the perpendicular. If the number of factors involved is small and limited, then this curve ought to rise to one or more symmetrical points. This is sometimes the case, especially in the motor reaction, according to the latest researches. It is evident, according to the last two of these, that the time of even the motor reaction can be shortened a good deal with practice, and the curves seem to show points at somewhat regular periods—these periods being, however, liable to minimal displacements when the nature or quantity of the stimulus is changed. It is also indisputably true, that the *class* to which any experiment is to be reckoned, is not determined by the nature of the experiment after it has been made, but by the nature of the given *preparation,* the direction of the attention to sensory or motor elements. Here, then, we have again differences between what we call the task and the mere tendency to reproduction or any physiological basis for the latter. A *motor reaction* is, therefore, merely the quickest and most constant reaction possible, which constancy and rapidity are achieved by simple and constant conditions of experiment and of task especially. The long-practised so-called *natural reaction,* in which the task directs the attention specially neither to the stimulus nor to the movement which is to be carried out, also shows a regular curve of distribution. It is evident that in this natural reaction, too, the factors involved are constant and regular. The *sensory reaction,* however, is not nearly so liable to be regular, and it is supposed that this lies in the *greater complexity of factors,* because the curve of distribution contains not one, but several high points. This is made probable by its being shown that, in the curves of distribution of the experiments made, the average times of most of the big classes of experiments found and distinguished on the basis of the records, lie under the larger rises, and *vice versa*. It is then likely that, if the conditions could be kept as constant as they are in the shortest possible reactions, the curves of distribution would be quite as regular for any set of conditions whatever. Peculiarities in the form of the curve of distribution would then be *symptomatic* of peculiarities in the reactions or in the factors which bring about these, and thereby an aid to discovery. The distinction between sensory and motor reactions is, therefore, *not physiological but psychological* in the prime instance, and is not an exact distinction. It has to be split up into its elements, and when this is done nothing new is found.

This result leads to a more decisive way of looking at those reactions which, through frequent repetition, are held by many to become *unconscious* or *mechanical.* It is evident that, if reflexes be excluded from this class, a task is always necessarily presupposed for the accomplishment of such a reaction. The task may not have been given before each experiment, but it must at least have become operative. The stimulus is given and the reaction follows without any conscious links intervening whatsoever. There is no need to appeal to the unconscious even when everything else falls away except the essentials, task and stimulus.

The *method of subtraction* of different sets of reactions from one another, in order to find the duration of an act of recognition, of distinction, and of association, is subjected to a criticism. In order to find the duration of elementary acts, it is no guarantee to suppose that the contents of all experiments carried out with the same task are the same. First of all, those experiments which are really similarly composed, must be collected with the help of the experimental data and the records. An ideally complete reaction, made up of bits out of many different reactions, is of no use for this purpose. The scheme which has been the basis of this method of subtraction is, besides, very mechanical, much too mechanical for any one to suppose it to be based on data which are true, or likely to be found true in physiology. But even if the number and nature of the elements in an experiment were experimentally determined, it has to be remembered that it is not yet settled how exactly the task affects each element which goes to make up the reaction. All this does not make the method impossible, but only for a long time purposeless.

If *association* be understood as the cause of the known fact and experience of reproduction, it may be *defined* as that by means of which it first becomes possible for one experience to be reproduced by another. Other definitions are found to rest on logical divisions, and to give no guarantee of unity in research. There can be only one kind of association, as far as we know, and on the basis of the previous results the later experience is never reproduced by the earlier by means of the *value* of the logical relations between them but only by the factors described above. The only conceivable condition for the origin of association is, that the two experiences shall have once been together or immediately successive in consciousness.

It is evident that, to form a *judgment,* the subject must have at the moment some experience, and, besides, some experience which consists of reproductions, because an absolutely new experience and nothing else could not be held to form a judgment by itself. An absolutely fixed and rigid system of reproductions, however, gives no judgments, but merely a succession of experiences under the one principle of association. Even the subjects themselves tend to decline the responsibility for judgments in which the reaction which constituted the judgment was determined by the overwhelming strength of a tendency to reproduction. The experimental conclusion drawn by Marbe is accepted, that if one confines oneself to the experiences between the stimulus and the reaction, there is no psychological criterion of the judgment. Outside of this limit, however, stands the *task* which, even if it is not identical in the sense of being always either visual representation or word-representation or the like, is yet *functionally identical*, and is the one factor which goes beyond the rigidity which the single tie of association would give. *The operation of a task makes the reaction* which is determined by or in spite of it, *a judgment* in reference to this task. This position must be met before the attempt can be made to set up hidden unconscious or rare experiences as the criterion of the judgment. It is also evident that the agreement of ideas with their objects, whether these be themselves ideas or not, can never be directly the aim in view. Such agreement, if it exists, can be only and merely the result of the operation of the factors enumerated, of which the one, the task, may of course include the conception agreement. For how would it be possible to proceed to obtain such agreement psychologically?

A *theory of thinking* has, then, to start from our experience as we know it. This presents to us no sharply defined states with beginning and end like printed letters, but only continued observation leads us to a more and more detailed and exact description of our experiences. By means of experimental data we can work ourselves out beyond this position and formulate our factors more precisely. We decline to accept choice and apperception or contrast and similarity as exact or useful scientific conceptions any further. The tendency to reproduction which realises itself, *ceteris paribus*, is that one which, by reason of more frequent actualisation, possesses a greater speed of reproduction. The task, which is no doubt itself a wider and stronger tendency to reproduction, has been sketched in detail as an operative force, and its sphere of operation is doubtless much larger than we have been able to

Experimental Contribution to a Theory of Thinking 199

determine it to be. Over against any tendency to reproduction, the task can only overpower a limited amount of force, a circumstance which makes false reactions possible. Any theory of association which operates only with associations between two experiences immediately following one another, is thus seen to be insufficient, though this much must be presupposed in any theory. Physiology can, perhaps, not offer us more than this at present, but a more exact definition of psychological factors and their sphere of operation can only be welcome to physiology, while the prospect that physiology and psychology will one day be able to give an account of their material which they will find to be much more intelligible to one another than it is now, is by no means excluded. It seems probable at present that the *variable factor* is the strength or rapidity of reproduction and *not the task*, which is supposed to favour in equal strength all tendencies to reproduction which come under its influence. The operations of these two classes of factors on one another, which seems to be confined to a small area which contains at least our fully conscious experiences, is what we know as thinking.

It must not be supposed that the picture of his mental experience given in a subject's record is by any means complete. We see from these results that besides mere suppression of parts of a record, which is not presupposed, the subject may have forgotten something, or the tendencies to reproduction and the tasks which would have enabled him to give a full and accurate record may not have been present, or, for want of practice, very poorly developed. Even if forgetfulness is put aside, we have therefore no right to suppose that what is not in the record was not experienced. But granting this, what can we say about that part of experience which does not come fully to consciousness in reproductions and judgments? A mere mechanical succession of events in consciousness seems to us obviously intelligible, as soon as it happens in fact. What we do not understand is the *meaning* contained in the reference of one experience to another, whether it reproduce or be reproduced by this other. The reaction refers to the stimulus, and, under the influence of the task, brings to fuller consciousness something which was latent in it, although, as we have seen, no other fully conscious elements need be found either in the record or by experimental investigation. There are, besides, several elementary experiences which cannot be further analysed into psychological components, but can only be rendered by one or many reproductions. Such experiences are the more indefinite conceptual states of consciousness, what is often called feeling (other than pleasure and pain). Such experiences may besides be introduced by representations, for example, word-representations, and they are then to be exemplified by conceptions and tasks. All this points to an *insufficiency of consciousness* to give a full knowledge of our subjective experience. The only means we possess for supplementing this deficiency, is to contrive that every part of our consciousness shall be operated on by tasks capable of bringing as much as possible to full consciousness in reactions or judgments. At the same time, this conception of the insufficiency of consciousness starts out from conscious experience and does not necessarily imply notions like the *unconscious*, which lie further afield and are as yet more or less indefinite and unsettled. The *great advantage of the experimental method* is, that it enables us, by grouping of data and by a more exact knowledge of the elementary factors of experience, to overcome the insufficiency of our direct introspection.

The thesis closes with a critical discussion of general representations and conceptions.

* * *

Whether or not Watt was ready to take the plunge into the unconscious, it was not long before others did. By the turn of the century the unconscious was part of the *Zeitgeist*. The new concepts of evolutionary theory, economic theory, and Freud's work in psychological theory were all eroding the supremacy of the conscious mind in determining thought and action. While the belief in the rationality of mankind holds sway, the conscious mind must remain king. But as the belief in rationality began to be undermined, other concepts rose up to fill the breach. Behaviorism found root in this soil, and so did the unconscious.

Messer, as we have seen in the last chapter, during his struggles to classify the *Bsl* came to the conclusion that much of the thinking process went on at an unconscious level. When he tackled the problem of the *Aufgaben,* he expanded the role of the unconscious, noting that their role was primarily an unconscious one. The importance of the unconscious, however, was voiced most convincingly by Ach in 1905. Working at the same time but independently of Watt, he developed the concept of determining tendencies. The concept is very similar to that of *Aufgabe* but placed within the framework of a more elaborate theory. The unconscious nature of the determining tendencies was dramatically illustrated by his use of posthypnotic suggestion, a sample of which is given in the following selection. Although the determining tendencies are similar in nature to the *Aufgaben,* there are some differences in emphasis and they play a more complex role in the thinking process. The concept is a more truly motivational one, in the modern sense of the term; that is, it is less an external stimulus than an internal condition of the subject. Its directing functions have been expanded; in one experiment, for example, Ach demonstrated that the determining tendencies could influence perception as well as the course of associations. He also pointed out that a determining tendency could form a new association or reproductive tendency where none was before.

* * *

Narziss Ach

Determining Tendencies

I. THE EFFECTS OF POST-HYPNOTIC SUGGESTION. The experimental findings of G. E. Müller and A. Pilzecker were the first to shatter

N. Ach, *Über die Willenstätigkeit und das Denken.* Göttingen: Vandenhoeck and Ruprecht, 1905, Chap. 4. This selection translated by D. Rapaport, from D. Rapaport, *Organization and pathology of thought.* New York: Columbia University Press, 1951. Pp. 15–24 reprinted by permission of the publisher.

the view of association-psychology that the train of ideas is governed solely by associative reproduction-tendencies. They have shown that perseverating reproduction-tendencies also may determine the contents of consciousness, and may under certain conditions even become dominant.

The investigations reported in this volume indicate that, besides these associative and perseverative reproduction-tendencies, there is yet another factor of decisive influence on the emerging state of consciousness: the determining tendency. Determining tendencies arise from the specific content of the goal-presentation, and define that state of consciousness so that it accords with the meaning of the goal-presentation. These determining tendencies are the basis of psychological phenomena long described as will-activity. The psychological processes that occur in the wake of suggestions are the most striking examples of these. Suggestions may become effective in the hypnotic state, or in a subsequent state of consciousness, either normal or hypnotic.

The literature reports many post-hypnotic suggestions demonstrating the existence of determining tendencies. Since they were given mostly for therapeutic reasons, I reinvestigated them in a fashion similar to my other experiments, carefully considering the psychological situation of the subject. The procedure was unknown to the subject.

The following suggestion was given to Subject G. in deep hypnosis: "Later on I will show you two cards with two numbers on each. To the first card you will react with the sum, to the second with the difference of the numbers. When the card appears you will immediately, and of you own will, say the correct number, without thinking of what I have now told you." This suggestion was repeated and, on request of the subject, its content retold. Thereupon G. was awakened from hypnosis. In order to make the procedure appear as natural as possible and to avoid the appearance of suggestion, I had already shown the cards to G. before the hypnosis, "incidentally" explaining, as it were, their use. Having terminated the hypnosis we went to another room, and after a few minutes of indifferent conversation I showed G. a card with the numbers 6/2. G. immediately said, "8." To the second card, 4/2, he immediately said, "2." The suggestion was, surprisingly, realized. I asked G.—showing him the first card—"Why did you say 8?" "Just happened to say it." "Did you not think at the moment that this is the sum?" "No. I had the need to say 8." "How about this one?" (showing the second card). "It was just accidental that I said 2." "But this is not accidental!" "I had to say that." "Didn't you think that $4 - 2 = 2$?" "No."

In order to allay the suspicion that a suggested amnesia might play a role here, I repeated this experiment, adding the following suggestion: "When questioned, you will be able to describe the experience exactly." The determination by the hypnotic suggestion was again manifest. The suggestion was to give the difference on the first card and the sum on the second. After hypnosis, the instant reaction to card 6/3 was "3"; to card 4/1, "5." Again the subject realized only later that the numbers he spoke were the difference and the sum. The experiment misfired only once: before reacting, the subject repeated the instruction itself. That is, to card 6/3 the subject said, "The sum is 9"; to card 4/1, "The difference is 3." The explanation is that in this case the suggestion was given not in precise form, but as follows: "Upon seeing the first card you will give the sum, upon seeing the second the difference." Indeed, this instruction was followed. A further experiment, using the precisely worded suggestion, yielded the usual results. . . .

The results are similar in the case of the following suggestion: "I will show you some numbers. To the first one, you will say the number that comes before it in the number-continuum, to the second the number that follows it. When you see the number, you will utter the correct number, of your own free will and without delay." G. repeats the instructions. A few minutes after hypnosis is terminated, he is shown the number 6 and answers immediately, "5." Now 6 is shown again and he answers immediately, "7." "What did you say after the first number?" "5." "Why?" "I don't know, it just came to my mind." "When I showed it to you the second time you said 7, why?" "I felt the need to say it, but I don't know why." Here, again, the idea corresponding to the meaning of the suggestion becomes directly over-valent. Executing a suggestion does not imply a mediation-process in which the number presented elicits the memory of the suggestion, due to which in turn the correct answer associatively arises. Rather, the determining tendency arising from the suggestion raises above the threshold of consciousness the idea which corresponds to the meaning of the suggestion.

This also explains the effects of negative suggestion. In another experiment I added the suggestion: "You will be shown a third card, but that one you won't be able to see." When shown this third card, G. was silent, moved his head to and fro, trying to look at my hand more closely. "What do you see?" "It looks like you want to show me something." "What do I have in my hand?" "Nothing." G. saw my hand, but not the card it held. . . .

It would be desirable to conduct experiments with time measurements on post-hypnotic suggestions. So far I have not been in a position to do that. My previous reaction-experiments with time measurements, in hypnosis or in a state of systematically narrowed consciousness, led to no results.

II. CONCERNING DETERMINING TENDENCIES. The influence of determining tendencies has been demonstrated in striking and extreme form by post-hypnotic suggestions, but it can also be demonstrated in reaction-experiments, particularly in those without coordination of activity. This reaction-form is quite variable. In these reaction-experiments there are five different ways in which the determining tendency arising from the goal-presentation manifests itself. The presentation to which the intention refers—in our case, the card with numbers—will henceforth be called referent-presentation.

(a) The goal-presentation was rarely reproduced at the time the referent-presentation appeared. When this happened, it was due to associative or perseverative reproduction-tendencies, and the goal-presentation had been in consciousness even in the preparatory period. With Subject B. this happened altogether three times, with C. only once. On these occasions . . . attention in the preparatory period was below its usual intensity. (b) Besides its reappearance due to perservative or associative reproduction, the goal-presentation became noticeable when it entered an *apperceptive fusion* with the appearing stimulus. The subject visualized a plus sign, and fitted the stimulus-numbers into the thus prepared schema. The result issued associatively from this apperceptive fusion. (c) The intention can be realized also by an apperceptive fusion between a presentation readied by it and the referent-presentation. In Subject C., for instance, we note a spatial displacement of the two numbers that correspond to the intention. When the intention is to add, the two numbers pull closer together; when it is to subtract, the smaller number appears to sidle toward the larger. When the result coincides with one of the two numbers presented, it issues from this apperceptive fusion, either associatively or directly. (d) In a fourth set of experiments, we again encounter an apperceptive fusion. Upon perceiving the stimuli, presentations readied by the goal-presentation fuse with those associatively reproduced. This was characteristic of the behavior of Subject A. throughout. When this subject intended to add upon the appearance of 5/2, his intention manifested itself by the internal utterance, "5 and 2 make 7." This occurred repeatedly with C. and once with B. (e) Finally, determination arising from the intention may become effective, so that tendencies readied by the goal-presentation reinforce the reproduction-tendencies which issue from the referent-presentation and correspond to the meaning of the goal-presentation. In these cases, the correct presentation appears in consciousness *immediately* upon the apprehension of the stimuli (referent-presentations). This was the usual procedure of B., and occurred with C. on the last two experimental days. . . . It is characteristic of all forms of determination that their realization is in accord with the meaning of the goal-presentation, whether or not their means be apperceptive fusion or the raising of the intended result over the threshold of consciousness directly through the referent-presentation. Only a few experiments were exceptions to this. The results so far available suggest that in these cases the necessary intensity of intention was not present. As already mentioned, the direct realization of the intention was most striking in posthypnotic suggestions. But even in simple experiments without coordination of activity, it was usual with Subjects D. and E. that the number corresponding to the intention came directly to consciousness.

Thus the stimulus alone does not determine the content of consciousness that follows its appearance: the same numbers may be followed at various times by different ones, depending upon the intention. For example, 6/2 may be followed by 8, 4, or 3, according to whether the intention was to add, subtract, or divide. *The same stimulus may lead to the reproduction of different presentations; in each case it is the presentation corresponding to the meaning of the intention which becomes over-valent.* It is due to determining tendencies that, of all the tendencies readied by the perception of the stimulus, those will become reinforced to overvalence which are associatively coordinated with a presentation corresponding to the given intention. . . .

There are yet other observations which indicate the decisive influence of determining tendencies arising from goal-presentations. When an intention to divide was followed by two numbers that would yield a fraction, the perception was accompanied by a state of surprise and an awareness of difficulty, connected with displeasure or with the immediate consciousness, "This doesn't work." No acoustic, kinesthetic, or other presentations occurred in these experiences. When, however, the calculation was easy, no awareness of difficulty or surprise was present. Such experiences were rather frequent. . . .

These observations indicate that the apperception and elaboration of the stimulus (referent-presentation) occur under influences corresponding to the meaning of the goal-presentation. If we do not assume that from the goal-presentation specific influences arise which are directed toward the apperception of the referent-presentation, then we find no content in the preparatory period of the examples here given which could explain this behavior upon perceiving the stimulus. Influences, arising from the goal-presentation and directed toward the referent-presentation, which determine the course of events so as to accord with the goal-presentation, are called determining tendencies. This term does not imply anything as to the nature of these curious effects, and expresses only the fact that mental happening is regulated by intentions, that is, goal-presentations. The distinction of these tendencies from associative and perseverative reproduction-tendencies will be discussed later on.

Thus, the ordered and goal-directed course of mental happening is the effect of determining tendencies. The independence of goal-directed mental happening from incidental external stimuli, and from the customary associative course of presentations, is due to the influence of these determining tendencies. We refer here to the fact of this independence, without discussing its limits. These determining tendencies may issue not only from existing intentions but from suggestive influences, from commands, and from tasks. Here we are concerned only with the effect and not with the origin of these determining tendencies.

The determining tendencies do more than merely establish an ordered goal-directed course of mental happening. They insure a certain independence [for the thought-process] by making possible the formation of new associations. Even though we are bound to the perceived presentation-material, the determining tendencies enable us to bring it into new, previously non-existent, associative connections.

* * *

The next step in building a consistent theory of directed thinking was taken by Otto Selz, but his developments do not belong properly into the history of the Würzburg school. That movement had done its work in a period of barely more than a decade. The isomorphism between conscious experience and the processes of thinking had been rejected and never again would psychologists insist that thinking must be amenable to detailed self-observation. Nor would it be possible for anyone to ignore the importance of directive influences on the train of thought. The importance of the Würzburg movement and the hopes for the future were summarized in 1912 by Oswald Külpe.

Oswald Külpe

The Modern Psychology of Thinking

The study of thinking, which in Germany has been nurtured primarily at the Würzburger Psychological Institute, belongs to [the] developmental phase of experimental psychology.

While earlier psychology in general did not pay adequate attention to thinking, the new experimental direction was so busy bringing order into the more solid institutions of sensations, images, and feelings, that it was quite late before it could devote itself to the airy thoughts. The first mental contents to be noted in consciousness were those of pressures and punctures, tastes and smells, sounds and colors. They were the easiest to perceive, followed by their images and the pleasures and pains. That there was anything else without the palpable* constitution of these

O. Külpe, Über die moderne Psychologie des Denkens. Appendix in O. Külpe, *Vorlesungen über Psychologie*, 2nd ed., edited by K. Bühler. Leipzig: Hirzel, 1922. This appendix was originally given as a lecture at the Fifth Congress of the German Society for Experimental Psychology, Berlin, 1912. It was first published in the *Internat. Monatsschrift für Wissenschaft, Kunst und Technik*, June 1912, pp. 1070 ff. Pp. 301–316 from the 1922 edition, transl. by George and Jean M. Mandler.

* Translators' note: In facing the troublesome problem of translating *"anschaulich"* and *"unanschaulich,"* we have generally translated the latter as "imageless" in keeping with traditional usage. However, the word *"anschaulich"* seemed more amenable to a variety of translations such as "palpable," "self-evident," "perceptual," and "specifiable." We have used these words in keeping with the context and have also, at times, substituted such choices as "non-perceptual" or "impalpable" for *"unanschaulich"* in order to point up the generality of the notion which relieves it from the suggestion of the visual that "imageless" implies.

formations escaped the eye of the scientist who had not been trained to perceive it. The experience of natural science directed the researcher's attention toward sensory stimuli and sensations, after-images, contrast phenomena and fantastic variations of reality. Whatever did not have such characteristics simply did not seem to exist. And thus when the first experimental psychologists undertook experiments about the meaning of words they were able to report anything at all only if self-evident representations or their accompanying phenomena made an appearance. In many other cases, particularly when the words signified something abstract or general, they found "nothing." The fact that a word could be understood without eliciting images, that a sentence could be understood and judged even though only its sounds appeared to be present in consciousness, never gave these psychologists cause to postulate or to determine imageless as well as imageable contents.

The prejudice upon which we have touched here has a long history. Aristotle declared that there were no thoughts without an image and during the scholastic period this position was held fast. The division between perception and thinking, between objects of the senses and objects of thought, made repeatedly by Plato, had never been psychologically pursued. In modern times one found words, and nothing but words when the perceptions were missing that were supposed to give them meaning and understanding. In the pedagogy of Pestalozzi and Herbart, perception was honored as the ABC of all mental development. Kant considered concepts without images as empty, and Schopenhauer wanted to base all of mathematics upon imagery; he even wanted to ban proof from geometry. Similar conceptions were added in poetry. Poetic art could only function through images; the more it tried to follow Horace and emulate painting—to create with the brush of perception—the more completely did it seem to fulfill its mission. . . .

What finally led us in psychology to another theory was the *systematic application of self-observation.* Previously it was the rule not to obtain reports about all experiences that occurred during an experiment as soon as it was concluded, but only to obtain occasional reports from subjects about exceptional or abnormal occurrences. Only at the conclusion of a whole series was a general report requested about the main facts that were still remembered. In this fashion only the grossest aspects came to light. Furthermore, the commitment to the traditional concepts of sensations, feelings, and images prevented the observation or labelling of that which was neither sensation nor feeling nor image. However, as soon as persons trained in self-observation were allowed to make complete and unprejudiced reports about their experiences of an experiment immediately after its completion, the necessity for an extension of the previous concepts and definitions became obvious. We found in ourselves processes, states, directions, and acts which did not fit the schema of the older psychology. Subjects started to speak in the language of everyday life and to give images only a subordinate importance in their private world. They knew and thought, judged and understood, apprehended meaning and interpreted connections, without receiving any real support from occasionally appearing sensory events [*Versinnlichungen*]. Consider the following examples. [There follow two examples, only one of which will be presented here.] The subject is asked: "Do you understand the sentence: Thinking is so extraordinarily difficult that many prefer to judge?" The protocol reads: "I knew immediately after the conclusion of the sentence what the point was. But the thought was still quite unclear. In order to gain clarity, I slowly repeated the sentence and when I was finished with that the thought was clear so that I can now repeat it: To judge here implies thoughtless speech and a dismissal of the subject matter in contrast to the searching activity of thinking. Apart from the words of the sentence that I heard and which I then reproduced, there was nothing in the way of images in my consciousness." This is not just a simple process of imageless thought. What is notable is that [subjects] stated that understanding proceeded generally in this fashion with difficult sentences. It is thus not an artificial product of the laboratory, but the blossoming life of reality that has been opened up by these experiments. [There follows a string of aphorisms and sayings to demonstrate examples from daily experience that produce just such thinking, e. g., Man is noble, charitable and good; that alone differentiates him from all other known beings.] Who would experience images here and for whom would such images be the basis, the inescapable condition of comprehension? And who wants to maintain that words alone suffice to represent the meaning? No, these cases provide proof for the existence of imageless conscious contents, especially thoughts.

But if thoughts differ from the images of colors and sounds, of forests and gardens, of men and animals, then this difference will also be found in their behavior, in their forms, and in their course. We know what lawfulness governs images. Everybody speaks of association and reproduction, of the appearance of an image, of its elicitation by others, of its connection with other images. We learn a poem or a new vocabulary. Here knowledge of content, knowledge of meaning is not sufficient; we must learn one word after another so that we can later faithfully reproduce the whole. We develop strong associations between the succeeding or coordinated members of a poem or a list of words, and for this we need a long period of time and a large number of repetitions. If thoughts are nothing but images, then the same tediousness should govern their memorization. Any reflection about the manner in which we assimilate the meaning of a poem shows immediately that the state of affairs is different here. One attentive reading is frequently sufficient to reproduce the thought content. And thus we progress through sheer mental exposure to such comprehensive feats as the reproduction of the thoughts contained in a sermon, a lecture, a dramatic production, a novel, a scientific work, or a long conversation. We not infrequently find to our sorrow how independent we are of the actual words. Sometimes we would like very much to be able to reproduce faithfully a striking expression, the pregnant form of a sentence, or an attractive picture. But even though the sense of what has been said is quite available to us, we cannot reproduce its form.

[There follows a discussion of some of Bühler's experiments.]

It is notable that one of the first results of our psychology of thought was negative: The old conceptual notions that experimental psychology had provided for descriptions of sensation, feeling, and imagination, and their relations, did not permit comprehension or definition of intellectual processes. But similarly the new concept of dispositions of consciousness [*Bewusstseins-*

lage] which was pressed upon us by factual observation, was not sufficient and only made possible circumscription rather than description. Even the study of primitive processes of thinking soon showed that the imageless can be known. Self-observation, in contrast to observations of nature, can perceive the presence and definite characteristics of what is neither color nor sound, of what may be given without image or feeling. The meaning of abstract and general expressions can be shown to exist in consciousness when nothing perceptual may be discovered apart from the words, and these meanings may be experienced and realized even without words or other signs. The new concept of conscious knowing [*Bewusstheit*] gave expression to these facts. And thus the inflexible schema of the previously accepted elements of mental life was extended in an important direction.

Experimental psychology is thus confronted with new problems which disclose many and varied perspectives. Not only do imageless states include known, meant, and thought objects with all their characteristics and relations, and states of affairs that can be expressed in judgments, but also the many actions whereby we take a position toward a given conscious content, whereby we order, classify, recognize or reject it. Although one once could use sensations and images to construct a mosaic of mental life and an automatic lawfulness of the coming and going of conscious elements, such a simplification and dependence upon chemical analogies has now lost its footing. Perceptual [*anschaulich*] contents could only persist as artificial abstractions, as arbitrarily isolated and separated components. Within a complete consciousness, however, they have become partial phenomena, dependent upon a variety of different conceptions, and it was only when they were placed in a complex of mental processes that they gained meaning and value for the experiencing subject. Just as perception could not be characterized as a mere having of sensation, no less could thinking be conceived as the associative course of images. Association psychology, as it had been founded by Hume, lost its hegemony.

The fact that thoughts are independent of the signs in which they are expressed, and that they have peculiar and fluid interrelations, uninfluenced by the laws of the association of images, demonstrated their autonomy as a special class of conscious contents. As a result, the area of self-observation has been extended to a considerable degree. Not only images and sensations and their characteristics and colorations belong to our mental life, but we can also include thought and knowledge, in which we can perceive neither color nor form, neither pleasure nor unpleasure. We know from daily experience that we have at our disposal a great spontaneity in our search for objects, their registration and comprehension, in our activity with and our actions upon them. Psychology has taken little notice of this activity of the mind. F. A. Lange coined the phrase about the scientific psychology without a soul, a psychology in which sensations and images and their feeling tones are the sole contents of consciousness. Such a psychology had to be watchful that no mystical force such as the ego should insinuate itself into this psychological world. More exactly, one had to say: "Thinking occurs," but not: "I think," and the process of such thinking consisted in nothing but the coming and going of images regulated by the laws of association. Even today there are psychologists who have not risen above this point of view. Their psychology can rightly be accused of unreality, of moving in an abstract region where it neither seeks nor finds entry to full experience. These are the psychologists who offer stones instead of bread to those representatives of the humanities [Geisteswissenschaften] who are asking for psychological justification; nor can these psychologists advise or help a biology that is seeking a connection with psychology. . . .

[The psychology of] thinking unlocked the door to the true internal world, and it was no mysticism that led us there, but the abandoning of a prejudice. Bacon already knew that the road to truth is paved with prejudices. In the present instance they happen to derive from the exact natural sciences, for whom in the last decades sensory observation meant everything and for whom concepts were only an expedient used to represent, in the simplest possible fashion, facts based on sensory experience. But now thoughts became not only signs for sensations but independent structures and values that could be ascertained with certainty just as any sensory impression. They were even more faithful, lasting, and freer than the pictures with which our memory and fantasy otherwise operate. But they did not, of course, admit to the same immediate observation as perceptual objects. The discovery was made that the ego could not be divided. To think with a certain devotion and depth and to observe the thoughts at the same time—that could not be done. First one and then the other, that was the watchword of the young psychology of thought. And it succeeded surprisingly well. Once a mental task was solved, the process that had been experienced became in all its phases an object of intensive determination by the retrospective observer. Comparison of several subjects and of several results from the same subject demonstrated that the procedure was unobjectionable. The pronounced agreement of our studies in the psychology of thought, whereby one could be built upon another, was a beautiful confirmation of our results. Once again it became clear why the previously used methods of observation could not find any thinking or other expressions of our conscious activity. Observation itself is a particular act, a committed activity of the ego. No other activity can be executed next to it at the same time. Our mental efficiency is limited, our personality is a unitary whole. But observation can take place after the completion of a function and can make it the object of self-perception. And now many acts were recognized which previously had not existed for psychology: attending and recognizing, willing and rejecting, comparing and differentiating, and many more. All of them were lacking the perceptual [*anschaulich*] character of sensations, images, and feelings, even though these phenomena could accompany the newly found actions. It is characteristic of the helplessness of the previous psychology that it thought it could define these acts through their symptoms. Attention was considered as a group of tension and muscle sensations, because so-called strained attention gives rise to such sensations. Similarly, willing was dissolved into images of motions because they usually precede an external act of the will. These constructions, whose artificiality immediately becomes apparent, were left without a leg to stand on as soon as the existence of special psychic acts was recognized, thus robbing sensations and images of their sole dominion in consciousness.

With the recognition of these acts another important innovation came to the fore. The center of gravity of mental life had to be moved. Previously one could say: We are attentive because our eyes are fixed on a particular point in the visual field and the muscles that keep the eyes in that position are tensed. It now became clear that this conception inverted the real state of affairs and that what it should rather say is: We direct our eyes toward a certain point and strain our muscles because we want to observe it. *Activity became the central focus,* receptivity and the mechanism of images secondary. . . .

The actions of the ego are always subject to points of view and tasks [*Aufgaben*] and through them are moved to activity. One could also say that they serve a purpose, either self-generated or set by others. The thinking of the theoretician is no more nor less aimless than that of the practitioner. Psychologists are used to taking this into consideration. The subject receives a task, a direction or instruction as to the point of view which he must adopt toward the presented stimulus. He may have to compare two light intensities one with another, to execute a movement upon a pressure or a sound, to reply quickly to a called-out word with the first word that he can think of, to understand a sentence, to draw a conclusion, and so forth. All such tasks, if they are willingly undertaken and remembered, exercise a great determining force upon the behavior of the subject. This force is called the determining tendency. In a sense the ego contains an unlimited variety of response possibilities. If one of these is to come to the fore to the exclusion of all others, then a determination, a selection, is needed.

The independence of the task and the determining tendency that was derived from it was also fateful for association psychology. Such a task is not some ordinary type of reproductive motive. It must be accepted, the subject must support it, and it gives his activity a certain direction. Sensations, feelings, and images are not given tasks; a task is set for a subject, whose mental character does not dissolve into these contents, but whose spontaneity alone can adopt the instructions and execute them. Since in all thinking such determining viewpoints play a role, since abstraction and combination, judgment and conclusion, comparison and differentiation, the finding and construction of relations, all become carriers of determining tendencies, the psychology of the task became an essential part of the modern investigation of thinking. And even the psychology of the task proved to have an importance that significantly transcended the narrower area in which it was developed. No psychological experiments are imaginable without tasks! The tasks must, therefore, be considered just as important an experimental condition as the apparatus and the stimuli that it presents. A variation in the task is at least as important an experimental procedure as a change in external experimental conditions.

This importance of the task and its effects on the structure and course of mental events could not be explained with the tools of association psychology. Rather, Ach was able to show that even associations of considerable strength could be overcome with a counteracting task. The force with which a determining tendency acts is not only greater than the familiar reproductive tendencies, it also derives from a different source and its effectiveness is not tied to associative relations.

* * *

The new findings from Würzburg were both startling and provoking to most psychologists interested in thought, whatever their theoretical stance. And while all this ferment was in progress the association psychologists could not and did not sit idly by. We have seen already how one sophisticated defender of the classical position—Titchener—reacted to the notion of imageless thought. At the time, the major defender of an associationist theory of directed thought was Georg Elias Müller. The following excerpt, in which he takes the Würzburgers to task, was published in 1913, that is after the major findings of that movement were available to him. Apart from chiding the association critics for prematurely jumping to conclusions, he quite properly indicated the vagueness of the concepts that psychologists such as Ach were trying to substitute for associative mechanisms. The tenor of Müller's critique of determining tendencies, for example, was to be echoed many years later in the criticism of so-called cognitive concepts, such as "hypothesis," by the S-R theorists of the 1940's and 1950's. The history of psychology in the twentieth century has repeatedly produced the phenomenon of the classical associationists keeping the "cognitive" rebels honest by demanding strict definitions and deductive theories.

* * *

Georg Elias Müller

In Defense of Association Psychology

I must describe as utterly incomprehensible Watt's remarks that any theory which attempts to make do with mere associations or reproductive tendencies is incompatible with his experimental results. This remark of Watt's runs completely counter to the conclusions of any attentive study of his own experimental observations. All his reports—about the way his subjects adjust the task [*Aufgabe*] in order better to handle it, how they behave after the appearance of the stimulus word, the number and type of false reactions he observed, his own remark . . . that the task produces a set [*Einstellung*] toward a specific group of representations favorable for its fulfillment—all of these show sufficiently that insofar as a solution of the task actually occurs in his experiments, this solution takes place not as a result of the action of mysterious determining tendencies, but rather on the basis of associative or perseverative reproductive tendencies that have been aroused by

G. E. Müller, Zur Analyse der Gedächtnistätigkeit und des Vorstellungsverlaufs, III. Teil. Z. f. Psychol., Ergänzungsbd. 8, 1913, 567 pp. Pp. 475–479, 484–489 transl. by George and Jean M. Mandler.

the psychic constellation (instruction and voluntary preparation, response opportunity [the occasion at which the response is required], preceding experiments, and so forth). The same goes for the expositions of Ach, who originated the term "determining tendencies." It must be stressed that neither in Watt's nor Ach's work, nor in the parallel statements of Messer, can be found the slightest trace of an experiment that really proves that considerations such as those presented by us are inadequate for an explanation of their experimental results. But it is after all an elementary rule of science that one should proceed to the postulation of new principles only after one has compellingly shown by intensive investigation that known principles, demonstrated with certainty to be valid, are not sufficient for the explanation of certain facts.

The assumption of determining tendencies, however, is not only utterly unsubstantiated, but also completely unsuited to provide a stimulus for an intensive psychological analysis of the phenomena of the will. We have seen that the solution of a task can come about in a variety of ways; for example, through the association, during the voluntary preparation, of the response opportunity with a particular state of attention or some other purposeful mode of behavior, or by the arousal of a set toward a particular group of images or through the cooperation of the task image, or by the controlling role of the task influencing those images which are produced haphazardly, so to speak, by the response opportunity or other factors. Nothing can be called less of a psychological analysis than, in all of these cases, to speak simply about the operation of determining tendencies.

The assumption of a determining tendency would only be worthy of consideration as an explanation of the phenomena involved if one were in the position to state specific laws that more closely define the character and action of these determining tendencies. Such laws should permit us to deduce why the solution of a task occurs in certain cases, why it is absent in others, why under certain conditions the solution of the task proceeds in one way, under other conditions in another way. If, however, one were to proceed with the establishment of such functional laws, one would find that determining tendencies lead to a solution of the task only insofar as the reproductive tendencies—which, according to the reproductive laws, become effective following the presentation of the response opportunity—can lead to such a solution. In the same fashion, the manner in which the solution of the task comes about is determined by the nature of these reproductive tendencies. In short, one would find that the assumption of a determining tendency would be quite superfluous. . . .

Therefore I come to the conclusion that the assumption of determining tendencies is unproven, that it is useless for the explanation of the phenomena involved, that it does not promote psychological analysis, and that its psychophysical consequences are incompatible with currently predominating views. If anyone does not agree with our assertion that the reaction experiments discussed can be adequately explained by the laws of reproduction, then let him describe clearly and unequivocally those phenomena that cannot be explained by the point of view that I represent, and let him show, in a logically adequate fashion, that these phenomena will not permit such an explanation. . . .

I am afraid that I cannot escape the unrewarding task of demonstrating and criticizing the manner in which certain circles have treated questions about the lawfulness of the train of thought. Külpe [in the selection on p. 208] cites as evidence for his statement that the influence of the task and its effects cannot be explained with the tools of association psychology, the fact that Ach "was able to show that even associations of considerable strength could be overcome with a counteracting task." The force with which the determining tendency makes itself felt was said to be "greater than the known reproductive tendencies." First it should be noted that in no way did Ach prove or even state that a determining tendency is stronger than the known reproductive tendencies. One would find, for example, that in all cases where the . . . goal to produce a correct response . . . creates, during the voluntary preparation, a strong association between the [subject's] image of the response opportunity and the appropriate orientation of attention, then, following the occurrence of the response opportunity, the accomplishment of the task proceeds on the basis of the associated orientation. Obviously, one would disdain an explanation of the accomplishment of the task . . . in terms of a peculiar lawfulness applicable to the function of determining tendencies rather than on the basis of [the laws of] association. . . .

I do not understand how one can prove that the effect of the task does not depend on association and perseveration by the fact that the voluntary preparation, occurring with high concentration immediately prior to the appearance of the stimulus syllable, supersedes in its effects a syllable association . . . that has not been similarly renewed during the foreperiod. By what investigations has it been determined that the advantage that the task must have had, according to the laws of association and perseveration, and that was developed . . . [with] high concentration immediately before the appearance of the stimulus syllable was not in fact greater than the advantage that many previous repetitions had given to the juxtaposed syllable association . . . ? I cannot understand how one can base a statement of such great import on such inadequate grounds. . . .

According to Messer,[1] the associative laws of similarity and contiguity "are not even remotely adequate to explain in any particular case why the arousal of traces which have been associated in manifold ways progress in just one particular direction." The reader is not told that decades ago association psychology stated that the decision which of two associative reproductive tendencies . . . will triumph depends on two factors: first, the degree of strength that accords to the competing association as a function of the number and distribution of the repetitions on which they are based, and second, the degree of readiness which the preceding experiences have transmitted to the representations corresponding to the competing reproductive tendencies.[*] The investigations undertaken by Pilzecker and me have, in certain respects, elaborated this principle and made it more precise.

The polemic against the "common association psychology" reaches unbelievable heights in Wreschner's paper.[2] For example,

---

[1] A. Messer, *Empfindung und Denken*. Leipzig: 1908.

[*] [This is the core of the constellation theory which Müller credits to Bain. Not only is the previously established strength of an association important, but prior instructions, e.g., the task or the image of what type of response is required will put into readiness the representations of one set of competing tendencies rather than another and thus produce additional strength for those reproductive tendencies at the time of responding — Eds.]

[2] A. Wreschner, Die Reproduktion und Assoziation von Vorstellungen. Z. f. Psychol., Ergänzungsbd. 3, 1907–1909, 599 pp.

we are told the following: "The theory of associated experiences pretty nearly excludes all invention, discovery, and every new combination from our train of thought." Even a beginner in psychology could advance the notion that whenever an image a is associated on one occasion with b, and on another with c, then the reappearance of c may, as a result of association, result in the appearance of the new combination $b + c$ or an associative mixed effect of novel character conditioned by the reproductive tendencies appropriate to b and c. Furthermore, according to association psychology, a subsequent strengthening of reproductive tendencies that have been aroused by quite different images may lead to a new combination of images, and even according to pure association psychology a goal representation directed toward something novel must be at work.

* * *

Even in his defense, Müller harks back to the atomism of the British associationists and in fact gives Bain credit for originating the constellation theory of directed thinking. However, the inadequacy of a position that tries to build complex thought out of simple associations is best illustrated by Müller's final argument that goal-representations (images) of the new are quite adequate to account for the appearance of novelty in thought. His argument here is just as vague and useless as some of the passages for which he excoriates the Würzburgers. However, Müller, like his antagonists, resorts to a concept (goal-representations) that, like tasks and determining tendencies, encompasses a much larger unit of consciousness—or behavior—than do images or sensations.

6

The Unit of Thought

At least since the days of Locke it had been assumed that mental life went from the simple to the complex, and that complex operations were painstakingly constructed out of elementaristic components. As we saw earlier, Hartley made quite explicit the notion that complexity = summation. This seemed such an obvious formulation that it was difficult to combat, and it was not until the beginning of the twentieth century that the proposition was seriously considered that complex units and operations may be acquired and used in one fell swoop.

Unhappiness with atomism had been around for some time, however, and it seemed patently obvious to some writers that thinking could not be reduced to a conglomeration of images and ideas. William James, for example, had clearly posed the problem in 1890 in relation to perception when he wrote:

> We certainly ought not to say what usually is said by psychologists, and treat perception as a sum of distinct psychic entities, the present sensation namely, *plus* a lot of images from the past, all "integrated" together in a way impossible to describe. The perception is one state of mind or nothing. . . .[*]

And in discussing the stream of thought, he cuts the Gordian knot that had made the concept of "relation" such a puzzle for the associationists by saying:

> There is no manifold of coexisting ideas; the notion of such a thing is a chimera. Whatever things are thought in relation are thought from

[*] W. James, *The principles of psychology*, Vol. 2. New York: Holt, 1890, p. 80.

the outset in a unity, in a single pulse of subjectivity, a single . . . feeling, or state of mind.*

No part of the new psychology of thinking produced a greater departure from tradition or a more revolutionary attitude than the notion that the elementaristic particles of association psychology could not in principle do justice to the problems of complex thought.† To abandon once and for all the conception of larger units of consciousness being glued and pieced together out of atomistic ideas and sensations meant to create a new vocabulary and new theories. Slowly the conviction that the mind contained such new and wondrous things as tasks, sets, and goal representations had gained adherents. Even the associationists admitted these new entities, though often in the role of *dei ex machina*. The new theories used these new units as their building blocks, not as crutches. Environmental inputs set into motion a vast apparatus of complexes, structures, and directing mechanisms, none of which were to be found in consciousness, many of which represented whole trains of ideas or sensations and replaced these particles with complicated hypothetical processes that restructured, organized, and molded the process of thinking.

Probably the major turning point in the history of thinking came with the work of Otto Selz. Although Selz studied with some of the Würzburg psychologists, his *magna opera* were written elsewhere and published in 1913 and 1922. Not only does he deal in these two volumes with the problem of directed thinking, but he is the first psychologist who is both willing and able to deal with the problem of productive thinking under the same rubric as reproductive thought. Neither his original two volumes of work‡ nor the summary of his theory of productive and reproductive think-

---

* W. James, *The principles of psychology*, Vol. 1. New York: Holt, 1890, p. 278.

† In American psychology it was John Dewey who carried on James' battle against elementarism during the early part of the century. His search for the functional unit of behavior, including thought, was to color much of the contemporary scene.

‡ O. Selz, *Über die Gesetze des geordneten Denkverlaufs*. Stuttgart: Spemann, 1913; and *Zur Psychologie des produktiven Denkens und des Irrtums*. Bonn: Cohen, 1922.

ing* received adequate attention during the ensuing years. Selz himself restricted his work in subsequent years, spent in a minor academic position in Mannheim, to a restatement of his position, and much of the psychology of thinking between 1920 and 1950 might have advanced faster had he been given proper recognition. He was killed during the 1940's in a German concentration camp.

Selz's primary reaction was against the constellation theory of the associationists. His major source of data and concepts can be found in the essentially descriptive work of the Würzburg school. However, he also represents the confluence of another point of view insofar as some of his ideas can be traced to the act psychology of Brentano and to Meinong in particular.† It seems plausible that one of Selz's main contributions—the notion of the actively processing mental apparatus—derives from the influence of the German philosophers, whereas the content of his theory is more clearly influenced by the psychology of association and the Würzburg school. Whatever his antecedents, Selz was the first voice in the early twentieth century to call for a psychology of thinking that dealt with primarily with processes rather than with contents. Instead of posing problems for a theory of thinking, he saw his task as the construction of a predictive and explanatory theory that related environmental events to the products of human thought. As de Groot has phrased it, Selz constructed "a conceptual model for thought processes. . . . [He] sounds much like modern model builders, who first of all strive for a system of general laws, logical consistency, and precision—if possible even in axiomatic form." ‡ This very search for precision and explicitness earned him the epithet "machine theorist" from some of his successors, such as the Gestalt theorists Benary and Koffka.

Starting with a critique of the constellation theory, Selz advances his theory of specific acts, responses that are specific to the structured complex of the task before the subject. Responses (thoughts) exist within systems which produce the missing links

---

* O. Selz, *Die Gesetze der produktiven and reproduktiven Geistestätigkeit.* Bonn: Cohen, 1924.

† A. v. Meinong, Über Gegenstandstheorie. In *Untersuchungen zur Gegenstandstheorie und Psychologie.* Leipzig: Barth, 1904.

‡ A. D. de Groot, *Thought and choice in chess.* The Hague: Mouton, 1964.

in reproductive thinking, and which attain the assimilation of new responses in productive thinking. The existing structure of responses in a sense *demands* a particular completion by the use of anticipatory schemas, rather than permitting a haphazard trial-and-error search in a welter of all possible response tendencies. Different systems, determined by the task and other experimental conditions, will be completed by different specific responses. Thus the unit of thought becomes a structured system of responses or thoughts, rather than a string of elementary particles.

The following selection is a summary of Selz's system published in 1927. Although some fourteen years had elapsed since the publication of his original work, this article succinctly summarized Selz's theory. In some passages he reads like a contemporary writer on thought (cf. his notion of operations on p. 231), and the modernity of his ideas is attested by some recent work which ties Selz's theory to contemporary work on computer simulation.*

* A. Newell, J. C. Shaw, and H. A. Simon, Elements of a theory of human problem solving. *Psychol. Rev.*, 1958, **65,** 151–166. See also A. D. de Groot, *Thought and choice in chess,* The Hague: Mouton, 1964; and de Groot's earlier exposition and use of Selz's theory in *Het Denken van den Schaker,* Amsterdam: Noord-Hollandsche Uitgevers Maatschappij, 1946.

* * *

Otto Selz

The Revision of the Fundamental Conceptions of Intellectual Processes

The revision of the fundamental conceptions of intellectual processes which the results of the modern psychology of thought

O. Selz, Die Umgestaltung der Grundanschauungen vom intellektuellen Geschehen. *Kantstudien,* 1927, **32,** 273–280. Transl. by George and Jean M. Mandler by permission of the publisher.

demand, may be summarized in the following basic thesis: Intellectual processes are not a system of diffuse reproductions—as association psychology thought—but, rather, like a system of body movements, particularly of reflexes, they are a system of specific reactions in which there is as a rule an unambiguous relation between specific conditions of elicitation and both general and special intellectual operations. When association psychology was concerned with doing justice to the intellectual processes, it arrived at the constellation theory of diffuse reproductions. . . . The reproductive tendencies of the associative links of the process diverge diffusely in all directions and they are said to enter into competition with the reproductive or perseverative tendencies of a goal-representation or some superordinate idea. During this struggle for existence among the competing tendencies, with its reciprocal inhibitions and facilitations [*Förderungen*], victory goes to that tendency which, according to the momentary constellation, is the strongest. The importance of the strongly perseverating goal-representations or superordinate conceptions in determining [the] direction [of thought] was explained by the assumption that the reproductive tendencies derived from them reinforce reproductive tendencies operating in a similar direction but inhibit those operating in a different direction.

However, even an analysis of *reproductive* thought processes shows the untenability of this theory of diffuse reproductions. For example, we set a subject a task of searching for the generic concept for some presented stimulus words. He is given the stimulus word "farmer" and the response "occupation" occurs without any mediating experiences. G. E. Müller, until recently the main representative of a constellation theory, proposed in his work on memory the following explanation for the solutions of such tasks. The task "generic concept" acts as a directional representation which reinforces certain reproductive tendencies of the stimulus word. The task puts into heightened readiness a wide gamut of representations—namely, the names of all generic concepts that have been previously acquired, such as "plant," "animal," and so forth. Among the names of generic concepts that have been made ready there is also the generic concept "occupation." Thus, among the several reproductive tendencies [associations] of the stimulus word "farmer," the task-relevant reproductive tendency "farmer–occupation" receives a reinforcement due to the favorable constellation produced for the association "occupation," and thus leads to a correct solution. This constellation theory, convincing as it is at first glance, would only be useful if reproductive tendencies other than the task-relevant ones were not favored by the constellation to the same degree. But the opposite is the case. Thus, in our example, among all the generic names that have been put in readiness by the task, there is also the generic designation "tradesman." The concept "tradesman" is furthermore also strongly associated with the stimulus word "farmer." For example, farmer and tradesman are tied together in every tax form. Thus the constellation favors the reproduction of "tradesman" in response to "farmer" in exactly the same degree as the reproduction of "occupation." A consistently applied constellation theory can offer no reason why the incorrect response "tradesman," which represents a coordinate instead of a superordinate concept, does not appear just as frequently as the correct response "occupation."

Such difficulties, into which any *theory of diffuse reproductions* inescapably leads, can be avoided in a rather simple manner by the *theory of specific responses*. This theory shows that the task "generic concept" and the relevant stimulus word "farmer" cannot be treated as factors acting in isolation, but rather that they act like the coherent question "What is the generic concept for farmer?" This question of the experimenter already anticipates schematically the knowledge-unit (or structure)* "Farmer is an occupation" which the subject has previously acquired. The question contains one member (A) of the known facts of the case and the relation (γ) to the other, sought-for member; in this case the relation is of species to genus. The question can, therefore, act as

---

* Translators' note: Selz uses as a central concept of his theory the term "*Komplex*." We have found it usually inadvisable to translate this term directly as "complex" since Selz's usage and obvious intention would be hidden by a term that does not do justice to the structural, unitary, and patterning implications of his term. We have preferred to use the terms "unit" and "structure" whenever possible, thus emphasizing that Selz's "*Komplexe*" — though constituted of elements — act as single units with their own specific structure.

an eliciting condition for the intellectual operation of knowledge-production [*Wissensaktualisierung*], whereby the uncompleted knowledge-unit ($A\gamma\,\square$) which the question represents, is completed by restoring the reproductive unit ($A\,\gamma\,B$). Instead of a diffuse play of competing reproductive tendencies, this theory offers a comprehensive process wherein the question acts as a unitary total task along with a uniquely relevant operation of knowledge-production. This operation can be shown to be a special case of structure-completion, since the fragmentary structure of the question is made complete by the operation of knowledge-production.

Just as the theory of specific responses differs from the associationist constellation theory, so does it basically differ from all superimposition theories. According to these theories, special directive factors, for example, determining tendencies or insightful acts of relational comprehension, are added to diffuse processes that are in themselves devoid of sense or direction. In this fashion, the ordered process actually is superimposed upon a state of affairs which, in reality or at least in general appearance, is unordered. In fact if one starts with the erroneous constructions of a system of diffuse reproductions, one needs a superstructure of factors to bring order into irregularity, resulting in the futile attempts of superimposition theories . . . to make sense out of a state of affairs that was senseless to begin with. If, however, we start with a system of specific responses, then we have from the beginning an ordered, instead of an unordered, system which needs no additions.

The replacement of the superimposition theories by the theory of specific responses also leads to important conclusions for a developmental theory of stages. A theory of stages using a developmental superimposition theory must be rejected. A system of diffuse reproductions in which the strongest association triumphs cannot be seen as a developmentally older stage to which insightful behavior is added at later stages. The identification of intellectual processes as a system of specific responses suggests rather the developmental integration of intellectual actions into an existing, more primitive system of specific responses; a theory of stages would then be concerned only with different developmental stages of a single system of specific responses. In this manner the auto-

Fundamental Conceptions of Intellectual Processes 229

matic acquisition of novel modes of behavior, Bühler's "stage of training [*Dressur*]," demands no system of diffuse reproduction but can be made comprehensible within the framework of a system of specific responses, as we shall show later.

Together with the theory of diffuse reproduction, a conception of intellectual processes as a mere running off of images must also be abandoned. It is not images, not even the awareness or thoughts that have sometimes been designated as imageless "elements," that make up the constituent units of our system of specific responses; rather these units are acts, intellectual operations that are just as needful of and amenable to analysis as the simple reflexes from which complex body movements are built up. These intellectual operations, together with their conditions of elicitation, do not form a closed system, but they are, just as are the body movements, links in the comprehensive system of specific responses that constitute the individual—a system in which all bodily and mental modes of behavior, and particularly those of the needs and affects, participate.

The fact that for such a long time intellectual processes or their assumed structure could be treated as a system of diffuse reproduction can only be understood in light of the fact that the principal difference between the associationist system of diffuse reproduction and a system of specific responses—such as reflex physiology has long envisaged—has been misperceived. Both systems try to link together the basic elements that previous analysis had discovered. The principal difference, however, consists in the uniqueness of coordinations in a system of specific responses. What happens in such a system is not decided by the momentarily strongest tendency arising out of some accidental constellation, but rather by the specific nature of the conditions of elicitation—the external or internal stimuli—on which the type of response depends. In contrast to a system of diffuse reproduction, partial processes in a system of specific responses, a system of reflex movements, for example, have a character that is relevant to the entire structure. The partial processes produce a specific fragment of the total output of the system and are, therefore, objectively appropriate and meaningful. For this reason, it is initially quite improbable that the higher processes of organisms, involving the intellect, should be dependent upon the accidental play of meaningless reproductive tendencies, while the processes in a purely reflexive organism are characterized by the relevance to the whole organism such as we find in a system of specific responses. Finally, a system of specific responses is characterized by the fact that a meaningful whole can be reconstructed synthetically from the basic elements that have been found in the course of analysis. The "inadequacy" of the synthetic procedure in psychology which recently Gestalt theory has reasserted, the inadequacy of the "pathway from the bottom to the top," is really relevant only to the inadequate attempts of a theory of diffuse reproduction, which tries to build the meaningful whole out of meaningless constituents. On the basis of a theory of specific responses, however, the synthetic construction of intellectual processes is in principle possible.

The utility of a theory of specific responses derives from the previously mentioned result of experimental self-observation, namely, that stimulus-word and task do not act in isolation, as the constellation theory of diffuse reproductions originally assumed. Rather, stimulus and task constitute the awareness of a total task, an awareness which even without express formulation has the directed structure of a coherent question. At the same time, within the indissoluble whole of the task or the question-unit, we must distinguish a *determining* and an *anticipating* factor. The determining or will-determining factor is part of each task or question as such, and it makes the conditions of elicitation of the intellectual operations a dynamic process. The anticipating factor consists, as we have seen, in the schematic anticipation of the complete structure of the solution by the total task acting as a question. The anticipating factor has a specific structure for each task or question and determines thereby the specific type and actual direction of the intellectual operation that has been initiated, as for example, the direction which the intellectual operation of completing a structure imparts to the phenomenological experience of [reproductive] reflection. In reproductive thinking the question acts, as our previous example has shown, as a fragmentary unit of knowledge, from which at least one part is missing. That missing part is categorically characterized in the formulated question by the interrogatories: what, where, when, how much, and so forth. The rising voice at the end of a question expresses through language rhythm the fragmentary nature, the functional incompleteness and need for completion of the question-complex. The schematic anticipation of the complete knowledge-unit, which is different for each question, makes the question a specific stimulus for the production of the relevant knowledge-unit. In this way, the knowledge-production at issue has the character of a specific response to the task.

Whenever several memory-units are relevant to a schematic anticipation, there may be a competition of several processes of unit completion. However, this competition, with the attendant inhibitions that are usually associatively interpreted, moves within the narrow range of task-relevant reproductions that have been fixed by the schematic anticipation. Only with a change of the specific task-stimulus, i.e., the awareness of a task and its after effects, do task-irrelevant reproductions arise, particularly in the case when the schematic anticipation is only partially effective.

In the course of experimental self-observation, the individual analysis of task-conditioned thought processes always shows an uninterrupted chain of both general and specific partial operations which at times cumulatively $(A + B + C)$ and at times in a stepwise fashion (B after failure of A) impel the solution of the task. These operations are continued until a solution is found or up to a momentary or lasting renunciation of the solution. Each one of these partial operations is tied to a specific condition of elicitation, for example: the success of a partial operation elicits the initiation of the next partial operation; the failure of one partial operation elicits the initiation of an alternative operation; the failure of a system of partial operations which cumulatively should lead to solution of the task elicits a new start and the potentiation of an alternative system; following the success of one partial operation, insight into the additional partial operations necessary for success leads to their elicitation in the order determined by that insight. Each attempted solution finally ends as a specific condition of elicitation for control [test] operations which terminate with the consummation or correction of the solution. Within these strictly directed and determined processes there is no room for diffuse reproductions. An occasional divergence from the task, as seems to be the rule in cases of flight of ideas, depends on specific responsivity to certain diverting stimuli and does not represent a negative instance for the theory of specific responses.

The failure of *reproductive thinking*, or reflection, that has been initially brought to bear upon a problem, due to the absence, for example, of reproducible task-relevant knowledge-units, represents the specific conditions of elicitation for the operations of *productive thinking*. The primary operations of productive thinking are the operations of means-production, leaving aside special cases such as a striving for originality. We are concerned here with the application of previously developed methods of solution to the mastery of a task in an analogous case, whereby a new product is developed. Should the operations of means-production fail then the operations of means-abstraction are initiated. They are designed for the dicovery of new methods of solution and are arrived at by analyzing the structure of the immediately given or reproductively restored problem [*Aufgabesituation*].

The posing of a problem in productive thinking also contains the schematic anticipation of the solution as a directing aspect. From among the previously developed modes of behavior only those are potentiated in means-production which lead to the schematically anticipated final state. In the case of means-abstraction, the schematic realization of the conditions of solution impress structurally lawful methods of solution on the problem. Or else, memory-units which are relevant to the schematically anticipated conditions of solution are called upon so that, for example, previously observed causal connections can now function as means. If the solution has to be abandoned for the time being, later accidental observations which conform to the schematically anticipated conditions of solution, can reawaken the latent problem and bring about the abstraction of the means-relations at a later time. In this fashion chance becomes a regular factor in the process of creation.

The overweening importance of schematic anticipation becomes developmentally comprehensible as soon as we realize that the most primitive drive in mental life—desire—contains within itself an anticipation of the final state, and this anticipation becomes schematic even when the partial conditions for reaching the goal are still unknown.

In the case of accidental means-abstraction which we have just mentioned, the reactivation of the latent problem-complex is possible only under the condition of undetermined (involuntary) reproductive processes. This undetermined process, however, does not justify a theory of diffuse reproductions since it acts only as a condition of elicitation of previously prepared specific responses. Due to the potential energy of the response dispositions, this process requires only a minimal amount of specific energy and remains, therefore, ineffective when no relevant response dispositions, that is, problem-complexes, are present. It is for this reason that accidental discoveries in the history of science and technology only occur after the relevant problems have come to the fore.

Through the operations of means-abstraction, new integrated [*ganzheitsbezogen*] modes of behavior, the new methods of solution, develop causally out of previously developed integrative modes of behavior, namely, the general operations of means-abstraction. Whatever we see in this insightful novel acquisition of integrated modes of behavior, we also see in the case of uninsightful automatic acquisition of such behavior. A new situation releases at first previously developed responses, for example, inherited instinctual movements or partially insightful trial-and-error movements. Among the movements initiated by these previously perfected responses, those that are successful in the new situation, that lead to a satisfying end state, are automatically selected. The selection is based on the schematic anticipation of the end state that is found in the desire for the goal. Thus on the basis of already existing responses, new specific responses can be developed for special situations. The system of specific responses that constitutes an individual carries in itself, therefore, the conditions for its growth through the assimilation of new integrative modes of behavior. All this assumes that, just as in the examples cited, the previously perfected integrative responses are of such a nature that under specific conditions of elicitation they occasion a lawful creation of new responses. In this fashion, the old vitalistic problem also seems to be nearer to a solution, to an answer to why the parts of a living system show this integrative character at each stage of development. It is characteristic of the structure of the whole, seen as a system of specific responses of the type described here, that the newly assimilated parts are always integrated. The integration of the parts of an organic system . . . becomes understandable at least insofar as we can, in principle, synthetically derive the later developmental stages of a primitive system of integrated specific responses, just as we can derive the later state of a mechanical system, e.g., the solar system, from a hypothetical initial state.

* * *

The line of development that stretches from the Würzburgers to Selz and to the Gestalt school is nicely illustrated in a dispute over priorities. In 1925 Koffka published an article on psychology[*] in a general handbook. In 1926 Bühler[†] and Selz[‡] critically evaluated Koffka's article and, in particular, charged that Koffka had "borrowed" his theory of thinking from Selz without giving the latter adequate credit. The attack was both strident and pertinent enough to move Koffka to publish a reply in 1927[§] in which he defended himself against the accusation on the grounds that "since Selz's theory is essentially . . . different from mine I cannot very well have borrowed my theory from Selz." The essential difference apparently lies in Koffka's insistence on the emergence of new qualities: "Meaning" is the essential quality of the natural process "thinking"; structure develops out of processes and is not produced by external factors. He calls Selz's theory a machine theory which

---

[*] K. Koffka, Psychologie. In M. Dessoir (Ed.), *Lehrbuch der Philosophie.* Band II. Die Philosophie in ihren Einzelgebieten. Berlin: Ullstein, 1925.

[†] K. Bühler, Die "Neue Psychologie" Koffkas. *Z. f. Psychol.*, 1926, **99**, 145–159.

[‡] O. Selz, Zur Psychologie der Gegenwart. Eine Anmerkung zu Koffkas Darstellung. *Z. f. Psychol.*, 1926, **99**, 160–196.

[§] K. Koffka, Bemerkungen zur Denk-Psychologie. *Psychol. Forsch.*, 1927, **9**, 163–183.

leaves little or no room for the inherent emergence of novel productions and processes. Forty years later, it seems that the difference is a minor one and that modern thought has tended to prefer Selz's "machine" position against the implied nativism of the Gestaltists. The growth of the psychology of thinking, however, need not be evaluated in terms of priorities; the important aspect is that a structural psychology of thinking was being developed in contrast to the constellation theory.

Starting with von Ehrenfels in 1890,* the notion of Gestalt qualities had made some inroads into sensory psychology, but it was not until the 1920's that Gestalt psychology became concerned with problems of thinking. We shall return to this aspect of the Gestalt movement later. For the time being it is useful to stress another aspect of the contribution of Gestalt psychology.

It is quite apparent that by the time Selz wrote his theory of thought, psychologists had abandoned the notion that all the concepts used to explain the thinking process must be found in consciousness. Tasks, determining tendencies, and anticipatory schemas were all theoretical notions constructed from the data available to the psychologist. But this development had taken place nearly unnoticed, and soon the Gestalt psychologists were to come along with Gestalt qualities and the laws of organization —none of which were even remotely "given" in consciousness.

With this step, the break with a tradition which demanded that thinking be explained in terms of introspective evidence was practically complete. However, one other traditional attitude had to be changed before psychology would come of age. In the following selection, Kurt Koffka argues convincingly for a distinction between descriptive and functional concepts. This introduction to Koffka's analysis of imagery, published in 1912, clearly states the difference between the data of immediate experience and the concepts constructed by the scientist. As Koffka points out, many of his contemporaries had been unable or unwilling to make such a distinction, which was to become diagnostic of the age when behaviorism was being born in America. The Gestalt school's

* C. v. Ehrenfels, Über "Gestaltqualitäten." *Vierteljahrsschr. f. wissenschaftl. Philos.*, 1890, **14**, 249–292.

commitment to this distinction is underlined by Koffka's prefatory expression of debt to Wolfgang Köhler and Max Wertheimer for many useful discussions.

* * *

Kurt Koffka

The Distinction between Descriptive and Functional Concepts

We are concerned with an analysis of concept formation in psychology, to be undertaken in the first instance with the use of a series of examples.

We shall start with concept formations that are feasible even within a prescientific psychology, and that have been undertaken by reflex psychology.

By imagining a great variety of different experiences, I am able to bring some order into them, in the first place by differentiating between images and feelings. Within these two groups, again by the sheer recreation of experience, I can specify new categories: I distinguish between perceptual and nonperceptual contents, between acts and appearances [contents], and within the latter I can distinguish colors and sounds, again distinct on the other hand from smells and tastes, etc. Within the colors I can, purely experientially, distinguish between the chromatic and achromatic ones, between saturated and unsaturated, between light and dark colors. An infinite number of such examples of concept formation could be listed.

On the other hand, I could make a series of observations of the following type: I hear a melody with great pleasure for the

K. Koffka, *Zur Analyse der Vorstellungen und ihrer Gesetze.* Leipzig: Quelle and Meyer, 1912. Pp. 2–16 transl. by George and Jean M. Mandler.

Descriptive and Functional Concepts 237

first time; it gives me pleasure even the second and third time that I hear it. The fourth time around, however, I seem to notice that my pleasure is less than what it was previously, by the fifth time my pleasure may have disappeared, and by the sixth time I may even feel some annoyance. As I reflect on this state of affairs, I may arrive at the concepts of adaptation and reversal of feelings.

Further: I remember an experience that has recently taken place. I am aware of each detail, I see the situation in front of me and can hear the people concerned talking. I do not think about it again for a whole year, until for some accidental reason I remember the occurrence; but despite all effort I am unable to recall every detail, even whole important sequences are irrecoverably lost and what is left has significantly paled and lost the distinctly perceptual character of my initial memory. Should I have available a direct report of that event, or a report prepared at the time of my first recall, I would be able to ascertain that much of what I now think I remember either never happened or did not happen in quite that way. Reflection on this state of affairs leads me to ascribe to time certain influences on memory. Concepts such as one about memory distortion may result.

As a third instance: Again and again I have the experience that, with increasing twilight, I am unable to find objects on my table because their color is indistinguishable from the background. However, I tell myself that as long as any light comes into the room it will be reflected by both the background and the objects placed on it. Thus, even with the weakest illumination, qualitatively and quantitatively different light is reaching my eye. I must conclude that this difference becomes so small that I do not notice it any more, and I have therefore arrived at the concept of a threshold.

Contrast these two types of examples. What is the relation between the resulting concepts and the experiences on which they are based?

In the first group the concept clearly contains only characteristics which can always be found in the experience from which it is formed. The concept of "achromatic color" includes a series of color experiences, just as the concept "color" includes all color experiences, and the concept "image" all images. All these concepts directly contain the experiences.

Just the opposite applies to the second group: I do not experience the adaptation or reversal of feeling, nor a distortion of memory, nor a threshold, the way I experience a color. Rather, I use these concepts to put experiences into relation with other objects, either with other experiences—as in the first two examples—or with stimuli as in the last example. Thus, these concepts contain characteristics that are not contained in the experiences from which they are derived.

All concepts that directly touch upon experience we shall call *descriptive concepts,* and all concepts of the second type we shall call *functional concepts.*

Since both types are derived from experiences, and from the same experiences, the difference between them can only have come about because the path that leads from experience to concept is different in the two cases. This difference must now be specified.

In order to do this, we shall again investigate concept formations, attending this time not to the goal of these concepts but, rather, to the path which the formation takes. However, in place of our previous examples, which were more or less related to prescientific thinking, we shall more suitably use some that are based on a skillfully worked out methodology. The road thereby becomes longer and offers more clues to be investigated, but it also becomes richer so that despite all variations the constant characteristics stand out more clearly.

We shall start with the descriptive concepts:

The path here is easily surveyed. . . . In the last analysis [even] an improved methodology can do no more for descriptive concepts than to produce the opportunity for experiences: The immediate experience, and the description of the immediately experienced, constitute the unavoidable condition for such concept formation. . . .

We maintain, therefore:

All descriptive concepts derive from simple perception and the description of experiences.

Descriptive and Functional Concepts 239

The path that leads to functional concepts is much more varied. Here we can be guided by examples:

The introduction of a definite task in the well known association experiment leads to a complete change in results. The reproduced words show . . . a certain relation to the task.

Given the task to name a superordinate concept for the stimulus word, the response to "thunder" might become "natural phenomenon" rather than the usual "lightning." The subjects' description of their experiences during the fore—and main—periods shows that in the early tests erroneous words and thoughts about the task frequently come into consciousness. Such interposed conscious contents slowly drop out and the subject responds to the stimulus word with the appropriate response word with full consciousness of the correctness of his response.

It is usually deduced from this state of affairs that the task has certain effects upon the reproductive process and the concept of determining tendencies is introduced in order to describe this effect.

Not stopping there, we can at the same time produce reproductive tendencies that vary in strength and then we can introduce a measure of the strength (i.e., the associative equivalent) of the determining tendency by finding out what strength of an associative reproduction tendency can be just overcome by the determining tendency.

Another example: We produce associations of equal or different strength between one syllable and two others. We then compare responses given to such double bond syllables with those given to single bond syllables, paying particular attention to response time and the subjects' report of their experiences. The results lead to the concept of generative and effective inhibition.

Or: One has subjects compare standard weights with various comparison weights and then determines from the distribution of judgments the differential threshold for the particular standard weights, using purely mathematical assumptions and deductions.

The physicist measures the amount of light I_1 that is projected onto a surface, and the amount of light R_1 that is reflected from that surface. He then measures a second pair I_2 and R_2 and he finds that the ratios I_1/R_1 and I_2/R_2, and as a matter of fact all ratios I/R, are equal, and thus arrives at the concept of reflectance. During all this, reflectance itself has never been observed. In the same sense, the differential threshold has never been observed in a psychophysical experiment. What have been observed are only experiences that end with a judgment. And the same is true for the concepts of generative and effective inhibition, and determining tendency.

What have been observed are only the sound of the stimulus syllable and the processes that follow it up to the pronunciation of the response syllable, processes that might well include experiences of tormenting emptiness. In the first example, again only experiences are observed, beginning with the foreperiod and ending with the response, and here too experiences may appear that could be described as goal-directed feelings of being driven.

Experiences such as the tormenting emptiness during the occurrence of an inhibition or the goal-directed feeling of being driven by a determination [determining tendency] might tempt us to argue with our derivation: both the inhibition and the determination are being experienced; there actually seem to be just such inhibition or determination experiences. But it is quite clear that this is inadmissible equivocation. An inhibition that I experience and an inhibition that I derive from the result of an experiment are just as different as color and light-wave, as sound and vibration of the air.

I do not mean the experience of inhibition when I talk about generative and effective inhibition, but rather the fact that a syllable that is associatively connected with another will show greater difficulty in forming an association with a third one than it showed in forming the original association. In other words, to reproduce a syllable in response to another syllable will be more difficult when the latter has been associated with two than when it has been associated with only one other syllable. An analogous argument applies to the determining tendencies.

The concepts which were illustrated in the analysis of the last examples quite clearly fall into the group of functional concepts derived above; they describe relations among experiences, not the experiences themselves.

Descriptive and Functional Concepts 241

Note the characteristics of the path that has led us to these concepts.

We were previously able to show a parallel between these concepts and physical concepts. Does this parallel also apply to the method whereby they are obtained?

The positivist will have no doubt about this, but proof can easily be provided even for a defender of realism.

What are the materials of concept formation in our physical example? Certain values of I and R. But these values are only an expression for certain observations, and in the last analysis these are again experiences, such as experiences of the equality of the intensities of two photometric surfaces. Not even the most stringent realism can deny that at the beginning—and even at the end—of each induction there is experience. . . . Even for the physicist the immediate material is experience, only what he makes of it is not an experience any more.[1]

Exactly the same process takes place in the formation of [psychological] functional concepts. Somewhere there are also experiences and they, too—whenever possible—are quantitatively apprehended: distributions of psychophysical judgments, number and distribution of responses as well as length of response times related to the number of repetitions, number of correct reactions and the reaction time of a conditioned reproduction. These objective data are the immediate starting points for our functional concepts. . . .

Maybe the great progress that modern psychology has made in comparison with the old psychology, especially in the area of the functional concept, can be derived from the great improvement in its objective stance [*Objektivierung*]. Only here does counting and measuring make any sense; the simple experience remains as ever unmeasurable.

In contrast to our proposition about the formation of descriptive concepts, we now state:

---

[1] Our derivation would not be disturbed in the least if instead of experience we say "thing," as most physicists would prefer. But even then it is clear that from "things" "non-things" are derived.

All functional concepts have as their basis experiences that have somehow been made objective. This kind of concept formation is of the same type as the formation of physical concepts.

Varying degrees of objectivity may be recognized not only in the precision and in the fine details of concepts, but also in their source.

While pure experience has been objectified in the reflex examples, in the methodological examples there is an objectively given [state of affairs] which more or less guides us to the goal of objectivity. Reaction and response times are purely objective; spoken reaction words, responses, and judgments have at least some objective aspect. If I depend solely upon expressive movement, as in some older applications of the expressive method and particularly in animal psychology, the material is already objective before I make use of it.

The objection will be raised that the preceding exposition is trivial. Why such a long disquisition in order to state the obvious? But this objection can be refuted, and the best way is to show what a disastrous role inadequate attention to our distinction has played in research.

We are only left with the task of showing in examples taken from the literature how descriptive and functional concepts have been confused in concept formation and, therefore, also in explanation. A good example can be found in the concept of attention.

In general this concept has the role of a functional concept: both absolute and differential thresholds depend on certain conditions, one of which may be called attention; the same can be said about the quality of learning and of memory and in respect to many other processes. Ebbinghaus and Külpe both based their concept of attention more or less clearly upon such a functional derivation.

On the other hand, there is a certain state of consciousness which can be called a state of attention so that a descriptive concept of attention is also possible.

Titchener most clearly represented such a derivation of the concept.

Thus it would be possible to give the name "attention" both to a functional and to a descriptive concept and it would be purely a question of nomenclature to decide which concept should actually be called by that name.

This would be the case if research were conducted not by human beings but by pure intellects. But since researchers are human beings, it becomes very easy to regard two concepts as *one* because they have the same name, even though at the start the concept is specifically defined in only one particular sense. That is what has actually happened and we can even say quite confidently that no psychologist can state with certainty that he has never been guilty of such a confusion. We want to demonstrate it in two places which are of great importance for psychological research—namely, in the great work of Wundt and in the most modern of all text books, that of Titchener.

Wundt says: "Apart from the coming and going of feelings and images, we can perceive in ourselves, in more or less clear variations, an activity which we call attention." According to this definition, attention would be a pure descriptive concept which could be shown in experience at any time.

On the other hand, there are statements about the effect of attention. "Only impressions which lie above the intensity threshold can pass the apperceptive threshold; but in order for this to occur the subjective function of attention must be added."

But this sentence is a functional sentence: Attention is the cause of an impression crossing the apperceptive threshold. Attention here is a functional concept since the causation cannot be experienced but only derived.

Wundt did not fail to see that he is dealing here with two different things, but still he did not appreciate that he has formed two quite different concepts:

From what we have said, attention and apperception are expressions for one and the same psychological state of affairs. We prefer to select the first of these expressions in order to designate the subjective side of that state, i.e., the accompanying feelings and sensations; we use the second one mainly in order to indicate the objective results, the changes in the quality of the conscious contents.

There is no question that Wundt puts greater emphasis on the unity of, rather than on the difference between the two concepts; the use of "prefer" and "mainly" leave no doubt about this matter. But what kind of unitary state of affairs is it which has a subjective and an objective side to it? . . . What we are dealing with here are two different concepts, one descriptive and the other functional. Obviously the confusion of these two has a series of important consequences, for example, the conception of apperception as a process of the will. The important point here is the adoption of a causal effect into a descriptive concept.

Turning to Titchener, he wants to use attention purely as a descriptive concept: "In the last resort, and in its simplest terms, attention is identical with sensory clearness."

But this author has no other way open to him; he knows only descriptive concepts in psychology: "Whatever attention is, it must be described in terms of mental processes, sensations and images and affections, and explained by reference to its physiological conditions."

That this author is completely unaware of the distinction we have made may be gathered from the fact that he leaves the decision among the various definitions of attention, functional and descriptive in our terminology, entirely to introspection. He does not even see the possibility of forming concepts with characteristics that are not to be found in experience, about which simple introspection cannot make any decision. Titchener's definition, therefore, leads unavoidably to an equivocal use of the word "attention" in which the functional concept eventually comes to the fore. In his discussion whether or not an increase in the clarity of a content parallels an increase in its intensity, we can find, for example, the following sentence: "You can hear, with attention, a faint sound that you cannot hear if you do not attend."

If we now substitute—which we obviously can—for the word "attention" the word "clearness" which, for Titchener, is identical, then the sentence reads: "If a weak sound is clear, you can hear it under certain circumstances; however, you cannot hear it when it is not clear."

It follows from this that under certain circumstances clearness can exist without the content which is supposed to be clear. What then is clear in this case? And, particularly, does Titchener's sentence say, after the substitution, the same that it says for most psychologists without the substitution? Not even Titchener would want to maintain that. . . .

The physiological concept of attention has no more in common with Titchener's psychological one than its name. But this concept quite clearly does what we expect the concept of "attention" to do; it explains, for example, the lowering of the threshold. But then it ceases being a descriptive concept and becomes a functional one.

We might have [one] physiological explanation that describes physiological processes which are synchronous with clearness, or [another] which describes processes that precede clearness. In fact we then have two quite different concepts, one descriptive concept, "attention" equals "clearness," and one functional concept, "attention" equals "facilitation and inhibition." But since Titchener did not differentiate these two concepts, he gets into a series of difficulties such as in his theory of voluntary attention which leads him to the consequence that the greater the effort the lower the degree of attention. It is not our present task to criticize Titchener's theory of attention; it only served to demonstrate that the distinction which we have introduced is not quite so trivial, and that its neglect may have dangerous consequences.

Instead of Titchener's theory of attention, we might have used his theory of association, where the same confusion of concepts may be found.

We want to add one other example from Titchener's book because his teachings here directly contradict the views which we want to defend later on—we refer to the concept of meaning. Meaning is said to be characteristic of all perception, in contrast to the sensations. What is meaning?

Meaning, psychologically, is always context; one mental process is the meaning of another mental process if it is that other's context. And context, in this sense, is simply the mental process which accrues to the given process through the situation in which the organism finds itself.

Originally the situation is physical (and thus not a mental process) and the meaning is kinesthetic: the organism reacts with movement to the situation and the characteristic sensations of this movement give meaning to the process that is in the focus of consciousness; these sensations are psychologically its meaning. One could well notice a contradiction here, but we would rather ask in principle: Is the concept of meaning still a descriptive concept which undoubtedly it would have to be?

As an answer, we will use another quotation in order to be quite sure about the author's opinion:

In characterizing perception, it is said that the context of perceptions has a fringe, a background, a context, and that this context is the psychological equivalent of logical meaning. But what does it mean to say that the context or background is the meaning of the content that stands in the center of attention? Is this meaning experienced? According to Titchener, only sensations, images, and feelings can be experienced. The sheer togetherness of context, vague perceptions, and central contents is not an experience of their togetherness. I can only experience A and B at the same time, not the connection between the two. Titchener denies just this. In his example about the primitive state, cited above, it says that the sensations of movement are the meaning of the most deeply conscious part of the situation. What is there more than mere succession or simultaneity?

Here, too, there has been a confusion between functional and descriptive concepts: on the one hand is the fact that words and other perceptual contents have a different meaning according to their relationship, and from this we deduce that the relationship has some influence upon meaning. But then "relationship" is being used as a functional concept. On the other hand, one can describe meaning in such a way that it is described as the fringe of perceptual contents; here we have a pure descriptive concept. Finally, even the relationship can be given as such in the fringe, and from these three states of affairs, two descriptive and one functional, arises the Titchenerian theory.

Generally, the consequence of Titchener's ignoring our differentiation is that his concept of the analysis of mental contents remains completely unclear and his concepts are, therefore, mostly neither pure descriptive nor pure functional concepts, but contain both elements in an unfortunate and concealing mixture.

* * *

Koffka's preoccupation with the nature and use of theoretical concepts was not only reflected in the work of the Gestalt school. In 1917, Claparède, for example, who was to stress the importance of "hypotheses" in problem solving, used a method of thinking aloud as an experimental technique. He was careful, however, to distinguish between these protocols and introspection, and he warned against treating them as such.*

In the same year, in *The Mentality of Apes,* Köhler made the subject-scientist distinction, although perhaps his subjects gave him an unfair advantage in arriving at this conclusion. Speaking of insightful solutions to problems given to his apes, he says:

... [It] often follows upon a period of perplexity or quiet (often a period of survey), but in real and convincing cases, the solution never appears in a disorder of blind impulses. It is one continuous smooth action, which can be resolved into parts *only by abstract thinking* by the onlooker; in *reality* they do *not* appear independently.†

In some ways, Köhler's book is more relevant to the studies of animal learning which had begun to appear in the early twentieth century than it is to the topic of this book. Much of his argument against blind trial-and-error behavior is focused on Thorndike's version of association theory, and even in 1917 it was already outmoded as an argument against associative models of human thinking. He did, however, formulate the concept of "in-

---

* E. Claparède, La psychologie de l'intelligence. *Scientia,* 1917, **22,** 353–368.
† W. Köhler, *The mentality of apes,* 2nd ed., transl. by Ella Winter. New York: Harcourt Brace, 1927, p. 191. The original work was published as: Intelligenzprüfungen an Anthropoiden. *Abhandl. d. Kgl. preuss. Akad. d. Wiss.,* Phys.-Math. Kl. Nr. 1, 1917. Quoted by permission of The Humanities Press, publisher of the 1951 edition.

sight," and in so doing laid out a battleground to be well littered during the next decade with the reputations of both human and animal psychologists.

In retrospect, much of the controversy seems to have been unnecessary, and was due in large part to an inadequate understanding of what was meant by the term "insight." Although Köhler himself later changed its definition, it is clear from the following passage what was meant at the time:

We can, in our own experience, distinguish sharply between the kind of behavior which from the very beginning arises out of a consideration of the structure of a situation, and one that does not. Only in the former case do we speak of insight, and only that behavior of animals definitely appears to us intelligent which takes account from the beginning of the lay of the land, and proceeds to deal with it in a single, continuous, and definite course. Hence follows this criterion of insight: *The appearance of a complete solution with reference to the whole lay-out of the field.* . . . How one is to explain that the field as a whole, the relations of the parts of the situation to one another, etc., determine the solution, belongs to the theory. Here we have only to exclude the idea that the behavior of the animals is to be explained by the assumption according to which the solution will be accomplished without regard to the structure of the situation, as a sequence of chance parts, that is to say, without intelligence.*

"The theory" was in the process of being worked out by Köhler, by Wertheimer, and by Koffka. Most of the work, both theoretical and experimental, was carried on in the field of perception, and on related problems of recall and memory. Throughout this time the theoretical tools were undergoing a profound change. A vocabulary of wholes and structures was in the making, but these were not merely new elements to be associated as sensations once had been, to be held together by directional forces such as the determining tendency. Directional concepts were to be allowed no special status. For example, in his treatise on problem solving, Duncker explicitly rejects this aspect of the work of N. R. F. Maier. Maier† had suggested that thinking consists of

---

* Köhler, *op. cit.*, pp. 190–191.
† N. R. F. Maier, Reasoning in humans, I. On direction. *J. comp. Psychol.*, 1930, **10**, 115–143.

combining previous experiences in new patterns under the influence of an organizing principle of direction. Duncker refuses even this remnant from the associationist approach:

> There exists as little fundamental difference between "direction" and "the elements to be combined" as between "direction" and "problem." For these elements combine with one another with only apparent simultaneity. In reality, they usually follow upon one another in a sequence in which each element possesses problem-character (thus "direction"-character) with respect to the following, and solution-character with respect to the preceding elements.*

The new units were to be basic, and the laws of association to be considered subordinate. The elements of any mental process are not discrete units combined into complex structures; the structures are given in the first place and the laws of association of any part with any other are determined by the laws of the total structure—not vice versa. As a result, association by contiguity is recast in the light of meaningful contiguities within structures, and problems of recall and other memory functions are based on association by similarity, which in turn is a function of the structural requirements of a percept. It is clear, therefore, that not the associative processes but the structures themselves needed study, and to this end Gestalt psychology turned primarily to the field of perception, secondarily to the study of changes in percepts over time, and only finally to other processes.

One of the early essays concerned with a Gestalt analysis of thought is Wertheimer's disquisition in 1920 on syllogistic reasoning.† The goal of this undertaking was most ambitious, Wertheimer wanted to know no less than "How does thinking really work"? In the following abbreviated version of this essay, the ambition sometimes outdistances explanatory achievement. However, whatever one might think of such terms as "recentering" and the "inner necessity of the whole," at a descriptive level Wertheimer's account challenges any theory of thinking. Gestalt theory may

---

* K. Duncker, On problem solving. *Psychol. Monogr.*, 1945, **58**, No. 5, p. 17. See selection on p. 262 ff.

† M. Wertheimer, *Über Schlussprozesse im produktiven Denken*. Berlin-Leipzig: de Gruyter, 1920.

not have significantly advanced our understanding of the structure of the cognitive apparatus, but its representatives did have the courage to tackle the most difficult problems. The following passage illustrates one such attempt.

* * *

Max Wertheimer

The Syllogism and Productive Thinking

When one attempts, in actual thinking, to use the *modus barbara*[1] of traditional logic, a curious discrepancy may arise. Like so many of the examples in textbooks of logic the *barbara* often appears empty, inadequate, and sterile. No wonder the *modus barbara* has been styled a *petitio*, or a merely classificatory device.[2]

And yet this is not invariably the case. Much clever thinking occurs in terms of this modus; very often one has the feeling that one's thinking *has* advanced. *What is really involved in such processes? How does it happen that the same logical operation can yield such diverse results on different occasions?*

Our aim here is to inquire into the nature of thought processes

---

M. Wertheimer, The syllogism and productive thinking. In W. D. Ellis, *A source book of Gestalt psychology.* New York: Humanities Press, 1950. Abridged and translated by W. D. Ellis from: Über Schlussprozesse im produktiven Denken. In *Drei Abhandlungen zur Gestalttheorie.* Erlangen: Verlag d. Philos. Akad., 1925. Original publication: 1920 (cf. above). Reprinted by permission of The Humanities Press.

[1] All men are mortal   M—P (Major premise)
Socrates is a man   S—M (Minor premise)

Socrates is mortal   S—P (Conclusion)

[2] Some logicians—notably John Stuart Mill—have maintained that the major premise is really an induction in disguise.

as they occur in actual affairs (not, as is customary, with regard merely to logical validity).

I

The syllogism should—on this everyone is agreed—lead in its conclusion to a "new" proposition. The extreme case of this requirement is expressed in the rule that the conclusion must not appear as a premise. This requirement is obviously justified, for if the conclusion merely repeats in a new way (i.e., as a kind of recapitulation) what was already known in the premises, the result is "meaningless." But what are the conditions imposed by the requirement?

In its essentials the situation before the process is this: I possess, somewhere in my knowledge, the judgments that are to be used as premises; I do not yet possess the judgment which will appear as conclusion. Later I do possess this.

Now how does this apply to Socrates? If the syllogism is to fulfil its essential conditions I must not know in advance whether Socrates is mortal or not. I write: S?P and then I proceed as follows. Somewhere in my knowledge I encounter the proposition that all men are mortal; elsewhere, that Socrates is a man. . . . Both of these *without* knowing whether or not Socrates is mortal. But is this possible? Are there really such cases?

The requirement of which we have been speaking sets forth that neither MP nor SM may, taken alone, provide any knowledge regarding SP. Neither may I know of Socrates that he is a man *because* he is mortal, nor that the mortality of "all" men would naturally include that of Socrates. The former condition is easily fulfilled. Of the latter, however, one is at once suspicious, for it is not true that I know about the mortality of *all* men; of many, yes, but not of all. Actually the major premise here is not universal but is an induction in disguise.

Now let us take an example which *does* satisfy both requirements. Socrates goes to pay his taxes. He inquires at the central office which sub-office he should visit. The attendant asks to which Tax Zone Socrates belongs. Socrates does not know; how should he? "Well," answers the other, "you must know the street where you live! . . . Good, you live in X Street (SM); and X Street is in Zone 426 (MP)—therefore . . . ."

The fact that Socrates lives in X Street does not trespass upon the fact of this street being in Zone 426, and hence the conclusion regarding Socrates is not gratuitous. The major premise asserts a civil regulation, not a piece of "knowledge"; it is an ordinance of the city government that for all cases having the property a, the property b *must* follow. Nothing is said about Socrates himself one way or the other; for purposes of the *ordinance* nothing need be known regarding any properties peculiar to Socrates. Indeed this is universally true and therefore holds also in cases where the major premise is a verbal definition or where it states something at least temporarily conceived of as subject only to human specification—e.g., an hypothesis tentatively set forth as presumably a law of nature. This was also accepted by Mill.

Everything seems to depend upon having the major premise universal without thereby presupposing any knowledge of SP. This brings up the ancient question of how knowledge can be universal without a prior determination of all particulars. Although this question is undoubtedly very important it may nevertheless be left outside our present considerations. I specify: P *is* known in all its particulars; the major premise *is* universal. Does it follow then that every syllogism is a *petitio*, a mere recapitulation of things already known? Are the foregoing requirements then impossible of satisfaction?

Let us consider how the requirement applies to the minor premise. Before the syllogism comes into being I must already possess SM but *not* SP. So far as SM is concerned the properties contained in P must be irrelevant. Thus neither S nor M in my minor premise may contain the property P. I can know a thousand things about Socrates, but I must not know that he belongs in Tax Zone 426. The formula, then, is that although any number of *other* characteristics may be contained in S, those appearing in the major premise must not appear in S.

It is a genuine question to ask: *How* does Socrates enter the syllogism? Do I mean here the Socrates who possesses *all* the possibly true characteristics (known and unknown) of the "object" designated by that name; *or* do I mean the Socrates whose *known and directly determinable characteristics* are actually given?

The Syllogism and Productive Thinking 253

The same holds for M. In the most simple case S is introduced as involving but one certain characteristic; S is defined, then, through *characteristic*[3] 1. Then to Sc1 there is added c2 [i.e., M], and this is the significance of the minor premise. Neither c1 nor c2 may contain anything of c3 [i.e., P] which appears as predicate of the major premise.

The major premise asserts (according to our formulation of its role, p. 252) that *all* instances of c2 are instances of c3 [i.e., all M is P]. But to assert anything of *all* c2's naturally involves asserting this of S [since all S is M]. Does this lead to a *petitio*? Not necessarily. Let us not overlook what has just been said regarding Sc1 and regarding the difference between the properties of S before and after the process carried out by the syllogism itself.

That there is such a difference seems obvious, and yet it is upon this basis that the charge of *petitio* is founded. This is particularly true in cases where S is defined by denotation, for then S is placed within a class in such a way that the *entire* S with all its characteristics, known and unknown, is thereby assigned its logical (denotative) locus. But if S already "contains" everything that could possibly pertain to it, then no "new" knowledge about it is possible. It is into this *impasse* that the traditional logic is predestined to fall. Such a logic is suitable only for one who already knows everything and needs only a system of classification; for a genuine advance in knowledge it is useless.

When, however, the foregoing is taken into consideration, an advance in knowledge *is* possible. What does it mean to say that S has already been examined with regard to P? The object S, yes, but is this already Sc1? Must I already know, must it be already stipulated that the given object (it is, namely, one of those containing c2) contains c1? Is it identical with the S which contains c1? As an object containing c2, S has necessarily already been examined. There is, however, *no* necessity that in this examination I should have established or known S *as* Sc1.

Here is the occasion upon which a genuine (and sometimes

---

[3] [Hereafter the word "characteristic" as used in this connection will be designated by the letter c.]

astonishing) advance in knowledge is possible—viz. when Sc1 reveals itself *as* a member of the group c3, which is already thoroughly known.

Two determinations are involved: I, that all cases having the property of c2 also have the property c3; II, that Sc1 is a member of the group characterized by c2. If I specify that determination I takes place in such a way that no recourse is made or can be made to c1; and, likewise, that in determination II there shall be no reference to c3, then I have a pure case in the desired sense.

Changing our example of the tax payment slightly we may illustrate this situation as follows. Suppose that each taxpayer is given a number and that all numbers between 1–1,000 have been entered in the ledger as paid. That such entries have been made has nothing to do with the fact that Socrates, who happens to be No. 43, is thereby involved. Conversely, the fact of *Socrates's* being No. 43, is not involved in the entry procedure.

In science, too, this form of procedure plays its role. Completely pure cases are not easy to find, however, since pure determinations are seldom available. An example, however, may be suggested. I investigate a liquid of unknown composition. I am interested in the relation between low specific gravity and low boiling point. I heat the liquid and note which gases are discharged. The first is yellowish, the second bluish, the third greyish. I observe that in the end the yellow gas floats on top.

> The first gas to be discharged is yellowish
> The yellowish gas comes to the top
> ———————————————————
> The first gas to be discharged comes to the top.

(I.e., the material of relatively lowest boiling point is also relatively lowest in specific gravity.)

II

But we must consider examples of a different sort if the significant aspects of our problem are to be discovered. A busy lawyer is in the habit of destroying the papers of cases so-and-so many years past. Consequently the records of Case A were recently burned. One day he is looking for a certain receipt connected with a current Case B. He looks in vain. He stops to think: what *was* it the receipt referred to? Suddenly he recalls that the *contents* of the receipt had to do with Case A—and the A papers have been destroyed! Now, expressed as above, we find: in the determination of the major premise the papers referred solely to Case A; not S and not Sc1, but Sc2. But Sc1 is a receipt referring to Case B. Their simultaneity does not of itself give rise to the conclusions, for in addition there must be a "click," so to speak, which snaps them together into the kind of inner relationship which *is* the conclusion.

Or to take another example. Peter and Paul have for a long time been members of the executive committee of their club. The committee meetings are dull and uninteresting and they have given up attending—except for the principal meeting once a year, when the annual Statement of Accounts is presented. One day Peter returns from a journey and finds a letter telling him of a decision unanimously reached in a recent committee meeting. He is incensed and starts to phone Paul when he reads further and finds: "The decision was reached at the annual Accounts meeting which was held earlier than usual this year. The Statement of Accounts was accepted on motion of Mr. Paul Brown."

It is from examples of this sort that one sees how S can suffer a radical upset. For a moment the premises are side by side, then suddenly there is a "click." A decision distasteful to Peter was reached; an Accounts meeting has been held. Suddenly they snap together. (What! Paul was there!—Paul too—is that *possible!* ——aha—ha—*so*—.) The whole concept S (Paul) suddenly undergoes a complete reorganization.

Such processes frequently occur in a study of history. Fundamental changes in one's judgment of an historical figure are often due to the discovery of some new facts about that person. The whole character is suddenly re-centred.

The objection might be raised that our examples of Socrates and his taxes or of Peter and his club raise only nominalistic issues, i.e., that the same object merely appears twice under different names. While not false, this objection is actually quite unimportant. One need merely consider the example of the lawyer in order to appreciate this fact. Here it is not true that the same object appears under two names; instead they are *logically different objects:* a memorandum among the papers of Case A is logically quite different from a receipt used in Case B. And viewing the matter in this light we see that the same applies to Peter and Paul. An abyss sunders the Paul of before and after the syllogistic process. The concept I have of a thing is frequently not only enriched but changed, improved, altered, deepened by the process itself.

Let us consider some further examples. We shall choose more modest illustrations whose determinations do not require so strenuous a purification in order to render clear the thought process involved.

In this square with a parallelogram strip across it (Figure 1) the lines a and b are given. Find the sum of the contents of the two areas. One can proceed thus: The area of the square is a^2, in addition that of the strip is . . . ? But suppose instead that one hits upon the idea:

[Sc1=] (square + strip) = (2 triangles, base a, altitude b) [=Sc2]

[Sc2=] $\cdots\cdots\cdots\cdots = \left(2\,\dfrac{ab}{2}\right) = ab\;[=P]$.

The solution has thus been attained, so to speak, at a single stroke.

Or, to take another example. Suppose, in the isosceles triangle of Figure 2 the equal sides are given and the angle between them is 90°. Find the area. One could work out from this what a and b are, divide them by 2 and solve the problem. On the other hand,

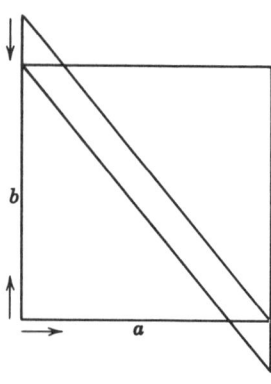 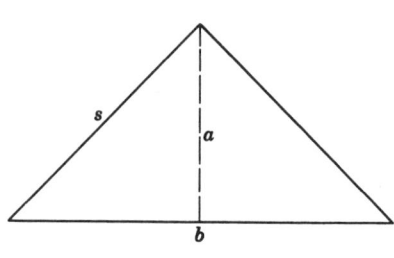

Figure 1   Figure 2

however, one might *see* that this isosceles triangle is tipped over—its base is really s; its altitude is also s. It is therefore nothing but half a square. Area $= \dfrac{s^2}{2}$.

Or again: Is 1,000,000,000,000,000,000,008 divisible by nine? The answer:—

$$(1{,}000{,}000 \cdots + 8) = (1{,}000{,}000 \cdots - 1) + (8 + 1)$$
$$\cdots\cdots = 999{,}999 \cdots\cdots\cdots + 9.$$

Similarly: Is $a^2 + ac + ba + bc$ divisible by $(a + b)$? The answer: $a^2 + ac + ba + bc = \overline{a\cdot a + a\cdot b} + \overline{a\cdot c + b\cdot c}$
$$= a(a + b) + c(a + b)$$

Another example: What is $\sqrt{a^2 + \dfrac{b^2}{4} + ab}$?

The answer: $\sqrt{a^2 + \dfrac{b^2}{4} + ab} = \sqrt{a^2 + \left(\dfrac{b}{2}\right)^2 + 2\cdot a\cdot \dfrac{b}{2}}$
$$= \pm\left(a + \dfrac{b}{2}\right).$$

A final example. It is reported of Karl Gauss that one day the teacher asked his class who could first give the total of $1 + 2 + 3 + 4 + 5 + 6 + 7 + 8$. Almost at once Karl's hand was raised. When the teacher asked how he had done it, Karl answered, "If I had had to add 1 and 2 and 3, it would have taken a long time; but 1 and 8 are 9, 2 and 7 are 9, 3 and 6 are 9, 4 and 5 are 9—four 9's, the answer is 36."

In general we see that in S?P the object (S), whatever it be, is given *as* Sc1—but there is no direct route from Sc1 to P. Upon further inspection, however, S proves amenable to a "recentring" away from c1—and in Sc2 I find the route to P opened. Now this procedure is enormously important in science, particularly in mathematics. It frequently occurs that the needed c3, exhibiting the required relationship to P, is only *possible* when Sc1 has been *re*-formed, *re*-grasped, *re*-centred in a specific way. And it is not less frequently the case that to effect this process *a deeper penetration into the nature and structure of S is required.*

Although illustrations of the steps which thinking involves are particularly obvious in geometry, we are dealing here with phenomena of a more general character. The hierarchy of properties in a concept may be subjected to the same treatment as has been suggested in the foregoing examples, for here too are involved certain structures and structural principles. And the same holds also for combinations of concepts. We are dealing no less in these cases than formerly with re-centring and the other operations already mentioned.

The history of science has provided many examples: comprehension of the nature of stellar movements ("falling" toward one another); the theory of the screw (i.e., seeing the screw as a wedge); the history of the conception of inertia. Until recently such accomplishments were thought of as essentially the results of "imagination," or "chance," or "the intuition of genius." But it is not these alone. *Formal* determinations, expressible in definite laws, are also involved. Crucial to many such cases is the fact that *certain* moments or characteristics of S are emphasized and brought into the foreground. In other cases the crucial step consists in a certain combination of factors.[4] In still other cases the essential process may be one of *centring*, where the important point is: *from the point of view of which part shall the remaining parts be seen?* Thus centring leads to a penetration into the essential content and hence to an apprehension of the concrete inner structure and inner necessity of the whole with which one is dealing. Manifestly there are other cognitive operations besides subtraction, abstraction, and classification.

In this connection it can be seen that neither the determination Sc2, nor the step Sc1:Sc2 is *arbitrary*. It is formally not a matter of indifference which of several possible reorganizations shall be employed, for the determination is carried out relative to the question "?P." We are dealing with S and P not as disparate juxtapositions; instead, they enter the operation as parts integrated according to definite formal determinations. Given S?P and no direct route leading to P, then the question arises: What is there in Sc1 (or, better, in the general range of things known about S) which is related to ?P ? On *what* aspects of S must I concentrate?

---

[4] Example: $a + b + c + d \ldots$ may also be seen as $[a + b] + [c + d] \ldots$ or, again, as $a + [b + c] + d \ldots$.

Or: *How must I apprehend S sub specie the task here before me?* How must I alter my former concept of S if I would see it in terms of ?P ? Expressed more formally: not everything in S, not every view nor every reorganization of S is equal with regard to ?P. There are, in other words, determinations of S which *themselves* point to the required solution.

The question of how Socrates combed his hair would be *meaningless* when we are interested in his mortality. Socrates too must be considered *sub specie* the question (of mortality) raised by P. And thus we come to the most important question of our entire study: When is the process meaningful, when meaningless? For the *modus barbara* we may say that over against S?P we have S⟶M⟶P in which M serves as a bridge. There are two extreme forms:

In the *first*, M has no other formal relationship than that of its *bare co-existence,* on the one side with S, and on the other with P. These are two relationships which merely involve general validity of the formal syllogistic procedure.

In the *second*, M is a bridge in the sense that its bridge-character is *meaningful demanded* by the question S?P itself. Here M (i.e., Sc2) stands *sub specie* S?P and it possesses certain formal relations within the whole process or situation.

In the first extreme form M is on principle *arbitrary*, and the most meaningless examples of M are (formally) as good as any other: All persons whose names end in *tes* are mortal, Socrates's name ends in *tes* . . . and so on. In the second form M is much more than a mere indicator of co-existence, and whereas the first form, asserting an empty fact of co-existence, leads to mere classification, the second accomplishes a genuine advance in knowledge.

* * *

Wertheimer's interest in "thought processes in actual affairs," just as Köhler's previous emphasis on insight, illustrates one of the distinguishing characteristics of the Gestalt school: a concern with the determinants and functions of intelligent behavior. Only recently has there been a revival of general interest in the mental processes involved in intelligent behavior, a field kept fitfully alive after the promising beginning made by such men as Binet and Claparède in the first part of the century. Piaget has probably been the most insistent among contemporary figures in promoting this view of intelligence. Ironically, Binet's very success with his intelligence test tended to obscure for many years his more fundamental concern with the problem of intelligence.

The most detailed and thoroughgoing attempts to extend Gestalt theory to the field of thinking were published by Karl Duncker in 1926* and 1935.†

Duncker started his analysis of productive thought processes within a framework very similar to Selz's. The latter had recognized the difficulties association theory faced in dealing with relations such as "part of," "cause of," and "equal to," and he had included these relations among the experimental structures to be learned, to be incorporated into larger complexes, and to be applied to new problems. Duncker used the basic units of Gestalt theory to handle these relations. He did not consider them as learned, but rather, for the most part, as dynamically and perceptually given by the nature of the problem and the structure of the mind. Although he granted that types or classes of solutions can be acquired and then applied by "resonance"—a term taken from Claparède and denoting association by similarity—to new situations, he thought that this approach left certain basic questions unanswered. If the solution is correct, how is it achieved, why is a particular schema brought to bear on the problem; and if incorrect, why has that particular mistake been made? Mistakes or successes *may* be traced to the blind applications of previously learned principles, but if we are to understand how, aside from chance, correct solutions are reached, we must discover what is demanded by the situation as given. In short, we must examine

---

* K. Duncker, A qualitative study of productive thinking. *Ped. Sem.*, 1926, **33**, 642–708.

† K. Duncker, *Zur Psychologie des produktiven Denkens*. Berlin: Springer, 1935.

the structural requirements of the problem if we are to understand the subject's behavior within that situation. Thus, Duncker's entire work becomes an explication of "insight," although he places no particular emphasis on that term.

Duncker applies the organization and dynamics of structures to problems of thought, but he is equally interested in the problem of the logical relation of a problem to its solution. He asks how human thought can obtain information about the nature of a conclusion from the nature of the premises. This is a very different question from that asked, for example, by Hume. Duncker's question is not an epistomological but primarily a psychological one.

We have touched only briefly in these pages on the relation of logic to thought, in part because it represents a different tradition from the one we are following, but also because until theories of thinking began to approach the sophistication of theories of logic there was little hope of disentangling the two. Interestingly enough, it was only when logic, thought, and logical thought were clearly demarcated in modern times that the real argument over the relationship of each to the other began. Only after the rift had become a chasm did it seem requisite to begin fitting them together again; this time, however, it was the psychologist who explored the nature of logical relations as they influence thought, not the philosopher using the psychology of thought (such as it was) to construct his logic. These problems have stayed with us until the present, influencing points of view ranging from Piaget's to those of psychologists interested in computer simulation.

In this sense, Duncker, as well as Wertheimer, was influenced more by Kant than by Hume. There is the implied assumption that the mind is constructed in such a way that certain logical relations are imposed upon the world, rather than being built up out of our experience of the world. While Duncker himself expresses the opinion that he differs from Kant on this point, the influences can be clearly seen in the following selection.

Karl Duncker

The Solution of Practical Problems

[NOTE: In this selection the author frequently refers to two experimental problems, the radiation problem and the pendulum problem. They are described in the introductory pages as follows:
Radiation problem: "Given a human being with an inoperable stomach tumor, and rays which destroy organic tissue at sufficient intensity, by what procedure can one free him of the tumor by these rays and at the same time avoid destroying the healthy tissue which surrounds it?"
Pendulum problem: "You know what a pendulum is, and that a pendulum plays an important role in a clock. Now, in order for a clock to go accurately, the swings of the pendulum must be strictly regular. The duration of a pendulum's swing depends, among other things, on its length, and this of course in turn on the temperature. Warming produces expansion and cooling produces contraction, although to a different degree in different materials. Thus every temperature change would change the length of the pendulum. But the clock should go with absolute regularity. How can this be brought about?—By the way, the length of the pendulum is defined solely by the shortest distance between the point of suspension and the center of gravity. We are concerned only with this length; for the rest, the pendulum may have any appearance at all."]

THE ASSOCIATION THEORY OF PROBLEM-SOLVING. The main contribution of the preceding discussion was this: the solution of a new problem typically takes place in successive phases which (with the exception of the first phase) have, in retrospect, the character of a solution and (with the exception of the last phase), in prospect, that of a problem. The problem we are considering takes therefore the following form: *How does a solution-phase*

K. Duncker, On problem solving, transl. by L. S. Lees. *Psychol. Monogr.*, 1945, **58**, No. 5, Whole No. 270. Originally published as *Zur Psychologie des produktiven Denkens*. Berlin: Springer, 1935. Selections reprinted by permission of the American Psychological Association.

The Solution of Practical Problems 263

arise out of the immediately preceding problem-phase? It is probably clear that the solution cannot take place reproductively by virtue of mere *"associations"* among the contents of the various phases. The explanation by association, moreover, becomes no more plausible if one adds the thesis that not these identical contents, but only similar ones, have been previously associated, and that this suffices. Let it be kept in mind that the classical concept of association has no reference to any such "material" relations[1] between associated contents as "cause of . . . ," or "solution of . . . ," but solely to temporal and spatial contiguity or similarity. But between a problem or its several parts and a solution there is no more spatial and temporal contiguity and no more similarity than between that problem and innumerable other contents, for instance, similar problems, or any circumstances accompanying earlier solution-processes, and so on. It follows that, according to the association theory, completely nonsensical errors should frequently occur in the solution of thinking problems. For example, the S should, in good faith, actually name as a solution some event which happened to take place on the occasion of an earlier solution, or he should mention a similar problem, *as though it were a solution.* From the fact that such errors do not occur, O. Selz has already drawn the necessary conclusions against the classical association theory of thinking, against the theory of "diffuse" association and reproduction.

FINDING A SOLUTION THROUGH "RESONANCE-EFFECT." A reproduction theory of the type of Selz's, in which room is expressly left for such relations as, e.g., "part of . . . ," "next to . . . ," "origin of . . . ," "solution of . . . ," deserves much more serious consideration. Without doubt, through experience, events can acquire the attribute, "solution of problem A," or at least, "leading to effect *a.*" Now if at some time something with the attribute, "solution of problem A" or "leading to effect *a*" is sought, the solution can be found *by virtue of the correspondence between the attribute desired and that which inheres in what is sought.* (Compare Selz's concept of "determined means-abstraction.") In contradiction to

---

[1] ["*Sachbeziehungen.*"]

the classical reproduction theory, the solution is here found by the "anticipation"[2] or the "signalling" of its specific solution- or means-properties in each case. (It need not even have occurred—or have become familiar—as a solution. It must merely have been experienced as "*leading to*" an effect similar to that which is now, for the first time, the goal. An example: For certain experiments in the psychology of perception, someone needs yellow illumination. There is no color-filter available. What to do? It occurs to him how, the other day, a blue folder reflected the light of a lamp as blue-tinted, "led to" a coloring. Aha! The reflection from yellow paper. . .)[3]

In agreement with Selz's theory of "schematic anticipation," we can write the general formula of such problem-solving as follows: The problem is: $?Rb$[4]; aRb exists in the thinker's experience; by reason of the partial correspondence with $?Rb$, aRb and therefore a are aroused. Thus this finding of the solution takes place ultimately through a kind of "excitation by equality" (Selz) or, better, of *resonance*.

Let us now ask ourselves whether the genesis of the solution of a new problem can be quite generally explained by the resonance-effect of an appropriate signal. That the problem and the solution are new, would be no argument against this. We have already seen that the solution need not have occurred before as "solution." Moreover, the several solution-phases might always represent familiar solutions, while their *combination* would be new. In our examples, the radiation problem and its solution are new, but the first solution-phase: "intensity small on the way, great in the tumor," represents perhaps, in its formal characteristics, a familiar solution of the more general problem: "Find a means to achieve at a certain place an effect which is to be avoided on the way." Do we not often decrease the intensity of some agent, when a diminution of the effect concerned is desired? And the "diffusion of the agent on the way," in its turn, would again be a

---

[2] In seeking, certain attributes of what is sought are "anticipated" or, as we should prefer to say instead, "demanded," "signalled."
[3] This "leading to . . ." is very often given as immediate perceptual experience.
[4] R signifies some relation, e.g., that of "leading to . . ."; therefore aRb signifies a in the relation R to b.

The Solution of Practical Problems 265

familiar solution of the problem: "a means to achieve less intensity."

Obviously, the theory of the "solutions by the resonance-effect of signals" deserves detailed examination. In point of fact, there are solution-phases everywhere which come about in such a way. At the end of a solution-process, for example, some appropriate object is often still to be found whose introduction into an already discovered procedure completes the solution. Thus in the radiation problem, one may be after a "free path to the stomach," and find the esophagus. Or a chimpanzee may look for something "long and movable" (with which to fish for the banana) and find a branch or a piece of wire or the like. Such parts of the solutions, no matter whether they are found in the perceptual field (as in the last example) or in memory (the field of traces), really originate by reason of the correspondence between the attribute desired and that inherent in the object. (?Rb would here mean that a thing is sought which has the attribute b. R would therefore symbolize the relation of an object to one of its attributes.) ...

At present we are interested only in this: Can the origin of even the earlier solution-phases, in which no definite real object but only the "procedure" is yet to be found, also and always be interpreted after the same pattern? It seems advisable to phrase the question thus: *Must* the origin of *all* phases be thus interpreted?

Of what aspects of a solution, then, does the theory just described really make use? If the solution meant nothing but "something which leads to the goal"—so that merely "if S, then G, and if not S, then also not G"—then such a theory of problem-solving would still be applicable. For this is all the theory requires. *Aside from this, under this theory, the contents of solution and of goal could be in any relation whatsoever.*

Suppose that we could interchange the solutions of two different problems (e.g., that of the radiation problem and that of the pendulum problem), in such a way that S_1 henceforth leads to G_2, and S_2 to G_1. A living creature who had never had experiences to the contrary would learn this; that is to say, for this creature, S_1 would acquire the attribute of being *a way to G_2*, and so on.

Suppose now that the finding of a solution required nothing but an anticipation of this leading-to character in question. When one day the problem arose to find a way to G_2, this creature would be able to find S_1 just as readily and in the same way as another creature with normal past experience would find S_2.

In other words, a theory according to which a solution is found by reason of the resonance-effect of a suitable signal would be equally applicable to any conceivable number of combinations of problems with solutions. The question arises: does the *actual* relation of a solution to its problem offer no other heuristic possibilities?

HEURISTIC METHODS OF THINKING: ANALYSIS OF THE SITUATION AS ANALYSIS OF CONFLICT. Let us investigate how a solution is actually related to its problem. We find that a *solution always consists in a variation of some crucial element of the situation.* Thus, in the solutions of the radiation problem, we find changed: either the spatial relations of rays, tumor and healthy tissue; or the intensity or the density of the rays; or the sensitivity of the tissue. And in the first case, the position either of the rays, or of the healthy tissue, or of the tumor can be varied. With this, the primary *conflict-elements* of the radiation problem are probably exhausted.

Thus every solution takes place, so to speak, on the concrete, specific substratum of its problem situation. For this obvious reason, quite apart from other factors, every solution of the radiation problem, *qua* solution of precisely this problem, is differentiated from every solution of, say, the pendulum problem. Solutions of the latter problem have to do with temperature and with the structure of the pendulum, not with tissues, rays, and the like. This is as important as it seems to be banal. For it follows from this that, in seeking a solution, one must bring the given problem-situation as clearly as possible into focus. He who merely searches his memory for a "solution of that such-and-such problem" may remain just as blind to the inner nature of the problem-situation before him as a person who, instead of thinking himself, refers the problem to an intelligent acquaintance or to an encyclopedia. Truly, these methods are not to be despised; for they have a certain heuristic value, and one can arrive at solutions in that fashion. But such problem-solving has little to do with thinking.

With the radiation problem as well as with the pendulum problem, it happened that Ss who were already dimly familiar with the solution asked themselves, "I must have heard of this before—now, how was it?" Every reader will already have experienced that such seeking-to-remember will often (say, in mathematical problems) disturb new thinking.

We can therefore say that *"insistent" analyses of the situation, especially the endeavor to vary appropriate elements meaningfully sub specie of the goal, must belong to the essential nature of a solution through thinking.* We may call such relatively general procedures, *"heuristic methods of thinking."*

The inquiry after elements which should be varied in a suitable fashion is identical with the question, *"Just why doesn't it work?"* or, *"What is the ground of the trouble (the conflict)?"* For, each component of the situation whose variation means a solution is in its original form a "ground of conflict" (e.g., the great intensity of radiation en route, or the spatial coincidence of rays and healthy tissue). To each solution corresponds a ground of conflict present in the situation. Analysis of the situation is therefore primarily *analysis of conflict.* In connection with the radiation problem, the S will ask himself, "Just why are healthy tissues destroyed as well? What elements of the situation are responsible for it?" In other words, he does not merely inquire after a way to avoid the accompanying destruction of healthy tissue, but *seeks to penetrate more deeply into the nature, into the grounds of the conflict....*

RESTRUCTURING OF THOUGHT-MATERIAL. Every solution consists in some alteration of the given situation. But not only this or that in the situation is changed, i.e., not only such alterations take place as one would have to mention in a simple commonsense description; over and beyond this the *psychological structure* of the situation as a *whole* or of certain significant parts is changed. Such alterations are called *restructurations.*

In the course of a solution-process, the "emphasis-relief" of the situation, its "figure-ground" relief, for example, is restructured in this way. Parts and elements of the situation which, psychologically speaking, were either hardly in existence or remained in the background—unthematic—suddenly emerge, become the main point, the theme, the "figure." . . .

Aside from the emphasis, the material properties or "functions" of parts are changed as well. The newly emerging parts of the situation owe their prominence to certain relatively general functions: this one becomes an "obstacle," a "point of attack" (conflict element), that other a "tool," etc. At the same time, the more specific functions also change. For example, the esophagus becomes a "passage for rays" or a triangle of matches becomes the "base of a tetrahedron."

Especially radical restructurations tend to take place in the *nexus or context of the whole*. Parts of the situation which were formerly separated as parts of different wholes, or had no specific relation although parts of the same whole, may be united in *one* new whole. For example, in certain solutions of the pendulum problem, the place of suspension may thus enter into some relation with the pendulum's length, while previously no psychological connection existed between these two parts. . . .

It has often been pointed out that such restructurations play an important role in thinking, in problem-solving. The decisive points in thought-processes, the moments of sudden comprehension, of the "Aha!," of the new, are always at the same time moments in which such a sudden restructuring of the thought-material takes place, in which something "tips over." . . .

But while, with undoubted justification, great stress was laid on the significance of restructuration or reorganization in thinking, another side of the problem was almost completely lost from view. *In what way* do these restructurations, and with them the solution, arise? *That* they take place, and that they happen more easily with one person, less easily with another, still in no way discloses *why* they take place, i.e., whence the directive "forces" derive which lead a thought-material from the old over into the new, adequate structuration.

The Solution of Practical Problems 269

In themselves, restructurations of a field can have the most varied origins. The psychology of perception is acquainted with a great number of reversible figures, which, simply through the fact that one lets them persist long enough in one of the possible structurings, tend of their own accord to "tip over" into the other, opposed structuration. Cf. the spontaneous interchange between front and rear in the perspective drawing of a cube, or a flight of stairs, etc. Here "satiation" is probably the origin of the restructuration.—Or, if one experiences in succession, or side by side, a series of partially identical complexes—whose objectively common component has not been made unrecognizable by camouflage—it happens under suitable conditions that the common part, the common aspect, becomes predominant, while in each individual case, taken alone, quite different aspects stand out phenomenally. Thus the restructuration here occurs through a sort of "precipitation of common elements" (Wm. James' "abstraction by varying concomitants"). —Or, one searches for something with definite properties, e.g., something long and solid, and now everything which objectively possesses such properties is "centered" accordingly. Here the restructuration takes place through the resonance-effect of an appropriate signal.—Furthermore, a restructuration may be caused by intentional alteration of given perceptual structures.

In its first two parts, the present investigation has the task of revealing the *causal (directive)* factors in the genesis of a solution. An exhaustive description of all occurring restructurations was not intended, the less since in this respect essential work had already been accomplished. On the other hand, the gestalt theory of thinking had not yet approached the causal problems involved. The theory of "closure" or *"prägnanz"* is much too general to be of any great use here. Of course, the solution-process continues until "the gap is closed," "the organization is complete," "the disturbance is removed," "equilibrium or release of tension is attained." And this is undoubtedly relevant from the dynamical or, more correctly, the energy point of view. But of what kinds of events this "tendency toward equilibrium" or toward *"prägnanz"* can make use, this is the problem which must now be investigated in the light of gestalt psychology. . . .

On Total Insight or Evidence

THE GRASPING OF GROUND-CONSEQUENCE RELATIONS AS NECESSARY TO PROBLEM-SOLVING. The past three chapters have already made sundry contributions towards answering the main question we are investigating: How does the solution arise out of a *Problemstellung?* We found, firstly, that the final solution is mediated by successive reformulations of the problem, and secondly, that these reformulations or solution-phases are in their turn mediated by general heuristic methods.

But this is still not a complete answer. As happens particularly with mathematical problems, the method of solution may consist, for example, in making appropriate deductions from the proposition or from the premises. But then the psychologist must still discover the psychological meaning of "making deductions from," must discover how, from one fact, thinking actually brings about the intelligent transition to another, new fact. Or the method of solution may consist in examining the situation for flexible conflict-elements—as happens especially with practical problems. Yet this observation in no way reveals how such a conflict-element makes itself known to thinking *as ground or cause*. To be a conflict-element means of course to be ground or cause of the conflict. And analogously, to be a solution means to be ground or cause of the realized goal. To understand a solution as solution accordingly means to understand the solution as ground of the goal.—But with this, analysis of conflict and grasping of the solution are involved in the whole set of problems concerned with the apprehension of causation. How does thinking succeed in reading off the cause from an effect, or the effect from a cause?

These two questions, namely, how thinking is able from the logical ground to apprehend the logical consequence and from the cause to apprehend the effect, we shall combine in one question and give the following generalized formulation: *Of what nature are the ground-consequence relations which are important for thinking in problem-solving?* Or, otherwise expressed: What possibilities has thinking of obtaining, from the nature of a ground, information on the nature of the consequence? The next two chapters will be dedicated to this investigation, which is fundamental no less to the psychology of thinking than to philosophy. (In this connection, something will also have to be said on the rational nature and the genesis of "heuristic methods.")

DEFINITIONS. *A connection of two data* a *and* b *may be called "totally intelligible," if it can be directly understood from* a *that, if* a *is valid, then* b *and precisely* b *is valid. (A connection is therefore "unintelligible" to the extent to which it is to be "accepted as mere fact.") A connection may be called "partially intelligible" if at least certain features of* b *can be understood from* a—*or are at least singled out by* a *in contradistinction to other possibilities.* In other words, a b may be called intelligible in respect to an a, if and in the degree to which b's real phenomenal characteristics, in contrast to other possible characteristics, appear *directly favored* by the phenomenal nature of a. By "directly" I mean: without intervention of further factors.—In the present chapter, only *total* intelligibility is to be dealt with.

The definition given above of intelligibility has reference to a fundamental statement from Hume's "Inquiry Concerning Human Understanding" (Sec. 7, Part 2): "When any natural object or event is presented, it is impossible for us, by any sagacity or penetration, to discover, or even to conjecture, without experience, what event will result from it . . . "—But suppose that, in regard to its characteristics, b is singled out by a in contrast to other possibilities. To the degree to which this occurs, one must also be able "to discover or even to conjecture" the b directly from the a, be it wholly or in part.

As prototype of entirely unintelligible connections we may cite one of those if-then relations which Thorndike imposed on his cats. If the cat licks itself, then the cage door opens, or if it presses on a certain knob, then the same happens. From the circumstance —to be understood quite literally—that a cat licks itself or presses on a certain knob, it appears in no way intelligible that the cage door should open.—Just as in the field of causation, we can find any number of cases of such unintelligibility in the province of coexistence. From the fact that a house belongs to a Mr. N, or that it has so and so many windows, it is in no way evident that it has a gray roof. (Be it noted that, in both examples, the premises should mean only what is expressly stated in them. Thus, for example, "Mr. N" is not an abbreviation for a definite concrete man with such and such characteristics, but means only: some man, purely and simply.)

In contrast to this it undoubtedly does happen that b *"follows"* from a, i.e., that b is completely intelligible from the content of a. For example, it follows from the circumstance: "the house is higher than the tree and the tree higher than the bush," that "the house is higher than the bush."—How is such intelligible connection of ground and consequence, such evidence, possible?

ON ANALYTIC AND SYNTHETIC EXPLICABILITY.[1] Two classic answers to this question are: Either b is already co-contained in a and may therefore be "analytically" explicated from a, or the faculty of reasoning is so constituted that it must always and everywhere connect a with b. The second formula, with which Kant believed he must and could insure the possibility of empirical knowledge, need not occupy us further here. It does not fully correspond to our definition of the intelligible, which required that it should be evident from a that, if a, then b. Simple necessity or generality of the connection is not sufficient; b must be evident "from the essence of a"—as Husserl would have put it.

The first answer, on the other hand, is to be inspected more closely. What does it mean to be "co-contained?" Something can be co-contained: 1) *as a constituent of the whole,* i.e., *so that it follows from the whole, but not from the other parts alone (constitutive co-containedness).*[2] Examples for this would be: a) (constitutive co-implication)[3] "The roan is reddish," or, "A straight line is determined by two points" (this statement understood as axiomatic *definition* of the straight line). Here the predicate, the reddish coloration or the being determined by two points, is con-

---

[1] [*Ablesbarkeit.*]
[2] [*Konstitutives Mitenthaltensein.*]
[3] [*Konstitutive Mitgesetztheit.*]

stitutively co-contained in the subject-concept defined by the statement, and indeed "co-implied."—b) (Constitutive co-existence)[4] "That house yonder has a gray roof," or, "The knowledge of the purpose and of the means belongs to the essence of action." Here the predicate, the gray color of the roof or the knowledge of . . . , is constitutively co-contained, "co-existent" in the full concreteness of the given.[5] Upon the fact that the parts and elements are given as such parts within a concrete experienced whole depends the usual evidence of inspection,[6] the "explicability" of the parts from the completely given whole.

One sees that constitutive co-containedness undoubtedly makes possible an evident "following" of the parts from the whole, that without doubt the conclusion here arises wholly intelligibly from the premises. But if no other connection between ground and consequence were intelligible to thinking than this analysis on the basis of a *constitutive co-containedness,* such thinking would be of little use in the world. Our question: "How is intelligible connection of ground and consequence possible?" calls for another answer.

And in fact, something can be co-contained (if one still wishes so to call it): 2) *as a consequence of the other elements of the whole (non-constitutive co-containedness).*[7] How about the example: "From $a > b > c$ it follows that $a > c$?" I can demonstrate the meaning of "greater" on all kinds of pairs of objects. With the help of the concept so obtained, a clear "paradigmatic"[8] situation: "a greater than b and b greater than c," can be constructed. From the situation so constructed, the fact: "a greater than c" may now

---

[4] [*Konstitutive Mitgegebenheit.*]
[5] In the last example it appears as if the predicated element already followed from the other elements (namely of action). This apparent following from the other elements always exists if a structure, a "strong figure" (Köhler), is present, in which all elements influence each other mutually. It is clear that then every element "follows" from these its "imprints" in the other elements. Nevertheless, each element can be entirely constitutive or indispensable for the whole.
[6] [*Anschauung.*]
[7] [*Nicht-konstitutives Mitenthaltensein.*]
[8] We shall call a situation "paradigmatic" if it is constructed for the mind's eye by the exclusive use of the concepts expressly contained in the premises.

be *read off. Yet—and this is the important point—this fact was not needed in the construction of the situation, the "foundation" from which it is now being read off. Therefore, in this case the conclusion is not constitutively co-contained in the premises.* (On the other hand, it would be reading-off on the basis of a constitutive co-containedness if, for example, "$b > c$" were explicated from the statement: "$a > b$ and $b > c$," or if from the concept "greater than," already defined as transitive, the transitiveness were explicated.) The reading-off of a fact which is *non-constitutively* co-contained we shall call "*synthetic explication.*" In this, a new aspect is "affixed" to the situation constituted in the premises (compare Kant's expression, "synthetic judgment"). The "extraction" of a *constitutively* co-contained element, on the other hand, may be called "analytic." ...

[Another] example: I try to have two paradigmatic "straight lines" intersect twice. Then I see, I read off, that in this effort they have become bent under my hands; more precisely: the being bent proves to be a new aspect, i.e., not utilized for construction of the situation: two lines intersect twice. With this, in conjunction with the principle of contradiction, the axiom: "Two straight lines intersect no more than once" is indirectly made evident.[9]

From these few examples it is already clear that, according to their direct meaning, the concepts "analytic" and "synthetic" are not unconditionally opposite, but are two sides of a definite relation. For, even "synthetic" reading-off is based on a definite form of co-containedness, and is therefore—in the widest sense—"analysis." The term "analytic" has, however, a special affinity to constitutive co-containedness, and the term "synthetic" to non-constitutive co-containedness. ...

DISCUSSION OF MODERN POSTULATIONAL THEORY. A concise discussion of modern mathematics should not longer be postponed. What attitude do the proponents of modern postulational theory take to the question of insight or evidence? For the modern mathematician, the straight line is that entity—originally undefined—which

---

[9] Of course, this could also have been done in the form of a direct proof: from the construction of two straight lines which intersect once, it may be read off that they do not meet again.

receives definition from the axioms about it, nothing more. And the relation: "greater than" acquires its transitiveness in mathematics merely by logical deduction from certain postulates, from the axioms about the relations: "between" and "congruent." In other words, in modern mathematics, propositions—relations of the form: "if a, then b"—which are not logically deduced from others are postulates, conventions (Poincaré), implicit definitions (Schlick). The evidence of these axioms is thus, intentionally, reduced to the form of a constitutive co-containedness (more specifically, co-implication) of b in the defined a, in short, to "analytical" explicability (tautology). Metaphorically speaking, the mathematician prescribes their "evidence" to the mathematical objects, thus sacrificing synthetic evidence. (By the way, nowadays the *logical* axioms, the principles of deduction, are also preferably regarded as mere postulates.)

There is no objection to this procedure. The mathematician and logician may proceed thus. As a matter of fact, mathematics and logic would "function" even if all principles were nothing but postulates. In short, "postulation" and "evident following from" are equivalent in respect to their logical achievements.

However, even though certain if-then relations *may* be treated as mere postulates, they can also be seen in a different light. Perhaps this other conception is irrelevant to the *purely logical* structure of mathematics. It nevertheless corresponds to actual facts in thinking. For, this other aspect of such if-then relations consists in precisely that synthetic evidence which we tried to demonstrate above with a few examples. Wherever mere postulates rule today, older forms of mathematical procedure demanded that such evidence be given. The demand has been relinquished by modern mathematics. Thus real evidence has been banished from the province of "pure" mathematics. To be sure, meanwhile evidence has acquired great honor in philosophy as the principle of so-called phenomenological knowledge, and has in this role been sharply contrasted with all merely inductive certainty. But if with reference to such knowledge the phenomenologists like to use the expression *"im Wesen gründen,"* they only hide with this expression the following fundamental problem: how can evidence arise from mere inspection of a subject matter? . . .

If, as we saw, neither pure mathematics nor the investigation of reality relies upon synthetic evidence, one could ask why synthetic evidence is necessary at all. The answer is threefold: 1) Whether necessary or not, it exists. 2) Even a maximally "formalized" mathematics still contains certain basic intuitions which cannot be eliminated, e.g., the concepts "element," "relation," "following from," as well as the principles of deduction. Should not what is right in the case of *logical* inspection or evidence be just as right in the case of *spatial* inspection and evidence? Further, if one believes that spatial inspection is unable to assure itself once for all and *per evidentiam* of its correspondence with the axioms of Euclidean geometry, then "pure spatial inspection" would be placed in the same epistemological position as "empirical reality." This appears to me extraordinarily erroneous, despite Reichenbach's attempts to this end. 3) Most important: As we shall see, without synthetic insight and evidence, productive thinking is nowhere *psychologically possible,* either in mathematics and logic or in the investigation of reality. More generally formulated: *The kind of experience in which synthetic evidence occurs represents the psychological medium of all productive thinking, postulational thinking included.* It is with this relevance of evidence for actual thought that we are here concerned.

HOW IS SYNTHETIC EVIDENCE POSSIBLE? Yet before we approach the proof for this more general proposition, something still remains to be done. Our question: "How is synthetic evidence possible?" has not yet been fully answered. Now, obviously—if we compare the examples [given above]—*synthetic evidence is possible for this reason. As a rule a situation may be constructed, or defined, by means of fewer facts than can afterwards be read off from it if new points of view are applied.*[10] *Not all possible aspects of a thought-object are necessary to its construction, just as little as all possible aspects of a visual object are necessary to the unambiguous comprehension of its structure. One and the same situation,*

---

[10] The term "to read off" is meant to express that here a "seeing," a "gathering" of something from a thing is involved. Insight is in fact a seeing, a becoming evident of something. Evidence, then, is the objective aspect of what in a more subjective sense is called insight.

paradigmatically constructed for inspection, may be considered a) from new sides, b) in new directions, c) in new structurings, d) for the first time as a whole, etc. It is this "aspect structure" of the thought-objects which makes synthetic evidence possible.

Examples for

a. the necessary curving of two "straight lines" which intersect more than once,

b. from "a greater than b" follows "b less than a,"

c. the transitiveness of the relations "greater than" and "divisor of,"

d. if there are in a room a person A and a person B and a person C... then there are *three* persons in the room.

Such aspects as are in this way explicable from a situation constructed heterogeneously, i.e., by means of other aspects, are designated intelligible "consequences" of the aspects used in the construction of the "ground." It will be seen that the classical criterion: "With the given ground, the consequence cannot be other than it is," follows with necessity from our conception of the intelligible relation of ground and consequence. . . .

INTERPRETATION OF SYNTHETIC EVIDENCE FROM THE VIEWPOINT OF GESTALT THEORY. In a synthetic explication, a change of aspect occurs along with retention of—yes, of what, really? What is really to be understood by the "foundations" of an explication? In this connection, let us consider the case represented in Figure 1. We are given a square and at a certain distance from it a line L, which one can consider as produced by the displacement of one side of the square so that it remains parallel to its direction. Here it may be read off that, if a point placed this side of the line L has the perpendicular distance α from L, it lies outside the square; that if it has analogously the distance β, it lies on the side of the square; that finally, if it has the distance γ, it lies within the square. Within each of these three

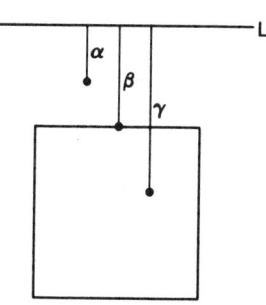

Figure 1

statements, a change of aspect of the point takes place. Each time, the point is first characterized only by a definite distance from the line L. Then, suddenly, it is characterized by its position in relation to the square. Therefore, by virtue of a new "point of view," it has now altered its aspect. In terms of Gestalt theory: *it has altered its concrete "function" by the fact that it has entered a new organization.*[11]

Now, one might be tempted to generalize from this and to say: Synthetic evidence obviously consists in the fact that the new characteristics resulting from a new structuring of given elements are read off from these elements. But with this one would at once have lost again the specific meaning of evidence and of "insight." For if one properly combines pure hydrogen and pure oxygen (thus bringing them into a proper Gestalt-nexus), and if one reads off the result: the explosion and the formation of water, then to be sure, something very important is read off, but certainly no synthetic evidence. Or suppose that, in an experiment on perception, the brightness b appears equal to a second brightness $b + s$, and this again to a third brightness $b + 2s$. If now in the comparison of b and $b + 2s$ inequality becomes apparent, something important is once more read off, but it contains no synthetic evidence. On the contrary, at first glance one is puzzled at such "lack of logic," even though one's own nervous system is here responsible.

In short, synthetic insight cannot consist simply in the fact that the result of a new organization is read off. In order to be comprehensible as an instance of synthetic evidence, the example of Figure 1 must therefore be otherwise interpreted. Actually, with the change of its "function," the point remains not only numerically identical—so do the hydrogen atoms and the brightness b, as well—but it remains identical also as to spatial location. *But this means that it remains identical in the respect in which it serves as "foundation" for the two successive functions.* The position in which the point had been put by its function in the first structuring (it had the distance a from L) remains unchanged

---

[11] One calls "function" or "part-property" that characteristic which appertains to an element only as a part of its concrete Gestalt-whole.

when in the second structuring the point assumes the function: "lying outside the square." We may express this as follows: The first structuring (the distance-relation to L) constitutes the foundation from which, in combination with further factors—such as the definite position and size of the square—the new aspect or new function is synthetically read off. "Foundation" therefore means a characteristic, constituted by the first structuring, which *must* be identically retained, if the new function is to appear evident in the new structuring. This foundation is what remains identical in the change of functions.—Incidentally, this identity brings about such characteristic phenomena as "following from" or "inner necessity." In reading off, one experiences how what is read off is founded exclusively on those properties of the situation which are constituted by the premises, and how it thus "follows from" these properties.

If this condition of identity be given sufficient attention, there will be no danger that the subject regard something as intelligible just because, in the moment of inspection, it happens to be apparent. Suppose, in the moment of reading off from: $a > b$ and $b > c$, the a were suddenly and maliciously to shrink (or turn red). Surely, under these circumstances the subject would not be doomed unsuspectingly to regard as evident from the premises that a must be less than c (or redder than c). For, foundations must enter into the new structuring with just those characteristics which they exhibit whenever considered in their earlier structuring.

Let us now summarize what has been attained in a final answer to the question of how synthetic evidence is possible: *Synthetic evidence is possible through the fact that from a situation given in a certain structuring and characterized by certain functions (aspects), without any change in essential foundations new functions (aspects) may be read off by virtue of new organizations.* By new functions, I mean functions which have not been utilized in characterizing the original situation.

With this, Kant's general question: "How are synthetic judgments *a priori* possible?" is answered, provided that "synthetic" is understood in the sense of following from non-constitutive co-containedness, "analytic" in the sense of explication through constitutive co-containedness, and "*a priori*" in the sense of intelligible.

Our answer to Kant's general problem is basically different from that of Kant himself, in that we do not reduce the synthetic *a priori* to prescriptions of reason incorporated into the object, but conceive this *a priori* as intrinsic in the nature of the objects themselves. Incidentally, concerning this point we are in agreement with Husserl's phenomenology. . . .

ON SYNTHETIC EVIDENCE FROM GIVEN, NOT FROM CONSTRUCTED, FOUNDATIONS. In the treatment of evidence so far we have dealt almost exclusively with foundations of evidence which were paradigmatically constructed from certain conceptual premises; in short, we discussed *constructed foundations*. However, it is clear that evidence is not restricted to constructed situations. Apart from the newly introduced "point of view," the foundations may also be simply "given," "found as existing." They need only to be "characterized" somehow. After all, what matters in synthetic evidence is only this: the original way in which the foundations, their definite "characterization," are given in a situation, should not already constitutively co-contain what is to be read off. What is read off must represent an aspect which is new in contrast to the original phenomenal aspect—not of course new in the sense of added material such as may be discovered by more exact observation.

Instead of further discussion let us have an example: Given a particular room with its furniture, etc. Here the following statement may hold, for instance: "If, in this room, one goes directly from the stove to the door, one passes close by a chest of drawers." This aspect need in no way be constitutively co-contained in the original way the room was given (as was, e.g., the presence of the chest of drawers); but it may nevertheless be read off from the facts comprising this room with the straight line drawn therein.—Another example, which involves an important component of almost all practical manipulations. There is given an object at a definite location P. Now if my body, my hand or a stick which I am wielding moves in a definite direction—not characterized with reference to P—it may be read off that my body (or hand or stick) will come into contact with the object at P, provided that nothing as yet unforeseen interferes.

The sole difference between these two cases and our earlier examples is that now the inspected situation is not constructed from any concepts, but for the most part is simply "given." [12] This holds in the first example except for the straight line and the consideration of its surroundings, in the second except for the movement in the particular direction. The reason for the emphasis in this chapter on the special case of reading off from a *conceptually constructed* foundation is simply: What is peculiar to synthetic evidence is more easily demonstrated if the foundation is conceptually "in hand" to begin with. About the pure state of being given, no communication is possible, and the "how" of such a state allows again of only conceptual characterization.—It contributed to this emphasis that I wished to facilitate the connection with older treatments of the problem.

When we are no longer limited to conceptually constructed (paradigmatic) foundations, the field of application of our concept of evidence increases tremendously. In daily life, we do not read off from explicitly established premises, but from given situations and from operations therein undertaken. In practical life, we are not interested in general statements which allow of general formulation and general understanding, but in the fact that something holds here and now. (Not to mention that, by the requirements of conceptually constructed foundations, animals would be excluded at the outset from the province of evidence, which would be unfair.)

---

[12] This does not mean that the foundations may not also be constructed, and indeed heterogeneously so, i.e., without utilization of the relation which is later read off. For this purpose, one need only characterize the positions of the different components of the room by means of their spatial coordinates in some reference system. And even though the translation of these various coordinates into the corresponding visual distribution within the room would constitute a relatively tedious process, this translation would still be of the same type as the translation of the expression $a > b$ into a perceptual model.

EXAMPLES OF SYNTHETIC EVIDENCE. In the following, a few further examples of synthetic evidence will be added, in order to demonstrate the range of application, the implications of the theory.

The first ... example involves not only a single reading off, as was the case till now, but a whole chain of evidences which terminates in a "final reading." In such a chain, the results of the earlier evidences enter into the construction of the foundations of the later ones, up to the final reading which gives the conclusion.

1. "An odd number plus an odd number equal an even number." "Odd signifies a quantity of pairs plus a half pair." In the first place, it may be read off that two quantities of pairs, combined, result again in a quantity of pairs. It may further be read off that a half pair together with another half pair results in a whole pair. Finally a third reading leads to the conclusion.[13] ...

[2.] Greater volume with constant mass means less density. From the expansion of a constant mass (e.g., of a gas), it may be read off as a "new aspect" of the situation that the substance concerned has become "thinner" throughout.

In conclusion, one more example, from pure logic:

[3.] The forms of logical conclusion as well owe their intelligibility to synthetic evidence. For example: From "all M are P" and "all S are M" (or, "this S is M"), it follows that "all S are P" (or, "this S is P").—Here the conclusion arises by means of a different relating of the terms; compare the representation by areas, after Euler, in Figure 2.

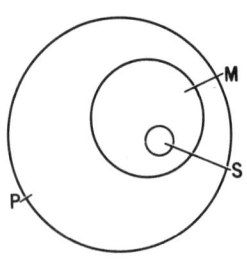

Figure 2

Incidentally, on the intelligibility of this procedure depends the intelligibility of the application of every general rule. I write the "formula of application" as follows: "From $f(a)$ and $a = b$

---

[13] The new aspect arises here each time through the fact that two parts are inspected "as a whole."

follows $f(b)$." E.g., to take (f) the longest object (a); the longest object is this wire (b); ergo: to take the wire $[f(b)]$.—If a human being or an animal, say, in a training experiment, has grasped the principle of the required conduct, e.g., "always to go through the door next to the middle," he will from now on act with insight in regard to that principle. Every intelligibility dependent on nothing but intuitive or logical deducibility from a general law, is exactly of the type of evidence involved in the above procedure of application.

APPLICATION TO THE PSYCHOLOGY OF THE UNDERSTANDING AND THE FINDING OF SOLUTIONS. This theory of total insight has purposely been developed without reference to the experimental material. It had to be mature in itself, before it was applied to the set of problems with which we are specifically concerned.

Let us begin with the most simple. In so far as analyses of goal and of situation consist in explications from the proposition and the premises, they are of the type of synthetic or analytic reading off.[14]

We have seen that the "point of view" in reading off is each time prescribed by the *Problemstellung* as a whole. Suppose that from the proposition that the prime numbers constitute an infinite series, it is read off that for every prime number there is always a greater one. In this the "point of view" of the reading is dictated by the wish to transform the proposition of infinity, which is not accessible to a finite method of proof, into a finite and general proposition. The realization that it is the infinity-factor which makes the original proposition incapable of proof is reached through the analysis of conflict. This analysis presupposes merely an awareness of what is really meant by proving something. And this again means a most general analysis of goal (of the type of analytic insight).[15]

---

[14] The expression, "analysis" of situation or goal, ought not to be confused with "analytic" reading off. Synthetic reading off, too, represents, as has been stated, an "analysis" in the broader sense of the word.
[15] We named a reading off "analytic," in the narrower sense, if it does not "affix" a completely new aspect to a given constitutive one, but merely explicates what inheres in this given aspect.

The role which such very general and purely analytic goal-explications play in problem-solving is as decisive as it is hidden. In the problem of prime numbers, the general nature of proof was to be analysed. In the following problem (discussed by M. Wertheimer) it is the general nature of measuring. Task: To express (measure) the side of the square in terms of the radius *r* of the inscribed circle. (See Figure 3.) Ideal solution: To measure means to make the measure coincide with what is to be measured. In the present case, the nearest approach to coincidence is parallelism and therefore rotation of the radius into the position parallel to the side. One sees now that the side of the square equals 2*r*.

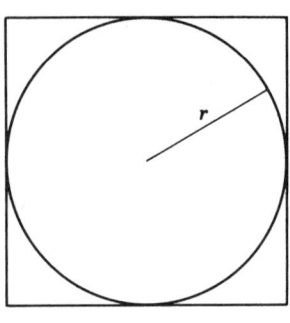

Figure 3

Through the special choice of the examples thus far used, the impression could easily have been given that synthetic evidence was pretty well restricted to the province of pure mathematics and logic. However, it is sufficient to bring to memory that so-called pure mathematics and logic is for the most part (i.e., with exception of the "artificial" axiom-systems and the theorems derived therefrom) embodied in reality; in other words, that everyday life is full of mathematical and logical situations. Let us take the two practical problems which occupied us at the very beginning, the radiation problem and the pendulum problem. In both cases, the understanding of the best solution involves synthetic insight at the decisive point. In the first case, it is decisive that more material exists at the intersection of several streams of material[16] than elsewhere. This accumulation of material may with perfect insight be read off from the model of the intersecting streams. The almost startling evidence of the solution by crossing

---

[16] For the sake of simplicity, a bundle of rays is here considered as a stream of material, i.e., by analogy with a river.

depends on this "synthetic reading off."—The best solution of the pendulum problem owes its evidence to the following synthetic reading off: "If p and q (in Figure 4) expand by the same length, then the distance d between their end-points remains constant."— Let the more material aspects of the effects, namely, that the rays destroy organic tissue, and that warming causes expansion, be as purely empirical and unintelligible as they please, the more "formal" aspect follows both times with entire intelligibility from the geometry of the rays or that of the pendulum, as contained in the solution.

It is generally a valid statement that facts (aspects) can be intelligible on the ground of synthetic reading off only in regard to their wholes. It is intelligible that the stick moved in this direction will strike the ball lying there, if the total movement of the stick, including the future part, be conceived as a nontemporal line, and if this line be related to the position of the ball. But what the ball will do when struck is by no means totally intelligible from the premises just named. The physical reaction of systems to one another contains, as we shall see, certain components which are "merely to be accepted," in other words, which are not intelligible.

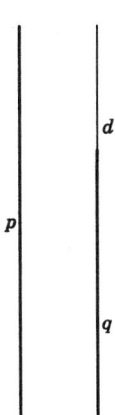

Figure 4

We have recognized that the intelligibility of the best solution of the radiation problem, as of the pendulum problem, depends on synthetic evidence within the given situation. Therefore, we are dealing here with a much more profound understanding of the solution than [takes place in a] more general form of understanding. There it was in principle sufficient for understanding if, in the form of "functional value," connection with a sufficiently simple and general causal relation between solution and goal had been established. This underlying causal relation in itself could be totally unintelligible.

Even the most general heuristic methods of productive thinking are of the type of evident explications, more particularly, of the analytic kind. Thus, for example, analysis of situation, where it consists in deduction from the given premises, itself derives analytically from the nature of proof. For, "to prove" really means nothing but deduction of what is asserted from the given premises. Still more generally: Both analysis of situation as examination of what is given, and analysis of goal as examination of what is demanded, these two fundamental methods of rational discovery, themselves derive analytically from the nature of problem-solving in general. For, to solve a problem involves making what is given serviceable to what is demanded.[17] That I must know what is given, in order to operate with it, and must also know what is demanded, in order to operate toward it, this in turn follows analytically from the nature of action. For action means acting, guided by knowledge of the purpose and of the means. This structure of action is no "definition," but an original and basic experience of mankind. Also the question, "Why doesn't it work?" or, "What should I alter to make it work?," in other words, what we call analysis of conflict, is evident—evident from the nature of "solution." For solution is ground of the realized goal, thus elimination of a possible obstacle to the goal.

But an important question yet remains to be answered. Assumed that the goal is intelligible from the solution, i.e., that the solution is entirely comprehensible as a solution. For this reason alone, could the solution already be found with complete insight? No, because for this, the solution in turn would have to be intelligible from the goal. After all, it is the goal which is given; the solution is yet to be found. But to the intelligibility in the direction from a to b, there corresponds in general no such evidence in the reverse direction. (Thus, for example, from $a > b > c$, $a > c$ may indeed be read off, but not the reverse: from $a > c$ it does not follow that $a > b$ or $b > c$.) Only in certain limiting cases, where goal and solution are equivalent to each other, does deducibility exist in both directions (cf. analysis of goal in the sense of a "reversible" deduction from the proposition given). But these are

[17] We may leave undecided whether this is actually "analytic" and not rather "synthetic" evidence. For, this depends on whether or not the situation in question was introduced (constituted) by another aspect; and this is to a certain degree a question of the particular psychological case.

exceptions, which—be they ever so important in their place—do not affect the rule that in most cases synthetic evidence has for thinking the character of a one-way street, which is not open to traffic in just the crucial direction: goal to solution. . . .

On Learning and Partial Insight

EMPIRICAL CONNECTION-STRUCTURES. According to the preceding chapter the intelligibility of many connections of the type: "if a, then b" rests on the fact that b can be read off when a is given. This evidence is either synthetic, i.e., b is a new aspect of the heterogeneously constructed situation a, or it is analytic, i.e., b is a constitutive aspect of the situation a, and therefore not "new." —Now questions like these arise: *Of what kind are those other if-then connections in which the "then* b" *can in no way be read off from the* a? *How are such connections accessible to a thinking creature? In particular: Does all intelligibility, in the sense of the general definition of the preceding chapter, depend on the possibility of such reading off?* Suppose that in a given case this possibility does not exist. Then the following other possibility must still be examined: Among all the phenomenal characteristics which b could assume, those which b really has may be directly singled out by the phenomenal nature of a. The term "directly" is meant to exclude the intervention of further factors.

Let us begin from below, i.e., from that minimum of "rationality" which functional connections in a world must exhibit if a creature is to be able to penetrate into this world by thinking, and thus to get along in it.

If the spatial and temporal connections among the events of the world were without any rules, were completely chaotic and thus absolutely a matter of chance, then thinking would have no practical significance at all. *Constancy* of connections is thus the minimum of rationality.[1] But since no event repeats itself quite

---

[1] The statistical conception of natural laws does not deny constancy in general, but only constancy on the microscopic level.

identically, a constancy of connection can prevail only among parts or aspects of events. For only such repeat themselves. For thinking, then, the problem arises of discovering what components of connected events have a constant connection, or—phrased somewhat more familiarly—what properties of given data are causally essential for an effect on which our eye is focussed.

Now in our actual world, such constant connections (laws) have for the most part not the type of a constant coupling of definite "elements," but that of a *constant structure of variables*. For example, there is no absolutely constant connection between the boiling of water and a quite definite temperature. But there is such a connection between the boiling of any fluid and that temperature at which the vapor-pressure of the liquid just exceeds the atmospheric pressure at the place concerned. In other words, the elements, such as the liquid, the temperature, the place, the pressures concerned, can vary, and yet the constancy of the connection is not thereby affected. On the contrary: Under altered conditions, events must occur which are altered in a definite way, so that the same connection-structure may be retained....

Not only in science, however, but everywhere in common life, man (and in principle, the same holds for the animal) finds himself confronted with the problem of grasping the constant structure of interrelated variables, *of "getting the idea."* For example, a chimpanzee will again and again promptly and sensibly utilize appropriate stick-like tools (e.g., a piece of wire, a wisp of straw, a shoe) when he wants to draw near a goal-object which is out of reach. He is capable of this only because he has grasped that the point is not the color, the original position or the absolute spatial direction of the tool, but purely and simply this structure: to move the goal within reach by means of a sufficiently long object.[2]

LEARNING OF CONNECTION-STRUCTURES. Now it is very important that the problem of grasping the essential can also be solved in cases in which the connection-structure as such lacks any intelligi-

---

[2] A few fine examples of use of a stick *without* understanding of this functional structure have been given by K. Gottschaldt.

bility; in which, therefore, for the subject in question any other effect could be just as well connected with the given cause as the actual effect. Nature allows its creatures to grasp all kinds of constant connections into whose inner necessity she still forbids them to penetrate. Among the philosophers, at least since Hume, there prevails the almost unanimous conviction that in physical nature none but such entirely unintelligible causal connections will ever be found.

We first raise the question: *How is it possible to grasp connections which are constant but in themselves totally unintelligible?* This question has already been answered by Francis Bacon and John Stuart Mill in the general form of so-called rules of induction. Their quintessence may be expressed as follows: *The essential cause of an effect b—or that which "leads to b"—can be grasped by the abstraction of those further factors which all b-situations have in common, and of those which all comparable non-b-situations lack in common.*[3] Such an "abstracting induction" takes place everywhere in the practical life of man and animal, only less systematically than in the sciences. Psychologically it means a process in which, out of a number of situations of a class, *the common aspect is "precipitated."* The result of such a "precipitation" is a *change of aspect* of the situations involved. This often occurs quite suddenly, possibly accompanied by an "Aha-experience."

Reorganizations of this sort may be very nicely observed in training experiments on man and animal. One can, for example, train chickens always to select their food from the lighter of two grey papers, whatever the absolute greys. Or one can train a person always to choose the box next on the left from the middle one, with varying position and number of the boxes offered. Such training often leads to sudden "insight." The principle of the required behavior is all at once clear, and the curve of errors exhibits that

[3] Huang's experiments bear eloquent witness to the degree to which this criterion is autochthonous. Huang, in experiments with children, brought about opposite effects by apparently the same event. For example, a needle laid on water sank once and did not sink another time. It is amazing how the most harmless differences between the two situations were promptly seized upon by the children as "cause" for the varying behavior of the needle.

famous and much-discussed *sudden drop*. Yet the principle *per se* may be as unintelligible as one pleases.[4] Therefore, paradoxically expressed, there may be insight in a connection which is totally inaccessible to insight. The paradox is resolved as soon as one realizes that here the term "insight" appears in two different references. By the grasping of the common principle of a number of situations, this principle—its inner Why—is not comprehended. What is comprehended is that once this common principle is given, *the individual situations must be just as they are and not otherwise.* The different situations, till then seemingly accidental, suddenly appear throughout as embodiments of a single principle. Therewith they acquire that "intelligibility" . . . which consists in nothing but *"reducibility to a general law."* This may be called "insight of the second degree."

Unfortunately, through this ambiguity of the term "insight," great confusion has arisen among psychologists. One speaks of the one meaning when he thinks he is speaking of the other. For the sake of unambiguity, I designate a connection of the type: "if a, then b" as intelligible, *not* if it is grasped as a principle common to a number of data, from which the latter can be derived, but if and in the degree to which, before other possibilities, b as such is directly favored or singled out by the a. This will be called "insight of the first degree."

VERY GENERAL CONNECTION-STRUCTURES. It is obvious that, with the help of abstracting induction, a principle will be the more surely and quickly grasped, the greater is the number of situations from which the identical principle may be abstracted. Now in this respect, the constitution of our world is relatively convenient. Let us consider the situation cited above, in which some stick-like object was utilized for drawing near a distant goal-object. This behavior presupposes, among other things, the general experience

[4] Among actual causal connections, those with which the experimentalist in medicine must so often be contented most nearly approximate the extreme type of totally unintelligible connections. (See in regard to this de Kruif's excellent book, *Microbe Hunters*, which is very rich in information about thought-processes, for instance, about the heuristic significance of chance.

that one thing is *movable* by another thing. Plainly, in order to have this experience, a subject does not need just the stick-goal situation and all sorts of trial-and-error reactions therein. Some other instance of communicated motion, not necessarily one related to a goal but perhaps a playful one, could demonstrate exactly the same to him. It is also unnecessary that it be the learning subject himself who directly or indirectly moves something; rather, transmissions of motion occur continually in our environment, as things push and pull each other. From this, time and again, the same lesson is to be drawn. To be sure, there are "objects" which are able to interpenetrate unhindered, as for example waves, shadows, and the like; but they are after all notorious exceptions.

Still much more general is the experience—realized, by the way, in both the radiation and the pendulum problem—that an effect depends also on the nature of the reagent (on its "sensitivity"). Even the infant, kicking and tossing about in his crib, experiences that it makes a difference whether one strikes the cover or the wooden railing. And it does not remain hidden to him that the mother reacts to crying differently from other people.

In summary: Everywhere in our world the particular causal relations participate in very general ones. But "very general" means: accessible in nearly every occurrence. Thus abstracting induction is surely not starved for material. . . .

On Solutions through Resonance

STATEMENT OF THE PROBLEM AND EXAMPLES. [A] solution can be found, or better, sought out, through the correspondence between the property demanded (anticipated, signalled) and that inherent in what is sought. The process by which, in the perceptual field or in memory (the trace field), an object or a situation is sought out through specific signalling, we then called *resonance*. The "finding of a solution through the resonance effect of a signal" was at that time only mentioned, in order temporarily to be set aside again as a principle which is obvious but much too limited for problem-solving in general. It is the most banal and least rational form of finding solutions, practicable in any world whatever, provided this world contains similarities and repetitions at all. Although the forms of evidence which were discussed [previously] permit more rational ways of finding solutions, yet this simple method is by no means made thereby superfluous. Wherever in the course of a solution appropriate means are sought for in the perceptually given problem situation, but above all wherever *previous experiences, learned structures, are included in a solution-process,* resonance effects through appropriate signals may well participate. It is therefore worthwhile to investigate more closely the nature of this finding by resonance.

As a preliminary, let us have a few more examples. . . . I look for a pencil on the table before me. My glance wanders around until it is finally "caught" on the pencil. We must thus distinguish between a signal or "model of search" (such as the approximate representation of the pencil) and a "region of search" (such as the table). Of course the region of search need not be in the perceptual field. Some memory field may be perused instead (with the "inner eye"). It may also happen that a particular region of search is completely lacking. That which is sought (together with its place of abode) then emerges directly "from memory."[1]

"Something of such and such a sort" can be sought just as well as some definite thing. For example, I seek something long like a stick (in order to get hold of an object which has rolled under the cupboard). In this situation I may look around for something suitable in perceptual space, or in some promising region of memory; or something of the sort (a ruler, an umbrella) may occur to me singly, and only afterwards may I ask where such a thing might be and whether it be accessible. One more example: Once I gave to several boys a problem in which they had to find a form

---

[1] One might be tempted to name a search with definite direction a "vector." However, the direction of such a "vector of search" would by no means be *spatially* defined. This vector would exist, if in a "space" at all, at any rate in some other "space" than, for example, the vector which is defined between the subject and the spatial location of the object when found.

of message which could under no circumstances be intercepted by enemies. The first solution-phase or reformulation of the problem—incidentally, analytic of the goal—consisted in that the children search with the model: "something high above," or "something invisible." (For what does "to intercept" mean?—in any case, to see and to touch.) To these demands corresponded the immanent properties of the proposals: airplane, submarine.

It need not be visual properties which serve as signal of what is sought, unless the search is in a visual field. When I need something with which to drive a nail into the wall, a hammer promptly occurs to me. Thus what is sought here is characterized by its typical function, not by characteristics of its appearance. Only if I look now for the hammer in my environment, does a visual signal come into play.

What is sought need not be a thing. It can also be a procedure, a way to. . . . The signalled property is then: "leading to effect so-and-so."

In such finding of objects and operations, it is of course unnecessary that the demanded or signalled property have at any time already been abstracted from the object. It need inhere in the object solely as a possibility or disposition. Otherwise, the object may occur in my experience for the very first time. It frequently occurs that a familiar object appears one day—under the pressure of a definite seeking—with a "new" property, i.e., one which until then I had never perceived in it. For example, I may look for something to weigh down papers—and a dictionary offers itself. Or the umbrella is suddenly claimed as substitute for a stick. Similarly, an event in my surroundings or in my memory may for the first time be claimed as means-to-the-goal. It is clear that, under the pressure of a definite seeking, very radical *recenterings of the object* can take place (see Wertheimer). Only the "disposition thereto" must be present in the object. Such recenterings of objects may be observed under the very simplest conditions. Let the reader make the following experiment: He is to scan the environment in his room or on the street, putting a stress on red, i.e., he is to seek out everything red which happens to be in the surrounding field. Then in the "relief" of his surroundings, which may be very familiar, an amazing alteration will take place. The structuration is in terms of "red," everything of a red disposition becomes unduly prominent, completely subordinated objects which earlier were hardly or not at all noticed (shop signs, book bindings, neckties) suddenly show off and enter into unsuspected connections with each other. It is not as if one gradually collected red things; rather what is red "leaps to the eye," becomes properly red and dominates the relief. Intellectual recognition limps behind. —For a change, one can also put the stress on "round." Then one suddenly sees quite new forms emerging, and the swarming of red is as though obliterated.

Similar signalling demands on the perceptual field may occasionally occur without our intention, namely, on the basis of so-called *sets* such as, for example, may remain after an intensive occupation with, and a seeking of, objects of a given kind. A personal observation which each time amazes me afresh: if for a while I have intensively read music, it often occurs that for minutes at a time I cannot afterwards look at a so-called homogeneous surface without having all accidental microstructures of this surface at once and inevitably grow into notes. If one realizes how varied are the symbols occurring in musical notation, it will be understood that countless accidental microstructures may be transformed into such symbols. (A larger oblique flaw, for instance, appears spontaneously as two heads of half or whole notes pressed obliquely against each other in the second-interval, or—if it be narrow enough—as a line connecting several notes.) Obviously this is not a case of hallucinations, but of changes in the perceptual field under a completely involuntary pressure in the direction of notation.

The conditions are somewhat different in experiments which K. Gottschaldt reports. By presentation of periodic series of visual stimuli, Gottschaldt produced in his Ss at definite positions in the series a specific expectation-pressure, under which a test figure, ambiguous in itself, was perceived in a correspondingly specific way....

DISCUSSION OF SOME EXPERIMENTS. The subject is to say what this is: "red, round—juicy—soft." After red and round, one subject reproduced "rubber ball," after juicy, "apple," after "soft" first "plum," then "tomato."—A second experiment: "long, pointed, cold." (An icicle is meant.) The Ss name at first things like "knitting needle," "sword." The experimenter then adds to the signal the property "brittle." Now the answer is more likely to be "icicle." If the model of search is further enriched by the property "hanging," the solution "icicle" seldom fails to appear. What have we here?

1. The individual properties given do not act "as pieces," as an aggregate,[2] as if each aroused its own trace, and as if then by superposition the trace common to a maximum of individual properties, or the trace preferred for another reason, were selected. Rather it can be directly shown as a phenomenal fact that the individual properties are joined into one unified "model of the thing," each in its specific position in the structure. In other words, the model of search "constructed" out of the given properties arouses as a whole appropriate trace-wholes. The process resembles, in this respect, the recognition of a perceptual thing, where again not individual properties arouse individually adequate traces, but the concretely structured thing as a whole establishes contact with a corresponding trace-whole.

2. But the model of search is no complete, sharply defined "thing." It is a partially undetermined, vague, fluctuating (or purposely varied) thing-schema with "gaps" which may be filled provisionally.

3. The model of search presupposes an understanding of the instruction, and this involves two phases: (1) Every single one of the verbally given properties must first be understood *per se*. This understanding occurs through arousal of the traces corresponding to the particular genus of property, by way of the proper word-traces. (2) From the aroused single traces, the model of

---

[2] See the "constellation theory" of thinking proposed by W. James, G. E. Müller, and Poppelreuter among others. This theory was refuted first by Selz theoretically and by Shepard and Fogelsonger experimentally, but still leads a somewhat vague existence (especially among psychiatrists). Cf. the alleged steering of the reproductive process by so-called "dominant ideas" (*Obervorstellungen*).

search with its character of a unified entity is then constructed through a process of "structural combination."

* * *

There is an aura of optimism hovering over Duncker's work, as if the hope of rationalism had again touched the psychology of thought. Both the world and the mind are constructed in such a way that the processes of interaction between the two can be laid bare by careful analysis. Thought, in its very nature, tends to be intelligent, that is, insightful, though it must be added that, as they are used by Duncker, these terms have lost much of their common-sense and therefore controversial meaning. Thought is insightful when it understands what it is thinking about, and the basis of that understanding is to be found by structural analysis. Although lip service is paid to the role of past experience, the history of the organism is underplayed in favor of analysis of current processes.

The aura of optimism becomes a positive halo in Wertheimer's *Productive Thinking*. Wertheimer, a major source of inspiration and concepts for the Gestalt school, after working on and off during his lifetime on problems of thinking, barely completed his theory shortly before his death. His book* was published posthumously in 1945, but unfortunately the conclusions that he reached were more programmatic and hortative than theoretical. The experiments reported in his book are similar in nature to the problems with which Duncker worked; indeed they formed the basis for much of Duncker's work. In any case, Wertheimer's influence on the history of thinking as such extends well beyond the period covered in this volume. As we have suggested earlier, Wertheimer posed problems and questions for the associationists of the mid-century just as Bühler had done for Wundt and his followers.

With Wertheimer, and some time earlier with Koffka,† the Gestalt theory of thinking had reached its peak of development—

---
* M. Wertheimer, *Productive thinking*. New York: Harper, 1945.
† K. Koffka, *Principles of Gestalt psychology*. New York: Harcourt Brace, 1935, Chap. 13.

and probably also of influence. The problems that Köhler, Duncker and the others had posed were to remain important goads for any theory of thinking. But the concepts of Gestalt theory have failed —certainly as of this writing—to catch fire. The reasons for this failure are probably threefold: first, the evidence failed to materialize that the Gestalt laws of perception could be easily incorporated into the theories of other areas of psychology; second, right or wrong the nativism of the theory was alien to the prevailing empiricism and genetic approach of the period; and finally, there was an increasing demand for theories that permitted unequivocal statements and elegant deductions, two demands that Gestalt theory could not pretend to fulfill. But the problems remained and the emphasis on structural factors and the intensive analysis of situational determinants was to be carried forward by other thinkers, just as Kurt Lewin's demands in these respects fruitfully influenced other fields of psychology.

In retrospect it is clear that the history of thinking from early associationism to the Gestalt period unfolded not only drastic changes in theoretical stance, but also in the kinds of questions that were being asked. From an examination of the flow of images and thought we have moved to the analysis of problem solving. With the departure of consciousness as the subject matter of psychology, it has become possible to conjecture what the processes might be that intervene not only between the asking of a question and the production of an answer, but also between the posing of a problem and its solution.

Just at the time that the results of the Würzburgers became common coin, the marriage between behaviorism and associationism produced a stream of development that was to interfere with the normal development of a psychology of thinking. Some of the battles that Müller and Selz fought were to be staged all over again some thirty and forty years later. But behaviorism also encouraged the interest in problem solving which seemed to be less tarred with the introspectionist brush than other fields of thinking.

Another area of research that slowly became identified with the psychology of thinking developed during this period—concept learning and attainment. Apparently acceptable to the behavioristic schools, the study of concepts soon shed the shackles of a misguided behaviorism that seemed to legislate content instead of objective method, and added valuable insights to our knowledge of the theoretical contents of the mind.

When we look retrospectively at the problem of thinking in the last four centuries, we can see that, like much of philosophy, it has fathered many independent empirical offspring and problems. Early theories of thought developed into problems of sensation and perception; nineteenth-century associationism gave rise to studies of human verbal learning; questions about the nature of intelligence gave way to the intelligence tests; the determining tendencies flowered into problems of motivation and attitude. Thinking about thinking has proved to be psychology's major springboard into many adventures, and yet somewhere there seems to be a core problem still to be solved, some grand design that will unlock the mysteries of the nature of thought.

To pursue our introductory theme, it seems reasonable to reconsider the history of thinking in the 1960's because another concerted attack is being launched on these elusive central problems. The field is alive with new ideas, from concept learning, problem solving, cognitive development, language learning, and many others. The notion of structure has gained acceptance, though the structures that Piaget, for example, finds in his subjects derive from the active interplay between organism and environment and not from postulated qualities of the mind. Rigorous theorizing has been made possible—and sometimes mandatory—by the availability of high-speed computers. The second battle over associationism is ending and the new theories of thinking have benefited from the various successes and failures of the psychologists discussed in the preceding pages. Some of these influences have been deliberately left aside for the moment, but an awareness of some of the old issues and battles might further an appreciation not only of the old, but also of the new.

Name Index

(Pages of selections are shown in boldface type.)

Ach, N., 5, 143, 151, **152–162**, 163, 165, 178, 184, 187, **201–207**, 216, 218–219
Aristotle, 5, 8, **9–13**, 25, 45, 70, 113, 134, 186, 209

Bacon, F., 213, 289
Bain, A., 69, 125, **126–129**, 131, 220–221
Baldwin, J. M., 172
Benary, W., 224
Berkeley, G., 7, 51, 65, 70, 168–169
Binet, A., 5, 134, 148, 260
Boring, E. G., 5, 70
Brentano, F., 224
Brett, G. S., 5
Brown, T., 91–92, 109
Bühler, K., 148, 162–164, 183, 211, 229, 234, 296

Claparède, E., 5, 247, 260
Clarke, H. M., 184

Darwin, E., 105
de Groot, A. D., 224–225
de Kruif, P., 290
Descartes, R., 14
Dewey, J., 223
Dilthey, W., 5

Duncker, K., 248–249, 260–261, **262–296**, 297

Ebbinghaus, H., 2, 147, 175, 242
Ehrenfels, C. von, 235
Erdmann, B., 150
Euclid, 48
Euler, L., 282

Fogelsonger, H. M., 295
Freud, S., 5, 200

Galileo Galilei, 14
Galton, F., 167
Gauss, K. F., 257
Gottschaldt, K., 288, 294

Hamilton, W., 8–9, 13, 168, 170
Hartley, D., 69–71, **72–91**, 92, 105, 112, 175, 222
Herbart, J. F., 155, 209
Hobbes, T., 3, 7–8, 13–14, **15–23**, 24, 70, 186
Horace (Quintus Horatius Flaccus), 209
Huang, I., 289
Hume, D., 7–8, 49–50, **51–69**, 70, 111, 175, 212, 261, 271, 289
Humphrey, G., 6, 166
Husserl, E. G., 5, 163, 272
Huxley, T. H., 168–170

Name Index

Jacobson, E., 184
James, W., 148, 222–223, 269, 295

Kant, I., 5, 209, 261, 272, 274, 279–280
Kessen, W., 2
Koffka, K., 3, 188, 224, 234–235, **236–247**, 248, 296
Köhler, W., 236, 247–248, 259, 273, 297
Kries, J. von, 178
Külpe, O., 51, 133, 163, 187, 207, **208–216**, 219, 242

Lange, F. A., 213
Lewin, K., 297
Locke, J., 3, 7–8, 23–25, **26–49**, 50–52, 69–70, 72, 75, 93, 168–170, 173, 222

Mackintosh, J., 8
Maier, N. R. F., 248
Mandler, G., 2
Marbe, K., 133, 135, 142, **143–146**, 148, 162, 165, 184, 198
Mayer, A., 133–134, **135–142**
Meinong, A. von, 224
Messer, A., 5, 146–147, **148–151**, 162, 178, 184, 200, 218, 220
Michotte, A., 50
Mill, J., 7, 69, 91–93, **94–125**, 129, 130, 142, 173–175, 186
Mill, J. S., 7, 69, 93, 115, 125, 130, 174–176, 250, 252, 289
Molineux, W., 34
Müller, G. E., 125, 187, 201, 216, **217–221**, 226, 295, 297

Newell, A., 225
Newton, I., 72

Okabe, T., 184
Orth, J., 133–134, **135–142**

Pavlov, I. P., 5
Pestalozzi, J. H., 209
Peters, R. S., 5
Piaget, J., 5, 260–261, 298
Pilzecker, A., 187, 201, 220
Plato, 209
Poincaré, J. H., 275
Poppelreuter, W., 295
Priestley, J., 8

Reichenbach, H., 276

Schlick, M., 275
Schopenhauer, A., 209
Schumann, F., 187
Selz, O., 5, 148, 207, 223–224, **225–234**, 235, 260, 263–264, 295, 297
Shaw, J. C., 225
Shepard, J. F., 295
Sigwart, C., 144
Simon, H. A., 225
Spencer, H., 7
Stewart, D., 8

Thorndike, E. L., 5, 247, 271
Titchener, E. B., 51, 138, 164–166, **167–184**, 185, 187, 216, 242–246

Vives, J. L., 8

Watson, J. B., 5
Watt, H. J., 178, 187–188, **189–200**, 201, 217–218
Wertheimer, M., 236, 248–249, **250–259**, 261, 284, 293, 296
Wreschner, A., 220
Wundt, W., 131–133, 144, 155, 162, 164, 173, 243–244, 296